LANDING IN THE
EXECUTIVE CHAIR

LANDING IN THE
EXECUTIVE CHAIR

How to Excel in the Hot Seat

By Linda Henman, PhD

CAREER
PRESS

Pompton Plains, NJ

LANDING IN THE EXECUTIVE CHAIR
EDITED AND TYPESET BY DIANA GHAZZAWI
Cover design by Ty Nowicki
Printed in the U.S.A.

To order this title, please call toll-free 1-800-CAREER-1 (NJ and Canada: 201-848-0310) to order using VISA or MasterCard, or for further information on books from Career Press.

The Career Press, Inc.
220 West Parkway, Unit 12
Pompton Plains, NJ 07444
www.careerpress.com

Library of Congress Cataloging-in-Publication Data
Henman, Linda D.
    Landing in the executive chair : how to excel in the hot seat / by Linda Henman.
      p. cm.
    Includes bibliographical references and index.
    ISBN 978-1-60163-153-4 -- ISBN 978-1-60163-673-7 (ebook)
    1. Executives 2. Leadership. I. Title.

HD38.2.H464 2011
658.4'09--dc22

                                                    2011010729

To all those who have worn the uniform, especially my father, Friday Henman, who flew in three wars. You have given your yesterdays and todays so that we can have our tomorrows.

We thank you.

Acknowledgments

A book is a production, much like a play or musical. Although the lead may draw the applause, many others deserve an ovation too. A large supporting cast helped me get this book on stage. I would now like to call them from the wings to thank them for their contributions.

First, I'd like to thank all those who guided the production to the stage, those who gave me interviews: General Richard Myers, the former Chairman of the Joint Chiefs of Staff; Lt. Col. Richard Cole, Jimmy Doolittle's co-pilot; General Bruce Carlson, Director National Reconnaissance Office; Mark Abels, the PR expert who helped after the loss of TWA 800; Navy Commander (Ret.) Patricia Beckman; Cathy Dunkin, CEO Standing Partnership; Tom Casey, the Raiders' manager; Dr. James Dennis, President of McKendree University; Alexandra Reed Lajoux, Chief Knowledge Officer for the National Association of Corporate Directors; Nell Minow, editor and cofounder of The Corporate Library; Maestro Antonio Pappano, director of both the Royal Opera House, Covent Garden in London, and the Orchestra dell' Accademia di Santa Cecilia in Rome; Tom Phillips, Owner Weekends Only Furniture; and John Stroup, CEO Belden.

Without their insight and guidance, I could never have captured so many perspectives on leadership, its nature, and its responsibilities.

Next, I'd like to thank those who helped in other critical ways. Air Force historian Dick Anderegg (Colonel, USAF Ret.) and author of *Sierra Hotel*, helped me contact Tom Casey, the manger for the Doolittle Raiders, and advised on all things military. Tom, in turn, helped me contact Lt. Col. Richard Cole, Col. Jimmy Doolittle's co-pilot during the raid over Tokyo. Todd Joyce, the son of Doolitle Raider Lt. Richard Joyce and the designer for the Raiders' Website, generously shared a picture of Crew One that included both Col. Jimmy Doolittle and Lt. Col. Cole.

Lois Standing offered immeasurable editing support, as did her daughter, Kelly Standing, author of the soon-to-be-released *I'm Still Standing*. My oldest daughter, Angela Origliasso, proofed. She and my other daughters, Sherry Shawver and Laura Bianca, gave both moral and emotional support.

Alan Weiss, my mentor, wrote the foreword, helped me crystallize my thoughts, and oversaw the writing of the proposal, which he subsequently sent to Jeff Herman, my agent. Standing Partnership, News Experts, and Julia Bishop-Cross directed the public relations and marketing. Chris Scavatto designed the set, which included process visuals in most chapters. I took many cues from this group of professional script writers and artists.

The team at Career Press choreographed and produced the book with a keen eye on the details. They painstakingly read the lines and prompted my best efforts.

As always, any errors—factual or otherwise—are totally the fault of one of the aforementioned people. The author can't be blamed.

Contents

Foreword by Alan Weiss, PhD 11

Chapter 1: F^2 Leaders: Fair but Firm 15

Chapter 2: Control the Hinges of Destiny:
Decision-Making and Problem-Solving 43

Chapter 3: Build Magnets to Attract Top Talent 71

Chapter 4: Strategize to Leverage Your
Competitive Advantage 101

Chapter 5: Turn Great Strategy Into Great Execution 129

Chapter 6: Plan Succession and Ensure the
Leadership Pipeline 151

Chapter 7: Lead a Team of Virtuosos 175

Chapter 8: Become a Star on the Board of Directors 201

Chapter 9: Become an Agent for and a Champion of Change 225

Chapter 10: Ten Lessons for Leading During Crisis 247

Appendix   269

Notes   277

Index   283

About the Author   287

Foreword

I've worked with leaders in the public and private sectors globally for more than 25 years. During that time, in my keynote speeches, I've been asked on perhaps a thousand occasions, "What is the primary factor in creating growth organizations?"

And my answer has never wavered: it's the person at the top.

If you don't believe that, take a look at the salad days at Apple, IBM, Southwest Air, and Google; then look at the forgettable days at Enron, BP Oil, Exxon, and Sears. The people at the top make the most profound difference of any factor.

You can observe this even within industries. Why did Southwest excel at the lower end of the airline market while Continental excelled at the high end, and everyone else took a bath? Because of Herb Kelleher and Gordon Bethune, that's why. The aircraft, federal regulations, and travelers were consistent for everyone. In every case of a failed airline, form Eastern to TWA, you will find a terrible CEO.

Within a single organization you can witness the phenomenon: Roy Vagelos led Merck to years of outstanding performance, including five consecutive annual citations of "America's Most Admired Company" from *Fortune* Magazine. His successor, Ray Gilmartin, created dismal results and was eventually forced out by the board. Hewlett-Packard has been a roller-coaster of high-level success and failure, with extremely adverse consequences for the stock and a well-deserved skewering by the media.

The "top" I refer to in all firms (except the "mom and pop" operations) includes a number of people. Those who lead subsidiaries, those with P&L responsibility, those heading large staff areas, executive and artistic directors of arts groups, and so forth. But like the old Roman legions, the person at the top directs the people immediately beneath, who in turn direct those below them, until the front line is well prepared for battle.

It's not only important for the leader to walk the talk, but also to "talk the walk." The top people must *communicate* what's important as well as *demonstrate* what's important. Jack Welch, whose term at GE is the stuff of management legend these days, moved the organization (virtually 12 separate, huge companies at the time) beyond scandals and erratic results by insisting on both top performance *and* adherence to a highly ethical value system in conducting business. When I watched him field questions from managers going through GE's training center in Crotonville, New York, he consistently stressed these traits, and then exemplified them. (The old "Neutron Jack" had disappeared.)

Linda Henman is no stranger to these dynamics. She's what I call (and am happy to be a part of) the "pragmatic PhDs" who use psychological aspects to support their practical advice about change and growth (and who don't insist that clients fit some esoteric conceptual model). She has brought her vast experience, in environments ranging from manufacturing to the Air Force, to bear with a laser-like focus on a pivotal issue: how can you prepare for, acquit yourself well, and exemplify the "change-agent-in-chief" best practices for your organization once you've been designated to lead it?

Her observations and advice on tough decisions, former peers who are now subordinates, executing strategy (where almost all strategy failure occurs), team building, board building, and self-building would normally merit a shelf of books. With finesse and style she has managed to assemble it all here in one highly readable book that will become for you an extraordinarily dependable reference.

No matter where you are in the hierarchy, if you personally aspire to increasingly senior positions—or, already at the summit, you desire to help others in the succession system—*Landing in the Executive Chair* is the only resource of its kind that can so smoothly guide you through the rapids of accession.

Linda will guide you to a graceful landing. And when you rise from that chair, you'll be standing tall.

—Alan Weiss, PhD

Author of *Million Dollar Consulting* and
The Consulting Bible

Chapter 1

F² Leaders: Fair but Firm

We didn't come here just to fiddle with the controls. We came to change the direction of the ship.
—Ronald Reagan

As the Baby Boomers look toward retirement, the Generation Xers look forward to filling the vacated corner offices. However, the next generation of executives will face unprecedented challenges in the war for talent, ones complicated by a challenging economy, more global expansion, and decreasing availability and readiness of employees schooled in science, finance, and advanced technology. The pool of average workers may tend to swell for the foreseeable future, but as job markets tighten, the buyer's market for "A" players is not likely to change—at least not for the better—for organizations wanting to hire them.

Unless they can enjoy a substantial gain, usually 20 percent or more, people prefer to stay with a trusted leader; but in a good economy, a disgruntled employee will leave for as little as a 5-percent increase. When valued employees depart, however, fewer top performers will surface to fill key positions. The loss of an average employee can cost your organization the equivalent of one year of that person's salary; the departure of an "A" player often costs four times that person's salary. The competition for top talent will continue to escalate, but only those companies who have hired magnetic executives that no one wants to leave will be able to vie in the global marketplace. To keep top talent inside their doors, executives are learning that they must better understand leadership, their changing responsibilities, and the forces that will stack up against them.

The decisions that executives, especially CEOs, make during their first few months on the job have far-reaching implications and a decisive impact on whether they will ultimately succeed or fail. The transition promises opportunity and challenge, but it also often brings a period of great vulnerability, especially if board members and other stakeholders expect immediate changes and improved performance. Executives promoted from within the organization face the challenges and frustrations of redefining their relationships with people who were once peers. When the company hires a top executive from outside, that person must quickly learn the organization, and sometimes the industry, as well as new customers and products, and an unfamiliar culture. Each person will offer a unique perspective, but best practices for becoming a magnetic executive who will attract, retain, and develop stars remain constant. New executives must set the right tone, make effective decisions, and establish credibility—all daunting tasks. Yet few resources exist to help them. They frequently flounder in their attempts to create a competitive strategy, work with the board, and keep talent from going elsewhere, all the while endeavoring to navigate unfamiliar and turbulent waters.

New executives aren't the only ones who need help; leaders who have held the job for a number of years need direction too. As companies expand and grow, the skills that led to an individual's success often won't sustain further development in a more complex, high-stakes environment. They need more. They need a roadmap to success.

In my work with hundreds of executives, especially CEOs and CFOs, I have observed the critical elements of success, both for the new leader and the one who wants to perform at the next level of success. Avoiding the pitfalls is one element; identifying a clear path for personal and organizational success is the other.

What Does It Take To Be an Executive?

Specifically, what does executive leadership require? As I explain in Chapter 6, executive leadership builds on the traits and behaviors that you needed when you walked in on your shiny new first day: good decision-making, results orientation, leadership talent, and people skills. However, with each rung on the leadership ladder, the manifestation of those traits and behaviors becomes more complicated. Being an officer of the company, especially a member of the C-suite, creates demands that don't exist prominently at other levels. For example, you can expect that:

◊ People will lie to you and cover up mistakes.

◊ It will be lonely at the top.

◊ The buck will stop with you.

Prior to stepping into an executive role, the advice you might have followed may have been, "Show up. Keep up. Shut up." Though extremely good advice for a golf caddy, one-third of it is extraordinarily bad for an executive. Now you need to know how to speak up. You need to understand better those forces that will propel you further into the arena of success, and those that will jeopardize your journey.

However, no universally accepted definition of leadership, much less executive leadership, actually exists. Here's what I know after studying leadership for more than 30 years: if you were to put thought leaders from psychology, sociology, history, business, and the military in one room and ask them to come up with a definition of leadership they could all support, they'd never, ever agree on a definition. So how do we begin an exploration of this? I'd like you to consider the perspectives of several people whose opinions I trust.

David McCullough, the noted historian, has written numerous accounts of successful and controversial leaders. In an interview with *Harvard Business Review*, he gave some of his own opinions about leadership, observing that the struggles, visions, and ideals of our nation's founders can serve as a constant source of inspiration. His work underscores his belief that, even in the darkest times, optimism, hard work, and strength of character endure. But he also encourages leaders to develop a healthy respect for luck, chance, the hand of God—whatever you choose to call it—because it stands as a real force in human affairs. For example, Washington might have been killed early in the war; he might have gotten sick; he might have been captured; he might have given up. Washington was lucky, but he also knew how to take advantage of lucky moments because he possessed good judgment.

Some historians who have studied the American Revolutionary War think a miracle caused things to turn out as they did. Had the wind in New York City been coming from a different direction on August 29, 1776, Washington's night escape might not have been possible, but fortuitous conditions and stellar leadership determined the outcome.[1]

Lady Luck will play a role in your success too. You won't have control of how economic and political leaders throw the dice; forces of nature will work in your favor, or not; other circumstances will overcome your plans, or they won't. As much as most successful leaders love control, fortune may or may not smile on you. Certainly, the harder you work, the luckier you tend to be, but learning to accept those things you can't control and to concentrate only on the things you can will serve as the foundation of executive leadership.

No one understands the importance of concentrating on things one can control better than a general leading a war. Colin Powell, Former Secretary of State and Chairman of the Joint Chiefs of Staff, honed his leadership skills in Washington, but he developed them during his distinguished military career. During his leadership journey, General Powell learned that "Great leaders know that asking the right questions unearths problems and yields tremendous understanding about their customers, employees, and operations." He further offers these leadership lessons:[2]

◊   Don't be afraid to make people angry.

◊   Make yourself accessible.

◊   Don't be buffaloed by experts and elites.

◊   Never neglect the details.

◊   Don't wait for permission—just get things done.

◊   Surround yourself with the brightest and best.

◊   Don't tie your self-worth to your position.

◊   Understand that perpetual optimism is a force multiplier.

◊   Have fun.

◊   Understand that command is lonely.

Another former Chairman of the Joint Chiefs, General Richard Myers, shared with me his perceptions of what he thinks it takes to be an outstanding leader and echoed some of General Powell's opinions. General Myers noted the importance of agility of thought and an unwillingness to get tied to dogma. Like General Powell, General Myers understands the critical role of listening and probing for understanding. General Myers, however, more directly stressed the importance of getting along with others and the significance of selfless service. As he put it, "showing you care about people as individuals, and being a good communicator and collaborator" are critical to successful leadership. According to General Myers, leaders need to realize that *people*, after all, are what will enable them to be successful. People won't follow a leader very far if they see him or her as self-serving and disinterested in the organization.[3] Neither general stressed technical expertise or the so-called "hard skills" of leadership. Rather, each emphasized the role of self-awareness and people skills.

Although the qualities traditionally associated with leadership, such as intelligence, toughness, determination, and vision are required for success, they don't offer a complete picture of what leadership requires. In my work with senior leaders, I have found direct ties between self-awareness, self-regulation, motivation, empathy, social skill—and business results. Common sense suggests, the two former Chairmen of the Joint Chiefs imply, and my personal observations confirm, that without a responsive, fair orientation, people can have the best training, an analytical mind, and an endless supply of great ideas, but they still won't make great leaders.

This should not be confused with popularity, however. Frequently, others do not immediately perceive stellar performance, even when it stares them in the face. For example, everyone knows that Lincoln's most famous speech was the Gettysburg Address. Few, however know that he was an afterthought. The committee initially invited Edward Everett to be their main speaker. At the time, Everett was a widely-known orator and prestigious former Secretary of State, U.S Senator, U.S. Representative, Governor of Massachusetts, president of Harvard, and Vice Presidential candidate. In short, Everett's speech was to be the day's principal "Gettysburg Address." His now seldom-read 13,607-word oration lasted two hours. The speech was well received as scholarly, moving, and well delivered, and his popularity was pronounced.

Not long after those well-received remarks, Lincoln spoke in his high-pitched Kentucky accent for two or three minutes. Lincoln's "few appropriate remarks" summarized the war in 10 sentences. Partisan lines divided reaction to Lincoln's speech. The next day the Democratic-leaning *Chicago Times* observed, "The cheek of every American must tingle with shame as he reads the silly, flat, and dishwatery utterances of the man who has to be pointed out to intelligent foreigners as the President of the United States."[4] Everett's popularity overshadowed Lincoln's in 1863, but before you read this, would you have even recognized his name? As an executive, the soundness of your decisions needs to stand the test of time too, not just the flavor-of-the-month litmus test.

Complicated and complex, the recipe for leadership greatness differs according to the person you ask. Some assert that leaders can learn emotional intelligence and the requisite behaviors that support it. Others, like the trait theorists, argue that leaders are born, not made. Some cite characteristics like intelligence; others contend that nebulous talents such as charisma separate those who can from those who cannot lead. Whatever your opinion, one thing seems certain. Executives need a new way to understand the elements of leadership they can control. They need to understand how their leadership style may be contributing to or detracting from their leadership effectiveness.

A New Model of Leadership: F^2 Leadership

What accounts for the difference between the leader who rises steadily through the ranks of an organization versus the derailed executive whose career mysteriously jumps the track short of expectations? If people find the fast track in the first place, they probably know how to get the job done, have shown themselves to be honorable, and offer enough intellectual acumen to succeed. When a leader offers all these and still fails, flawed leadership *style* may be the culprit.

The Situational Leadership Theories of the 1960s started the discussion of leadership style, offering that effective leadership depends on a particular set of circumstances that should guide leaders to determine the optimum amount of direction and socio-emotional support they must provide. These theorists dispelled the notion that task and relationship define either/or styles of leadership. Instead, leadership style could be viewed as existing on a continuum, moving from very authoritarian leadership at one end to very democratic leadership behavior at the other.

Each theory differs slightly, but they collectively contend that the successful leader adapts to the unique demands of an ever-changing organization by diagnosing the needs and wants of followers and then reacting accordingly, remembering all the while that the group is becoming more experienced and less dependent on direction. However sound in their foundation, the theories are somewhat less than pragmatic in their approach, so beleaguered executives, looking for a model to help them, are hopelessly lost. What's a leader to do?

The F^2 Leadership Model explains the *behaviors*—not skills, talents, attitudes, or preferences—executives need to display to be effective. F^2 leaders have a balanced concern for task accomplishment and people issues. They are *firm* but *fair* leaders whom others trust, leaders who commit themselves to both relationship behavior and task accomplishment.

The model, which reflects the contributions of the Blake Mouton Managerial Grid, sets tension between opposing forces—firmness and fairness—to provide understanding and direction. In general, the model simplifies the way we think about the dynamic and complex dilemmas that characterize leadership style. In other words, it challenges us to ask ourselves how to have both a clear task orientation and an appreciation for the people who achieve the results.

The F^2 Model urges the student of leadership to use this framework to explore—to gain deeper meaning and arrive at more informed choices about leadership style. This model is truly more follower-driven than leader-driven. It keeps the leader's focus on those who count—the people in the organization who will define success. It helps leaders figure out whether they are losing balance, tending to act like Genghis Khan or Mr. Rogers.

The four-quadrant model is both *prescriptive* and *descriptive*. It allows leaders to understand their own behavior relative to their direct reports, but by its nature, it implies a preferred way of behaving. In other words, the model explains what leaders *should* do to be effective instead of merely describing what they tend to do or prefer to do. It explores two key dimensions of leadership: relationship behaviors, such as fairness, and task behaviors, such as firmness. When leaders lose the balance between fairness and firmness, they lose their effectiveness and compromise that of their direct reports. The model helps them analyze what they're doing and then make choices to move toward F^2 behavior. Keep in mind, the model addresses behavior and represents an ideal, so no person fits into one quadrant all the time. Leaders who want to be more magnetic strive for F^2 behavior, but they occasionally drift into one of the other quadrants. When this happens, problems occur, but awareness offers the first step toward remedy.

	Aggressor	**F^2 Leader**
	◊ Overly task-focused	◊ Firm but fair
		◊ Assertive
	◊ Controlling	◊ Responsive
	◊ Domineering	◊ Results-oriented
	◊ Insensitive	
Firm		
	Quit 'n' Stay	**Accommodator**
	◊ Apathetic	◊ Harmony-seeking
	◊ Not task-oriented	◊ Too friendly
	◊ Not people-centered	◊ Eager to please
	◊ Passive/aggressive	◊ Not task-oriented

Fair

The Aggressor

The upper-left quadrant represents leadership behavior that is too forceful and aggressive. The person whose behavior fits into this quadrant displays too much dominance and control and general insensitivity to others. Often aggressors justify their behavior because, in the short run, it gets results. Ironically, leaders often find themselves in this quadrant because of their own ability and success on the job, overlooking the fact that the performance of other people will now define their success. Although they recognize that they are practicing an autocratic style of leadership, they see no reason to change. They fail to notice anything detrimental about their behavior, even when they start to experience high turnover and have trouble retaining star performers.

The Quit 'N' Stay

The lower-left quadrant represents people who commit neither to task accomplishment nor to building relationships. People who display quit 'n' stay behavior too much or too often usually don't make it to the level of executive because they are cautious, unassertive, secretive, or submissive. They draw a paycheck, but they have retired on the job, often years before they actually walk out the door. They tend to drag their feet on decisions, take forever to accomplish a task, and avoid changes that will cause upheaval in their lives. Occasionally, burnout will cause an otherwise effective leader to start to display quit 'n stay, but unless he or she recovers quickly, this quadrant represents the surest and fastest way to fail.

The Accommodator

The lower-right quadrant describes the accommodator, the person who is highly sociable, overly optimistic, talkative, and eager to please. Notice that in all three quadrants, other than the F², the behaviors in question are *too* overboard. Being sociable and optimistic are arguably positive, endearing traits. But when they cause a person to gloss over conflicts, ignore troubling facts, give in for the sake of harmony, or spend inappropriate amounts of time socializing at work, they stand in the way of effective leadership. Leaders who can't make tough decisions or who won't give negative feedback fit into the accommodator quadrant. They are pleasant to work for and often engender affection and loyalty, but when the results are tallied, they fall short.

The F² Leader

The upper-right quadrant describes successful, magnetic executives. These leaders tend to be collaborative and democratic in their leadership style. They are highly skilled in task accomplishment, but they don't throw people under the bus to get the job done. They consistently show a greater capacity to look ahead, to define purpose and direction, to coordinate the activities of others, and to support the organization's strategy better than leaders in the other quadrants. Direct reports, peers, and other leaders value F² leaders because they not only get things done, but they do so in a manner that motivates the people around them. Their balanced leadership style brings out the best performance in others, and accounts, in large part, for their success. F² leaders challenge others to deliver their best; they stay focused, and demand excellence. They allow the situation, not their own mood or tendencies, to determine the degree of forcefulness they will use.

Therefore, the basis of F² Leadership—equal parts of fairness and firmness—involves the constant realigning of these two concerns and serves as the cornerstone of effectiveness. F² Leadership requires the ability to do what needs to be done, when it needs to be done, whether or not you want to do it. It involves a desire to lead, the intelligence to learn quickly, the analytical reasoning to solve unfamiliar, complex problems, a strong action orientation, integrity, and people skills. With the exception of people skills, most of these are both resistant to change and difficult to develop. The good news is that though flawed interpersonal skills often cause leadership derailment, leaders who possess the other characteristics can learn these interpersonal skills, the one set that will have the greatest impact on their success. Therefore, becoming a firm but fair leader that others trust is at the heart of sustaining effective leadership.

But none of it is easy. Probably the toughest aspect of developing better interpersonal skills involves the aforementioned tricky balance leaders face between concern for people and a focus on results. Without a strong bias for action, leaders don't succeed. Effective leadership demands dominance, the exercising of control or influence. It means being assertive, putting forth ideas, and striving to influence the way others turn ideas into action. Dominant leaders take charge, guiding, leading, persuading, and moving other people to achieve results. Instead of *letting* things happen, they *make* things happen.

But without a strong concern for the people who can deliver the results, leaders aren't effective either. Balancing dominance and responsiveness requires constant recalibration, a challenge with which even the most seasoned leaders struggle. The F² Leader who wants both results and strong professional relationships should strive to keep the following in mind:

- ◇ Demand results through involvement. Set tough goals and insist on analytical approaches.

- ◇ Get to know your people, their strengths, their weaknesses, and their motivators, and then deal with each person as a unique individual.

- ◇ Maintain an "us-centered" mentality.

- ◇ Demonstrate concern and responsiveness. Rather than merely trying to please direct reports for the moment, work with them to uncover their concerns, and then balance these with the needs of the organization.

- ◇ Put disagreements and problems on the table as soon as you perceive them. Don't wait until you are angry or until a crisis is brewing to talk about them.

Sustaining a dedication to excellent results and a commitment to your people will be a huge step toward building trust, an essential component of F² Leadership. Although essential for creating a trusting, trustworthy organization, personal integrity isn't enough. Developing *behaviors* that indicate you have integrity is also crucial. Like interpersonal skills, the behaviors can be taught and learned.

Building trust within an organization, a complicated and fragile process, requires unwavering attention on the part of the leaders at all levels of the organization. Employees need to have trust in the people who lead the organization. They have to believe that decision makers have the vision and competence to set the right course, allocate resources intelligently, fulfill the mission, and help the company succeed. They want to feel confident that processes are well designed, consistent, and fair. Does the company make good on its promises? Research demonstrates that links definitely exist between trust and corporate performance, and common sense indicates that, all other things being equal, people will stay with the trusted leader.

Just as importantly, employees want to trust their own leaders. When determining if their boss merits personal trust, people ask themselves, "Does my boss treat me and others fairly? Does he or she consider the employees' needs when making decisions? Will he or she put the company's needs ahead of personal desires?" The answers often shape both the nature of the trust and the quantity of it.

But what can a boss actually *do* to build this climate of trust with direct reports? Obviously some aspects, like organizational trust, might be outside the purview of a particular leader, but there are many things the boss can do:

◊   Send consistent messages. One of the fastest-moving destroyers of trust—inconsistent messages—can occur at any level of the organization. Often leaders can't do anything about the strategic or organizational trust issues in their companies, but they can certainly make sure they don't send mixed or inconsistent messages. Predictability defines the heart of trust, and direct reports expect it. They want to know they can trust their leaders to do what they say they will; they won't overlook a leader's tendencies not to follow through.

For instance, when I coached Nan, her direct reports told me though she frequently told them how much she valued them, she didn't keep scheduled appointments with them. She took calls when they met for performance reviews and showed up late for meetings with them, each act sending the loud and clear message that indeed they were *not* important to her. Employees who have this kind of boss can be counted on to disengage, to focus on rumors and politics, and to update their resumes. Nan created an environment in which her direct reports did not trust her, but as we continued our work together, I discovered she didn't trust them either. The reasons for high turnover in Nan's department didn't stay a mystery for long.

◊ Trust others. One of the phenomena of human behavior is that *trustworthy* people are also usually *trusting* people. As the saying goes, a man only looks behind a door if he has hidden behind several himself. If leaders can't trust their direct reports, one of two things is wrong: either they simply won't trust because of their own exaggerated need for control, or the direct report has given them reason not to trust.

For example, I worked with Mike, a vice president who routinely worked a 70-hour week. He complained that he had no life balance, and his wife was tired of shouldering all the family responsibilities herself. When I probed more, I learned some of the reasons he worked so many hours on a consistent basis. He failed to delegate because he wanted to ensure quality— an exaggerated need for control—and he didn't trust at least one of his direct reports to account for expenses accurately. Therefore, Mike worked too much, primarily because he suffered from both trust afflictions: he wouldn't delegate full responsibility for projects, and he reviewed expense accounts to make sure no one cheated.

To remedy this situation, Mike needed to face two separate issues, but trust related to them both. First, he needed to let his direct reports know that he trusted them to do their jobs, their way, without his micromanagement. Second, Mike needed to let them know that he expected integrity in their expense reporting. One of his direct reports had previously cheated on his expense report by taking his wife to dinner on the company. This sort of violation should result in the direct report being punished with either a stern, formal reprimand, or dismissal. Mike should not have punished himself by taking on the additional duties of reviewing all expenses, something an administrative assistant can usually handle.

⬥ Keep policies and standards uniform. When leaders play favorites and allow a few pet performers to bend the rules, others notice. Consider the boss who doesn't like confrontation. He turns a blind eye to the fact that a select few do not adhere to the company's rules regarding flex time, signing in and out, using work time for doctor's appointments, etc. If you establish a rule, everyone should be required to uphold it. If you don't consider an issue important enough to have a company policy about, don't bother with it. The "hot stove" form of leadership applies here. No matter who touches the stove, it's hot, and the person touching it will get burned, no matter the person's position in the organization or the favor the boss feels for the person who touches it.

In other words, don't have a policy about something unless you are willing to fire your most valuable employee for violating it. If you think a problem important enough to make a rule about it, consider it important enough to fire or discipline the company's star for violating it.

⬥ Expect competence, high-quality performance, and decent behavior from everyone. Whether the person is a genius, technical expert, top salesperson, rainmaker, or company curmudgeon, the same standards should apply, but often they don't. Leaders tend to overlook people who operate at one end of the continuum or the other. Too often top performers get away with volatile behavior and tantrums, both appalling behaviors in any organization. On the other hand, leaders often close their eyes to the under-performer's unacceptable behavior simply because they don't want the confrontation that may occur when they address it. Once again, others notice, and they resent the company's tolerating problematic employees.

◊ Give honest, balanced feedback. How many times have I had conversations with frustrated human resource managers because obviously a person needs to be fired, but the recent performance reviews were glowing? A legitimate question a lawyer would ask in a wrongful termination hearing might be, "If this employee was bad enough to fire, how do you explain these scores on his last appraisal?"

In addition to causing headaches for the company, this kind of dishonest feedback fails to help the direct report develop skills or take actions to better performance. Similarly, if everyone receives the same bonus and raises, what incentive do people have to work hard for stellar performance? Motivation may come from within, but only for a while. People tend to object to unfair treatment that they can't control. The boss who engages in flawed feedback, which is neither fair nor firm, invites others to weigh in by voting with their feet as they walk out the door.

Why It's Tough to Be Fair

Fairness costs little and pays handsomely. Why then don't more leaders manage to behave fairly? In a nutshell, fairness and responsiveness take time—the non-renewable commodity that so many executives hold most dear. Jumping in to fix problems, telling people what to do instead of mentoring them, and maintaining your action orientation involve less time than keeping your concern for people as high as your concern for task accomplishment. Magnetic leaders do well to understand the role fairness plays in their ability to attract and retain top talent. Ultimately, each person decides whether you have behaved fairly, but you can take steps to stack the deck in your favor.

But it isn't about making popular decisions. Well-supported decisions don't usually define great, much less adequate, leadership. As an executive, you will be called upon to weigh the pros and cons and make the decision that serves the company best. However, the *process* you use to arrive at it can determine whether your employees see you as fair or unfair.

Perhaps the most important step in establishing a fair process involves seeking and considering input from stakeholders. People realize you can't and won't always give them their first choice, but if you never bother to find out what that would have been, you can't possibly respond to their issues, much less create the perception that you are behaving fairly. Listening takes time in the short run, but it pays in the long run.

At a recent retirement party of an Air Force four-star general, I asked one of the guests what he most appreciated about the general's leadership. Without hesitation, he responded, "He is a listener. He hears all sides of an argument before he makes a decision." I doubt this man liked every decision the general made, but because this general consistently engaged his people and truly considered their opinions, he created a fair process that made his decision-making both predictable and transparent. At the same event, one of the generals in the four-star's chain of command told me he would miss working for someone who is "such a gentleman." He went on to explain that no matter how contentious the subject or how bad the news, this general never raised his voice, lost his temper, or treated the people in the room disrespectfully.

This illustrates the basic premise of the importance of fair leadership. Even if people don't agree with the outcome and even if they don't get what they want, if they think you have heard them and have treated them well during the process, they will usually support you and the decision. Common sense suggests, and research confirms, that people who are treated fairly embrace rather than sabotage organizational change. Disgruntled employees seldom produce innovative solutions, and they almost never stay with a leader who disgruntled them in the first place. As Winston Churchill responded after his countrymen castigated him for his deferential tone in his declaration of war to the Japanese, "When you have to kill a man, it costs nothing to be polite." Indeed, fairness costs less than little; it costs nothing.

Why It's Fair to Be Tough

When I introduce the F^2 Leadership Model to groups, one of the first reactions I usually hear is, "Linda, sometimes you can't worry too much about being nice. Sometimes you just have to get the job done." Although solid in its foundation, this philosophy misses the essence of the model. Leaders should never compromise toughness. Leadership involves a continuous diet of making one difficult decision after the next, and yes, sometimes you just have to get the job done. But never do you need to do it unfairly.

Several years ago I was coaching a CEO, Jack, who needed to establish some boundaries with one of the members of the board of directors. He had scheduled a dinner to outline for this director his plethora of complaints. The trouble Jack faced was that he had waited so long to address these issues that he was really angry. He had shot right past firmness to aggression. If he had pursued the conversation as he had intended, he would have done irreparable damage to his relationship with this director, and possibly to the board in general. After a lengthy discussion of his emotions and thoughts, Jack realized his goal: to address the director's behavior and request a different path for the two of them. When he was able to do this—to put aside the anger in favor of toughness—he had control of the conversation, and ultimately of the outcome. Like many others, Jack had trouble balancing fairness and firmness, or in this situation, nonassertive behavior and aggression. Firmness demands forcefulness, directness, and assertiveness. It does not require domination, aggression, bad manners, or losing your temper. A piece of advice that I heard early in my career is one I pass on to each of my coaching clients: remember, if you lose control, someone else will have it.

I seldom encounter a low degree of toughness in my coaching clients, but it does happen. Usually the executive knows the best course of action, but because that path will require upsetting people, making unpopular choices, or terminating someone, they put off rather than address the problem. Here's something I've observed and believe: bad news seldom gets better with age. Gathering data and considering multiple perspectives are laudable; dragging your feet because you don't want to make the hard call is not. Here are some of the questions I use with my coaching clients to help them make a difficult decision:

◊ How much longer can this go on before you experience more negative consequences?

◊   What else would this person have to do before you'd think firing was warranted?

◊   What adverse effects might occur if you do nothing?

◊   What opportunities might you miss if you do nothing?

Answering these for yourself when you face the tough call can often help you view the situation dispassionately and objectively, rather than emotionally. When you can deal with the facts and put aside your irrational feelings, you will have taken a huge step. It truly is lonely at the top, and often you won't enjoy popularity while there, but if you and your organization want success, it is fair to be tough.

Derailers: Executive Mistakes That Interfere With Success

Leadership style, personality traits, and emotional intelligence account for much of an executive's success or lack thereof. But executives can engage in other destructive behaviors that will cause them to compromise or damage their own chances for success, too. Although somewhat counterintuitive, I've seen irrefutable evidence that one of the major reasons for executive ruin is the tendency to overuse a strength to the point that it becomes a weakness. To wit: overachievers, at some point, can run amok, focusing too intensely on achievement while demolishing trust and morale. Gregarious leaders build enviable relationships but fall short of hitting targets. Brilliant thinkers analyze data adeptly but then fail to find out if anyone else will support their ideas. Here are some more specific examples of how executives can play a role in their own demise:

An Imbalance of Fairness and Firmness

Consider Bill, the CEO and owner of a small consulting firm that sold about $10 million a year of services. Bill's professional staff of nine included the best and brightest in the field, but he lost about one of these top performers a year, chiefly because none of his direct reports knew which Bill would show up to work: the aggressor or the accommodator. On a given day, Bill would scold a person in front of others, raise his voice, and charge through the office like a bull who carried his own china closet with him. On another day, avuncular Bill would engage in solicitous conversation with each member of his team, often distracting them from the task they needed to do, causing them to have stay to late or to take work home.

When you consider that each person who left the company cost more than $100,000 in turnover expenses, and add the loss of corporate memory and client relationships, conservative estimates put Bill's losses at about a quarter to half a million dollars a year, a considerable chunk of the firm's annual billing. Yet Bill refuses to change, so he continues to derail both his own success and that of his company. Many things could explain Bill's behavior and failure to advance, but I have always suspected Bill lacked fundamental self-awareness—the fact that he never solicited feedback from his direct reports and never changed his behavior based on mine—thereby removing any chance of gaining the perspective that would have helped him advance.

Lack of Self-Awareness

When I begin a coaching relationship with clients, my first goal is to build on the self-awareness they possess and to provide new insights. When I give feedback about assessment results or multi-rater feedback, people seldom register dismay. More often they wonder how I could know that much so quickly. As the coaching progresses, I look for the clients' willingness to grow in their understanding of their emotions, strengths, weaknesses, motivations, fears, and values.

Frequently people know certain things about themselves but lack the understanding of how to use the information to change their lives. Self-aware people tend to be more honest with themselves and others, so they start from a position of knowledge. On the other hand, people who lack self-awareness don't know where to start.

Consider Louise, a smart woman who understood neither her strengths nor her limitations. She had the ability to think analytically but lacked empathy. She could solve unfamiliar problems, but because she had such regrettable people skills, she couldn't build cohesion, much less collaboration.

She failed to recognize how her feelings affected her, other people, and her job performance.

Once Louise concentrated on self-awareness, she was better able to leverage her strengths to mitigate her limitations. She better understood the kinds of situations that caused her frustrations and angst and how to develop ways to avoid situations that caused her to perform at less than optimum levels. When people like Louise learn to assess themselves realistically, they avoid the inner turmoil that comes from treading on their values or putting themselves in situations where they can't possibly succeed. Self-awareness means having a deep understanding of one's self, a celebration of talents and an acceptance of limitations. Self-awareness implies a balance of self-perception, not unhealthy self-love.

Narcissism

Narcissism describes the trait of excessive self-love, based on self-image or ego. The term comes from the Greek mythology of Narcissus, a hero renowned for his beauty. He was exceptionally cruel, however, in that he scorned those who loved him. As divine punishment he fell in love with a reflection in a pool, not realizing it was his own, and perished there, not being able to leave the beauty of his own reflection.

In adults, especially successful leaders, a reasonable dose of healthy narcissism allows people to balance their needs in relation to those of others. It spurs them on to greatness, because they expect it of themselves. Taken to a pathological extreme, however, it causes people to have a grandiose sense of self-importance, a preoccupation with power, a belief that rules don't apply to them, a need for excessive admiration, a sense of entitlement, and a lack of empathy. Their tendency toward grandiosity and distrust creates their Achilles' heel, and often their demise.

Narcissists thrive in chaos, so they tend to create it. They crave control, so when they feel it slipping away, they create turmoil and then save the day with their efforts. Considering themselves bullet-proof, they disregard caution and listen only for information they seek. Sensitive to criticism, narcissistic leaders shun emotion and keep others at arm's length. They don't care what others think and won't tolerate dissent.

History provides numerous examples of social and political leaders who created their own downfall because they allowed ego or a sense of importance to cloud their judgment. Clinton's lies under oath, Nixon's Watergate cover-up, and Kennedy's infamous Bay of Pigs invasion all showcase how a leader, sometimes one who has otherwise led impressively, can create his own permanent or temporary collapse. More recent examples of narcissists fashioning their own ruin grace the pages of the *Wall Street Journal* nearly every day. The permanent or temporary nature of the downfall often has to do with whether a person can learn from mistakes. For example, unlike many others who continued on the path of narcissism, after the Bay of Pigs invasion, President Kennedy admitted his mistakes, accepted full responsibility, and altered the course of history in his stellar leadership during the Cuban Missile Crisis.

Often narcissism shows up early in a career, but from my experience, it frequently surfaces later, sometimes in someone who has been fabulously successful for decades. In these cases, it causes the person to derail at the critical time before he achieves executive status and wreaks havoc at a critical juncture. Phil, a career military officer, offers a perfect example of how this can happen. The golden boy of his ROTC wing in college, an honors graduate from Undergraduate Pilot Training, and the distinguished graduate from his advanced training class, he showed nothing but promise. Yet, as his confidence grew, so did his symptoms. In social settings, his grandiose sense of self-importance induced him to dominate conversations. His self-absorption caused him to lose his family and friends; but his heartfelt belief that the rules didn't apply to him brought him down, both literally and figuratively.

For the first 10 years of his career, Phil made modest attempts to hide the ways he violated the Uniform Code of Military Justice, which forbids adultery and relations with enlisted women. Later, however, he flaunted the rules, almost daring someone to challenge his power and authority. In all fairness, Phil did get away with breaking the rules for almost 20 years, and at the time of his forced retirement, he was being considered for a major promotion. But then he derailed.

The first strike to Phil's house of cards came from a general who noticed the aberrant behavior seven years before the forced retirement. When the squadron transitioned to a more advanced aircraft, the general did not allow Phil to retrain. But the coup de grace did not come until several years later, when a disgruntled enlisted woman disclosed that, in violation of protocol, she and many others had engaged in inappropriate relations with Phil. To avoid the publicity of a court martial, the senior leaders asked him to resign. He lost his job, his marriage, his children, and the regard of many friends. Narcissists like Phil often enjoy a long run of success, but when they begin to flounder, they founder soon after, and their recklessness often causes them to crash and burn beyond recognition. Sometimes their egos orchestrated the crash; at other times recklessness played a role.

Recklessness

Recklessness and the headstrong desire for self-fulfillment it brings have caused many leaders to strike a Faustian bargain that led them in a diabolical direction. Recklessness, an identifiable behavior among narcissists, explains how and why leaders can fall prey to stunningly poor lapses in judgment. It has contributed to the ruin of religious leaders such as Jimmy Baker and Jerry Falwell, and corporate titans like WorldCom's Bernard Ebbers and Enron's Kenneth Lay. Like Icarus, who disregarded his father's advice and soared too high and too close to the sun, these once-admired leaders became reckless and fell. But how do you attempt to soar above competitors without melting the wax on your wings? Smart risk takers define the playing field for everyone else by taking calculated risks and anticipating the future, not by idiocy and folly.

In his best-selling book, *First, Break All the Rules*, Marcus Buckingham advocated a contrarian view of conventional business thinking, but he never intimated that rules are for fools. Certainly, creative thinking challenges paradigms, but it needn't threaten integrity. In a never-ending attempt to bring about improvement, thought leaders consistently and constantly challenge traditional approaches. They experiment, theorize, press for new solution, and pioneer innovation. Yet, effective leaders never lose sight of the value of convention, even while pushing for change. Challenge the status quo, but don't crush it for the sake of doing something different or a desire for excitement. To continue the playing field metaphor, every basketball player realizes that if you never foul, you aren't playing hard enough; however, five fouls will land you on the bench. Your team deserves better than a leader who fouls out or fails to deliver.

Lack of Empathy

Another hallmark of narcissism, a lack of empathy, explains further reasons executives fall and fail. Almost all narcissists lack empathy, and by definition, all sociopaths and psychopaths do, but not all those who are un-empathic are narcissists or mentally ill. Some lack insight. Others just don't care.

Empathy builds on self-awareness, because the more people are open to their own emotions, the more adept they will be at reading those of others. However, when people are confused about their own feelings, they are absolutely bewildered by those of others. During interactions, they lose the nuances of conversation—the notes and chords that weave through the exchange often communicate far more than the actual words themselves.

All empathy is not created equal, however. In my work with executives, I have found they often display one or both of two kinds of empathy. The first kind is what I call "no dog in the fight empathy," which occurs when a person has no vested interest in the outcome. This sort of empathy requires no true understanding or compassion. It allows people to excel at expressing the appropriate reaction to someone's bad news, dutifully show up at funerals, send flowers to congratulate, and generally display social astuteness to match the occasion. Almost everyone has some degree of this kind of empathy. People who only possess this kind of empathy don't lack sensitivity in all circumstances, just ones that involve someone contradicting them. They can appear very attuned to others' feelings—just not when those feelings represent a threat to the narcissist's world view.

The second kind of empathy causes people to identify closely with others and their problems. People who exhibit this kind of empathy are truly concerned about others, value close emotional ties, celebrate others' triumphs, and feel upset by their misfortunes, even when feeling these reactions is not convenient. From a business standpoint, people who demonstrate this kind of empathy tend to be able to put themselves in another's shoes, even during conflict, and to imagine what another person might feel or fear in any interaction.

Lack of empathy, probably the most rampant of the derailers, manifests itself in a variety of destructive ways. Often it shows up as a complete inability to listen to, much less consider, an alternative point of view. At other times, those who have difficulty feeling or displaying empathy appear emotionally aloof. They do not allow feelings to intrude on their decision-making and prefer impersonal relationships to close ones. Generally unresponsive to those around them, they display little compassion for other people's problems, especially if the problems create a threat to work accomplishment or some other stake the leader has in the ground. Executives who cannot or will not express empathy regularly put their relationships at risk, causing those around them to question whether they want to stay. The remedy, listening, is easy and painless, but unfortunately, not widespread among those who suffer from an empathy affliction.

Failure to Listen

Active listening provides the surest and more effective antidote for lack of empathy. If you truly listen to another—not just stay quiet while he or she speaks—but truly listen for both facts and feelings, you will have taken a giant step for mankind. When I conduct multi-rater feedback interviews, the number-one weakness direct reports identify in their leaders is a failure to listen. Direct reports tell me their leaders usually display some sort of telling behavior that indicates the end of the conversation, or at least a reduction in empathy. For instance, the boss will start looking at papers on the desk, glance over at the computer, interrupt, or produce audible interrupters such as the hurried "uh huh," all sure-fire signals that the boss is too busy or simply doesn't care. The importance of listening will be a recurring theme throughout this book, but I'd like to address it here as a derailer.

Successful leaders take the time to understand the issues, their people, and the underlying emotions. They invest the time to probe for understanding and then patiently work through solutions that help both the quality of the decision and the development of the direct report. Executives who are too busy to do either often find themselves acting as talent repellents instead of talent magnets.

Failure to Hire the Best and Brightest

In Chapter 6, I will go into more detail about the importance of hiring the best and brightest to support your strategy, but at this juncture, let me mention that failure to do so will contribute to your personal failure and that of your organization. A Players want to play on a team with other A Players. They will tolerate a B Player but won't suffer a C player too long or too much, and they will often leave if you force a D Player into the mix.

Often, however, decision makers fear that a stronger player coming in may usurp their position. They want to guard the sovereignty of their role and not give those above them reason to question who should be in charge. Then too, companies often don't want to pay the premium of hiring the best and brightest.

Derailed executives often have a knack for not selecting and attracting talented individuals. They fail to establish their organizations as a place where people can maximize their skills and abilities with minimal bureaucratic interference. That's one explanation for the failure. Another is that they forget they must commit to the continuous and constant task of selecting, molding, and grooming of top talent. It costs money, it takes time, and it takes courage. But failure to do so dooms your company to mediocrity.

For example, while working with a COO, Jane, I commented that the turnover at her company was unusually high and her staff strangely undercompensated. In spite of the enormous sums the company paid each year in turnover costs and temporary agency charges, Jane refused to authorize raises, commenting that "we pay the average." I pointed out that they had hired me to make sure they didn't hire average people, and the turnover costs in one year would more than fund the raises to attract and keep A

Players. Jane doomed herself and her company to run-of-the-mill results because of an unwillingness to pay top talent its worth. Whether fear of competition, refusal to pay a competitive salary, or just plan inability to recognize talent explains your situation, if you don't attract and keep the best and brightest in your industry, your competitors will.

Failure to Be the Best and Brightest

When coaching executives, I frequently encounter a widespread and nefarious trend—they have begun the process of stagnation. School is behind them, they have met the continuing education requirements, or they think they are simply too busy to spend time on learning. People who spent thousands of dollars a year pursuing a degree to get them where they are hesitate to spend hundreds a year on continued development.

Some industries change more quickly than others, but no matter the nature of your work, you need to be learning about your industry, leadership, the world, and people. Formal training and classes often help, but so does reading. Protecting time each day for learning and steadfastly pushing yourself to improve are the first steps. They will help you in your own advancement, but they will also make you a better judge of the talent you encounter. Continuous learning should be a priority for you and those you lead because, in general, it will equip you to set better priorities.

Failure to Set Priorities

Peter Drucker once said, "There is surely nothing quite so useless as doing with great efficiency what should not be done at all," which highlights the confusion between effectiveness and efficiency—between doing the right things and doing things right.[5] In Chapter 4, I will more directly address the necessity of prioritizing goals to support the strategy, but a failure to set priorities defines a more basic derailer.

Productive managers realize they can't do it all. We are each limited by the hours in the day, our energy level, budgets, and the support we receive—just to name a few. Prioritizing, the sense of what's mission-critical and what's nice to do, therefore, separates those who rise to the top and those who fall. Several reasons explain an otherwise effective leader's inability to prioritize: a belief that everything's equally important, an addiction to activity, poor time management, or an unwillingness to set boundaries. Without clear priorities, leaders tend to create activity traps for their direct reports. In these cases, everyone works long hours trying to make virtually everything perfect, but nothing of importance actually gets done—largely because everyone is too worn out from addressing inconsequential activities to work on the important ones. Even though a commitment to excellence distinguishes the average executive from the successful one, an inability to make distinctions among tasks and a predisposition to perfectionism create the slippery slope for a leader's derailment.

Perfectionism

Perfectionism, an overuse of detail orientation to the point that it causes analysis paralysis, contributes mightily to failure. Successful executives have a keen eye for the critical details but don't usually concern themselves with the unimportant ones. They zero in on what needs to be done and demand accuracy and precision on those things that truly matter but don't squander their time and that of others on the inconsequential.

Few things in life need to be perfect—brain surgery and taxes being the exceptions. Yet many focused and determined people mistakenly believe the adage, "If it's worth doing, it's worth doing well." Most things don't need to be done well; some things just need to be done. When you're 80-percent ready, move. The time you will spend gathering the data for the other 20-percent accuracy may be the critical time it took your competitor to launch the new product, initiative, or service. Think of perfectionism and recklessness on a continuum, neither extreme offering the best course of action. Neither folly nor precision defines great business decisions; bold innovation does.

Conclusion

When I ask people what they think it takes to be a great leader, their first response is usually "vision." Without question, effective leadership requires a strategic focus, but remember, people in mental institutions have visions, too. Seeing into the future is not enough; magnetic leadership requires more. Talent magnets understand they must lead better than their competitors; they need to inspire loyalty through firm but fair leadership; and they ought to avoid the pitfalls that will force an end to their own success. Even though their personalities and management styles may differ, executives who make it to the top, and stay there, share some common traits: they have a sense of proportion in their leadership styles and lives; they possess a high degree of self-awareness and self-regulation; and they maintain a long-term focus. They are willing to delay reward for the bigger payoff. Daunting? Probably. But remember the lessons of the "Rule of 70": If you improve 1 percent a day, in 70 days you'll be twice as good. Once committed to your own excellence, you can grow exponentially.

Chapter 2

Control the Hinges of Destiny: Decision-Making and Problem-Solving

Choices are the hinges of destiny.
—Edwin Markam

When senior leaders consistently make good decisions, little else matters; when they make bad decisions, *nothing* else matters. Effective decision-making stands at the center of executive leadership. As you climbed the stairs to your current position, others called on you to solve problems and occasionally to make decisions. But now you define most of your day by these two critical functions—decision-making and problem-solving—the hinges of your destiny and that of your organization. Each time you engage in either, you stand at a pivot, a turning point that will take you in directions that will contribute to your success or demise. Influencing the lives and livelihoods of others makes each of your calls more important. Thus, learning more how to use both defines the very essence of your continued success.

If decision-making and problem-solving were predictable, static events, they would involve more science than art—something that could be taught, learned, and controlled. They're not. Successful decisions involve a systematic evaluation of alternatives and realistic actions. Much depends, however, on the leader understanding the dynamics of decision-making, which include the elements that contribute to, and detract from, individual and group decision-making effectiveness. More knowledge of how to improve the process will better ensure a profitable outcome.

The Differences Between Problem-Solving and Decision-Making

Actually, you've been solving problems all your life. By definition, problem-solving involves the process of finding a solution to something that needs to change or a deviation from what you expected to happen. It involves a multistage process for moving an issue or situation from an undesirable to a more advantageous condition, and typically involves a process for answering the following questions:

◊   What changed? When? Why?

◊   What is the tangible evidence that you have a problem?

◊   How can you measure the magnitude of the problem?

◊   What caused the change?

◊   Is this change or deviation consequential enough to spend time resolving it?

Once you have the answers to these questions, you can start to evaluate alternatives and to overcome the obstacle that stand between them and a satisfactory resolution. There are many ways to do this, but these are among the most effective.

The Steps of Reflective Thinking

In 1910 John Dewey introduced the "Steps of Reflective Thinking," a systematic approach to problem-solving and a solid foundation for decision-making. The following sequence creates a kind of "map" of the problem:

◊   Define or identify the problem.

   ♦   What is wrong?

   ♦   What are the symptoms?

   ♦   When did this happen?

   ♦   How big is it?

- Whom does it affect?

- What have we already tried?

- What will happen if we do nothing?

One of the most successful ways to help groups begin the analysis process originated with Sakichi Toyoda, who developed a technique that Toyota Motor Corporation later used during the evolution of their manufacturing methodologies. The architect of the Toyota Production System, Taiichi Ohno, described the "5 Whys" method as the basis of Toyota's scientific approach. According to Ohno, by asking "why?" five times, the nature of the problem and its solution become clear.[1]

The "5 Whys" have become almost catechistical for many organizations, especially those in manufacturing, and the technique is now used within Kaizen, lean manufacturing, and Six Sigma initiatives. When someone presents a problem, the "whys" begin: Why can't we fulfill that order? Why are we out of stock? Why did we let the inventory get too low? As the questions continue, the group moves close to the core issue, which is, How do we balance the need to respond quickly to customer requests with a need to keep inventory low? Once everyone agrees about the nature of the issue, the individual decision maker or group can then plan implementation of the best solution using the following process:

- Analyze the problem and set criteria for possible solutions.

  - What conditions led to the present problem?

  - What criteria must a satisfactory solution offer?

- Brainstorm possible solutions.

- Evaluate potential solutions.

  - What do the experts say?

  - What risks and rewards does each possible solution offer?

  - How well do solutions meet the established criteria?

  - How practical is the solution?

⬧   Select the best solution.

     ◆   How do we execute this decision?

     ◆   What timeframe makes sense for solving this problem?

This approach has been modified and questioned through the years, but one principle remains clear: a structured approach to problem-solving increases the chances that you and your team will arrive at a workable resolution.

Surviving decades of scrutiny, Dewey's approach has stood the test of time because it offers a reasonable start to almost any problem-solving situation. When groups use this technique singly, however, they too often stop at symptoms rather than digging deeper to root causes. Further, the members' current knowledge and inability to ask the right "why" questions can limit their analysis. Fortunately, other methods like the 2 × 2 Matrix, can challenge the group to go beyond obvious answers and simple solutions.

The Magic of the 2 × 2 Matrix

The purpose of the 2 × 2 Matrix is to look at two variables influencing something that matters to the organization, like profitability and time. Placing these two on a standard x-y grid enables you to analyze the tension between opposing forces. The horizontal axis represents a This/Not This (low/high, past/present, etc.) issue that stands in tension with the vertical axis that characterizes another This/Not This situation—cost versus benefit, product versus market, or change versus stability, etc. Thinking in a 2 × 2 Matrix recognizes the power of exploring competing forces as we challenge ourselves to think at a higher logical level and to put aside emotional ties to solutions. It helps us see both sides of an issue, even when we face a paradoxical situation.[2]

The 2 × 2 Matrix represents, perhaps, the most notable analytical tool ever to emerge in business. It has, however, been much-maligned, mistrusted, and misunderstood, chiefly because the people using it didn't understand it. Like any other tool, it can only be as good as its least able workman. For instance, when tactical thinkers use the 2 × 2 Matrix, they find themselves frustrated because they can merely generate a colossal list of stuff that lacks perspective on the underlying factors that contribute to the problem. Or, they miss the links that connect various principles or phenomena. So, the first step in capturing the magic of the matrix is to include strong strategic, analytical thinkers in the exercise. (For a list of how to spot strategic thinkers, see Chapter 4.)

In Chapter 4, I introduce a 2 × 2 Matrix to help decision makers better understand how to explore and unearth the inherent tensions between strategy and tactics. The act of focusing on these variables does not simplify the analysis. On the contrary, decision makers can gain deeper understanding of their issues and learn more about their challenges when they break business down to manageable components and discuss competing priorities, in this case of tactics and strategy.

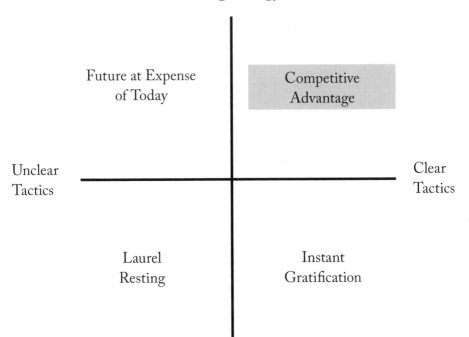

When you and your team face a problem, tools such as the 2 × 2 Matrix can help you and your team restore things to what they were before the problem arose. Remember, however, that reinstating the status quo won't take your organization forward; it will just keep you from slipping backwards, often a vital first step.

Too often senior leaders allow themselves and their team to focus on the past. In futile attempts to rewrite history, they concentrate on corrective or adaptive actions—activities that will keep everyone busy but won't really move the organization forward. Preventing problems before they arise, or planning for contingencies if they do, would be time better spent. But, too frequently, reinstating or maintaining the status quo sets the agenda, as decision makers overlook ways to move toward renewed success. Therefore, the next step is to learn to use the 2 × 2 Matrix as an instrument for making better decisions.

Decision-making, as opposed to problem-solving, involves choosing from among several alternatives to move the company forward, to change what you've been doing to support a strategy that promises innovation and growth. *Managers* fill their days with problem-solving; successful *executives* know they have to do more. Even though decision-making usually only takes a small fraction of their time, it defines one of their specific tasks: to make decisions that have a significant impact on the entire organization, its performance, and its results. Effective executives do not make a great many decisions; instead, they concentrate on the important ones. They focus on the highest level of conceptual understanding to think through what is strategic and generic, rather than tactical and problematic. However, the actions needed to carry out the strategic decision should be as simple as possible, otherwise the decision will degenerate into a good intention.

Executive vs. Group Decision-Making

Before deciding whether to make the decision alone or to involve others, determine if a decision must be made at all. Deciding not to decide should not be equated with indecision, which occurs when a leader *should* make a decision but opts not to. So how do you know? First, ask yourself whether the situation will deteriorate or improve with the decision. If nothing will change, you might not need to make a decision at that juncture. Then, ask yourself what will happen if you do nothing. Will the situation resolve itself? Go away? Compare the effort required to make and implement a decision to the risk or lost opportunity of doing nothing.

If a decision appears necessary, the next question becomes, Who should make the decision? Sometimes you will need to stand alone in your decision-making; at other times you will want the input of your direct reports. Three options can help you decide how to decide:

1. Act alone. Ask for information if you need it, but make the call and tell others what your decision is.

2. Convene a group, actively explain the issue, and ask for input. Interview people individually for their opinions, consult experts, and seek advice. Challenge your team to produce the highest-caliber thinking they can, but make the decision yourself.

3. Involve the group directly, and encourage them to work for consensus. Assure them you will endorse their decision.

Sayings such as "two heads are better than one" express a folk wisdom that reflects accumulated knowledge about human behavior in groups. When individuals join each other to solve problems and reach decisions, synergy occurs. Group members share knowledge, resources and experiences, and, usually, better decisions result. Although individuals can make decisions more quickly than groups, the quality of a group's decision will usually be better. When group members use time and resources well, they can pool knowledge to solve problems, and ultimately reach a better thought out conclusion. While few "certifiably correct" decisions exist, group members, working together, will typically outperform or match the efforts of the individual.

Should you, therefore, involve others in all or most of your important decisions? Although no sacrosanct rules exist to determine when you should make the decision by yourself and when you should include others, circumstances will dictate when to do each. In general, you should engage others when the following conditions exist:

1. You need to make a risky call. Because of the blame or responsibility that occurs if an extreme course of action fails, usually one person working alone exercises too much caution. Obviously, as the leader, you will incur the blame no matter who makes the decision, but if you include others, you will hear and entertain more radical points of view.

2. You need multiple perspectives. Frequently, there are many parts or steps to the problem, or a great deal of expertise, credibility, or creativity will be required to reach a conclusion. When this happens, no single person will have the resources that a group can provide.

3. The individuals involved will be affected by or responsible for the consequences of the decision. When you need the understanding, cooperation, and commitment of a group, soliciting input from them will increase the likelihood that they will commit to carrying out the decision. Also, if executing the decision will demand coordination of resources, a division of labor, or interdependence, the group members will be able to determine the role that each will need to play in implementation.

4. When people hold diverse or passionate attitudes about the problem and are likely to resist a solution you impose, asking them to reach their own conclusions often engenders their cooperation.

In the aforementioned four cases, you will achieve more success by including others in your problem-solving and decision-making. On the other hand, circumstances sometimes indicate that an individual, rather than a group, should make the call. As the leader, you will often be the one to make the decision, but at times you will want to delegate it to the most qualified among your direct reports. An individual should make decisions in the following situations:

1. If time is short. If you have all the available data, you will make the decision more quickly than a group could.

2. If one or two people will determine the outcome. Sometimes one or two group members tend to dominate discussions and cause social pressure within the group to conform. Circumstances like these can reduce the discussion to a debate or an intimidating situation. When leaders perceive this kind of situation, making the decision alone or assigning an individual the task of deciding can help to prevent the pessimism and destructive conflict that might surface during a group meeting.

3. If one member of your team has the expertise to make the decision alone.

4. If the group as a whole lacks the qualifications of an individual member, that person should hold sway.

5. If the information needed to make an informed decision is confidential, only those people who need to know the data should be involved in the decision-making process.

Situations will determine the advisability of group decision-making, but in general, assigning this task to a group will have a better result. People often feel more motivated to make high quality decisions when they have an audience because social interaction plays a role in their wanting to "measure up." In groups people frequently emulate more motivated and skilled individuals and, by so doing, raise the standard. A word of caution: The single biggest mistake I see senior leaders making does not involve their reluctance to involve others in decisions. It has to do with their eagerness to make *popular* decisions. A well-liked decision and a well-thought-out one differ significantly. The former will seldom prove to be the best one; the latter often will.

Any decision, no matter who makes it, will have three elements: objectives (what you want to do), alternatives (possibilities for doing it), and risk (the uncertainty involved). Disagreement about any one of the three elements will cause conflict in the group, but if the members can't agree about *what* they are trying to decide, they doom the process before it begins. When individuals lack clarity about the goal of their decision, they confuse their thinking, procrastinate, and pick an alternative they end up hating. *What* needs to change defines the central and pivotal question in all decision-making circumstances.

For instance, I worked with a group of senior executives who wanted to refine their strategy vis-à-vis their marketing plan. Immediately, one of the group's members started discussing what products they would introduce, what new markets they should enter, and the increases to the sales force they would require. This person instantly jumped to alternatives and risk before the group had decided whether or not this was the year to expand or maintain the status quo. When I asked, "What is your goal?" the group realized that disagreeing about alternatives and risk made no sense when they hadn't even decided what a viable solution would look like.

When setting the objective, the group should also separate "musts" from "wants." Too often I've seen clients frustrate themselves, create conflict, and retard progress by elevating a "want" to the status of a "must." Any marketing plan *must* address areas of profitability and capability, but the sales force may *want* to do business with previous clients, in good climates. As every good negotiator knows, never sacrifice a "must" for a "want," and don't let the "wants" create the hill you'll die on.

Of course, everyone agreeing on the status of a "must" versus a "want" won't happen every time or automatically. Expressing these different perspectives allows members to consider many different points of view, to have fewer fixations on one course of action, and to consider risky alternatives. This discussion of different positions enhances members' involvement with the issues, a situation that becomes more significant when the decision the group is considering is a radical one.

The quality of the decisions will further depend on the interaction patterns among the members and the information exchange they experience. Participants listening to each other and encouraging every person's contribution will coordinate knowledge, thereby correcting errors or blind spots. This usually results in the group recognizing and rejecting incorrect solutions. So even if you opt for a group decision, as the senior leader you will still need to influence and monitor the group's processes, oversee the methods members use to make the decision, and understand who will have authority to make the final call.

Who Owns the Decision?

Quality, speed, and execution of decisions set top performers apart from everyone else. However, at every level of the organization, ambiguity over who owns decisions can create bottlenecks and turf wars that stall the process. Verdicts about ownership of decisions start at the top, as CEOs negotiate with the board of directors those decisions the CEO will make independently and those that will involve the board.

From there, CEOs determine how members of their team will make decisions for the company. In large organizations, often the first question of ownership centers around functional heads making the calls for their areas versus general managers making them for their businesses. One of my large clients struggled with this for years, until a new CFO candidate determined the outcome. After a daunting process to find a qualified CFO for this $1.5 billion company, the board and CEO were amenable to demands of the most promising candidate. In short, he would not accept the role unless he owned the finance function throughout the organization. Prior to this, each general manager held sway over the decisions of his lead finance person, who then had a dotted line reporting relationship to the company CFO. The entering CFO reversed that. Once the CFO claimed responsibility and control of his functional area, the CEO realized that the rest of the organization should follow suit. This formula won't work for all organizations, but the lesson remained clear. The buck has to stop someplace with someone. Those stopping points need to be transparent, even if stakeholders don't agree about them.

Unclogging decision-making bottlenecks requires clear roles and responsibilities. In a perfect world, the leadership team at each level of the organization would agree about who has input for decisions and who has ultimate responsibility for them. However, not too many companies represent perfect worlds. Consensus represents a worthy goal, both when deciding areas of accountability and when making the decisions themselves. But consensus involves time, which can be an obstacle to action, and for the most part, decision makers do not eagerly abdicate control. Therefore, if you can't unclog the bottlenecks, then make the tough call, and decide who owns the decision. Before you do that, though, you might want to try accountability charting. As I mention in Chapter 3, done well, it has power at all levels of the organization. When people understand what others expect of them, they tend to take responsibility for outcomes. Fear of overstepping can delay action as often as the turf wars do. I will give more detail about accountability charting in other chapters, but here's how it works.

Developing your accountability chart is a two-phase process. First, ask each group member to identify the major decisions he or she makes. The completed list should include all major responsibilities as they relate to the group's involvement. Then, each person assigns the appropriate code letter to signify the level of involvement he or she thinks the boss and others should have in the decision.

Second, in a team meeting that includes the boss, the group member shares these perceptions. If everyone agrees about the level of responsibility, they agree to operate under this agreement until further notice. If group members disagree, they negotiate parameters under which they will operate. Often this will take the form of the leader assigning boundaries for decisions.

Groups do not provide the perfect arena for solving all problems or for making all decisions. Working in groups presents difficulties; however, when the leader manages these challenges and when the group leverages the talents and resources of each member, groups have tremendous potential. When participants understand decision-making dynamics and the pitfalls that accompany them, the group has taken steps to a conclusion. But the insidious fiend called indecision can still lurk.

How to Conquer a Culture of Indecision

If clear areas of responsibility and accountability don't exist, you have the first ingredient in the recipe for a culture of indecision. Making sure the senior team and all their direct reports have well-defined roles and responsibilities, which leaders link to rewards and evaluations, certainly defines the first step, but it's just the beginning. Triumphing over indecision will take more concentrated efforts simply because some leaders just can't make up their minds. In fact, they are very decisive about avoiding decisions, and in time, indecision itself can become a decision. But as the senior leader, your job is to take steps to make sure uncertainty does not engulf you or your team. Here are some ways to move toward incisiveness and creativity.

Encourage Dialogue, Not Monologue

The primary tool for combating indecision is interaction—dialogue between leaders at the top of the organization and those who will implement decisions. Through the exchange of ideas, people challenge assumptions, put new ideas on the table, and through synergy, create ideas that never would have existed if individuals had tried to go it alone. In other words, conversations bring coherence to fragmented ideas and encourage the laser focus that decision makers need to move ideas to action.

One of the surest ways to promote indecision and quash robust discussion involves appointing a "talking head," especially one that likes to overuse PowerPoint. When a senior leader assigns someone the task of preparing a presentation, the "more is better" paradigm begins to shift into place, and the spirit of shared decision-making dies. Often the person responsible for the production will spend an inordinate amount of time trying to put magic actions into a PowerPoint. Three things occur in this scenario, none of which moves the group toward better decisions.

First, the person preparing the information wastes time that should be spent on his or her primary responsibilities. I recently had a conversation with a military colonel who told me he had spent two full days preparing 50 slides for a presentation to a general. I asked him if that was the best use of his time. He answered, "No, but that's what the general expects." Contrast this situation to one that occurred with another CEO client, Jack, who had a "two-slide rule." Because he would view only two slides in a presentation that lasted less than an hour, Jack's direct reports became very adept at streamlining their messages and focusing their efforts on the critical aspects of a given problem. Jack didn't reward "dazzle them with data" behavior, so he didn't have to tolerate it. He also didn't have to put up with indecision.

The second problem occurs when the overuse of PowerPoint or any other method of solo presentation encourages group idleness. When the presenter spends days preparing bells and whistles to present information, those in the room tend to shut down, drift off, and engage in group laziness. Interrupting a peer who has clearly worked so hard to astound seems at cross purposes with teamwork and cohesion—plus, if people do interrupt, they run the risk that they'll make their peer look bad in front of the boss, or worse, cause him or her to retaliate when it's their turn. Ambivalence often arises, but outright resistance from those who might have to implement the decision can also happen.

Finally, when you advocate monologue and one person taking too much responsibility for guiding the group's discussion, you sacrifice openness and candor. Conversely, when you establish a safe haven for dialogue, you create an atmosphere that encourages spirited debate, learning, and trust. When people can express their real opinions and take collective ownership of problems, without fear of reprisal or rejection, they become more willing to speak the unspeakable and to identify the elephant that frequents so many corporate meeting rooms. Only then can you hope for a sincere search for answers.

Support a Sincere Search for Answers

As I have mentioned before, when senior leaders speak, they encourage echoing, which in turn prompts waffling—an ingredient in, and first cousin of, indecision. On the other hand, if you, as the senior leader, refuse to offer an opinion until each member of the leadership team has expressed one, you will invite a full range of views, unpleasant truths, and better-informed decisions. Others echoing your thoughts isn't the only problem that can fuel indecision, however. Sometimes others filtering information and failing to give you hard truths can also play roles in the breakdown of decision-making.

At some point in the pipeline, leaders become the recipients of what others think you want to hear. The remedy? Get rid of the filters. Ask members of your leadership team to invite to decision-making meetings those who hold the keys—those people who can answer you directly. If you don't demand this, it won't happen. Like well-tuned flow valves, throughout history people have guarded and controlled the stream of information to the top—occasionally to justify their own existence; at times to maintain control; and sometimes to cover their own incompetence. You decide: what information do you need, and where is the horse's mouth in your organization?

Filtering the data through the chain of command has its place, but supporting a sincere search for answers needs to happen when you have to hear the information directly. At a recent symposium, I heard a four-star general lament the passing of days when people would give him information directly. Now that he's one of 13 senior Air Force leaders, too many people have the opportunity to influence what information he receives and what he doesn't. Like the tasters of Medieval times who decided what the king could and could not eat, these people do a type of information triage. Unless you establish a clear line of communication between you and those in your chain of command, you won't get sincere information either, which can compromise your confidence and promote vacillation. Even though it may seem counterintuitive to involve more rather than fewer people in decision-making processes, failure to include everyone who needs to add relevant information to the decision actually clogs the process and wastes time. And you don't end up with sincere answers; you end up with sanitized data that can often interfere with your capacity to move ideas to action.

As critical a role as sincere dialogue and accurate information play in decisiveness, they represent only a good start. If the open communication doesn't turn into action, you've gained nothing. Follow-through is the coin of the realm of execution. Therefore, as I mention in the strategy chapter, each time the leadership team meets, everyone, or at least the key players, leaves with assignments and deadlines. If you fail to establish the follow-through, you will destroy the discipline of execution and invite indecision both for the current situation and those in the future. These assignments then play a role in your formal assessment of each of your direct reports and influence compensation and promotion. If you fail to make this link, people aren't sure about what decisions they own, and if you don't give feedback, you will lose the battle against indecision in your organization.

How to Sidestep the Hidden Traps of Decision-Making

The best leaders get most of the important calls right. They exercise good judgment and make the winning decisions. All other considerations evaporate because, for the most part, at the senior-most echelons of any organization, people won't judge you by your enthusiasm, good intentions, or willingness to work long hours. They have one criterion for judging you: do you show good judgment? Therefore, leveraging your strengths in this arena and avoiding the hidden traps of individual and group decision-making define two of the surest ways for you to improve in your own decision-making and to influence the effectiveness of your team.

When group members make effective decisions, they can do so because they have used time and resources well, resulting in correct, or at least well-thought-out, conclusions that they can easily carry out. Problems, however, can interfere with this process. Here are some to look out for:

- ◊ Lack of group maturity. Not enough time together as a group, or inexperience with the task, can cause the group to select an inappropriate course of action.

- ◊ Insufficient time to complete the task, inappropriate group size, and ineffective leadership will further reduce the likelihood of reaching an effective decision.

- ◊ Pessimism, another enemy, causes group members to perceive a "no-win" situation that, in turn, causes them to procrastinate or stall. Dismal hope about reaching an objective further contributes to fears of blame and can cause members to shift responsibility, or to "pass the buck."

- ◊ Self-centeredness and conflicting goals can trigger participant's failing to use information, knowledge, or resources. The desire to shine or stand out often results in the group being impaired.

- ◊ Agreement-seeking will often occur when the group lacks heterogeneity, or differences. The homogeneity of the group is particularly problematic when there is a dominant leader of a powerful subgroup, because the already cohesive group is particularly vulnerable to these strong influences. Groupthink is likely.

The Groupthink Trap

In 1972 Irving Janis, a social psychologist, first identified groupthink as a phenomenon that occurs when decision-makers accept proposals without scrutiny, suppress opposing thoughts, or limit analysis and disagreement. Historians often blame groupthink for such fiascoes as Pearl Harbor, the Bay of Pigs invasion, the Vietnam War, the Watergate break-in, and the Challenger disaster. Groupthink, therefore, causes the group to make an incomplete examination of the data and the available options, which can lead the participants to a simplistic solution to a complex problem.

High cohesion, a positive group dynamic, creates problems when the group has excessive amounts of it. When groups become too unified, the members, especially the insecure or weak ones, allow loyalty to the group to cloud their ability to make effective determinations. Often, these weak participants engage in self-censorship because they perceive that "the group knows better." This, coupled with their fear of rejection and the stronger members exerting direct pressure to conform, discourages the voicing of dissenting ideas and leads to mind guarding.

Mind guarding routinely takes place in these highly cohesive groups. Through subtle or overt pressure, powerful members create an atmosphere of intolerance. The group discourages dissension and prevents the raising of objections. The absence of obvious dissent leads members to conclude that the others concur; they assume everyone agrees; and they engender the *illusion of unanimity*. Mind guarding and high cohesion can further lead to *collective rationalization*, the process through which members invent justification for their actions, causing them to feel they are acting in the best interest of the group. A "safety in numbers" mentality develops and can lead to excessive risk taking when the group feels accountable to no one.[3]

The decision-making that led to the Challenger disaster illustrates how each of these causes of groupthink can lead to a tragic outcome. The Challenger blasted off at an unprecedented low temperature. The day before the disaster, executives at NASA argued about whether the combination of low temperature and O-ring failure would be a problem. The evidence they considered was inconclusive, but more complete data would have pointed to the need to delay the launch.

Cohesion and pressure to conform probably explain two of the primary causes of the groupthink. The scientists at NASA and Morton Thiokol felt the pressure of their bosses and the media to find a way to stick to their schedule. Because the group discouraged dissenters, an illusion of unanimity surfaced, and the collective rationalization that allowed the decision makers to limit their analysis led to their favoring a particular outcome—to launch on time.

Due to an extraordinary record of success of space flights, the decision-makers developed an illusion of invulnerability, based on a mentality of overconfidence. After all, NASA had not lost an astronaut since the flash fire in the capsule of Apollo 1 in 1967. After that time, NASA had a string of 55 successful missions, including putting a man on the moon. Both NASA scientists and the American people began to believe the decision-makers could do no wrong.[4]

Any one of the causes of groupthink can sabotage decision-making, but in the case of the Challenger, they created a tragic outcome by displaying most of the symptoms. When you're in the throes of groupthink, you can't always see or understand what's happening. That's why you need to take steps to prevent it before it rears its ugly head.

High-quality decision-making depends on groups preventing group-think by structuring a systematic approach for evaluating alternatives. First, you can serve as an impartial leader who refrains from expressing a point of view. You can further enhance the evaluation process by assigning one of the members the role of *devil's advocate* or *devil's inquisitor.* Inviting outside experts to examine information further contributes to higher-caliber decisions

The chance to rethink a decision occurs when you set a second-chance meeting. The group can then avoid feeling "under the gun" by agreeing they will make no final decision during the first meeting. Time and distance from the information will allow group members to avoid impulsiveness and quick-fix methodology.

The Failure-to-Frame Trap

When you or your organization faces a significant decision, as the senior leader, one of your primary responsibilities will be to frame the problem for yourself and others. Like a frame around a picture, this can determine how we view a situation and how we interpret it. Often the frame of a picture is not apparent, but it enhances the artwork it surrounds. It calls attention to the piece of work and separates it from the other objects in the room.

Similarly, in decision-making, a frame creates a mental border that encloses a particular aspect of a situation, to outline its key elements and to create a structure for understanding it. Mental frames help us navigate the complex world so we can successfully avoid solving the wrong problem or solving the right problem in the wrong way. Our personal frames form the lenses through which we view the world. Education, experience, expectations, and biases shape and define our frames, just as the collective perceptions of a group's members will mold theirs.

Because people often react unconsciously to their frame of reference, in your role as senior leader you can help your group become aware of the frames they bring to the table. When facing a major decision, here are some ways you can do that:

⋄ Put the problem or decision into one sentence that does not imply a solution. (If it can't go into one sentence, or frame, you have more than one issue to resolve. Frame each separately.) Begin the sentence with "The problem is..." or "We need to decide whether..." This simple discipline will do two things. First, it will keep you focused on the objective or strategy before you start discussing alternatives—inside the frame is important to this discussion; outside is not. Second, it helps reduce mental clutter and achieve agreement about critical areas before you move ahead.

⋄ Whether you offer the initial frame or someone else does, don't automatically accept it. Instead, try to reframe the problem in various ways. Ask, "Is this really the issue?" Force yourself and others to get to the core of the problem without being distracted by symptoms, indications, causes, or effects. For example, in many of our public schools, drop-out rates are high, teacher readiness is low, parents don't get involved, and inadequate funding impedes improvement. While true, none of these gets to the root of the problem, which is that too many children can't read or do math at grade level. So, to frame the issue in one sentence, "The problem is that a large number of the children in this school district can't perform at grade level." The group can then define the objective: to increase student performance. Starting with any other frames takes the group in a direction that won't get to the heart of the issue, and therefore, won't ultimately solve the problem. You should:

◊   Ask questions that test the frame. Force new perspectives by encouraging comparisons:

  ♦   Are you dissatisfied with _____ or _____?

  ♦   How would you compare _____ with what has happened before? What is different?

  ♦   When something like this happened before, what worked?

  ♦   What resources will you commit to this?

  ♦   To what extent are you willing to change the status quo? Structure? Reward system? Reporting relationships?

◊   Frame the issues from different reference points, and discover the frames of those who disagree with you. What biases do you and they reflect? What agendas might they promote?

◊   To circumvent bias, use neutral, concrete language to frame the problem.

◊   Challenge assumptions and examine underlying causes. Ask yourself how your thinking might change if your framing changed.

People who understand the power of framing also know its capacity to exert influence. They have learned that establishing the framework within which others will view the decision is tantamount to determining the outcome. As a senior leader, you have both the right and responsibility to shape outcomes. Even if you can't eradicate all the distortions ingrained in your thinking and that of others, you can build tests like this into your decision-making process and improve the quality of your choices. Effective framing offers one way to do that.

The Complexity Trap

Effective framing can help you embrace "Occam's razor," a principle attributed to the 14th century English logician and Franciscan friar that states "Entities should not be multiplied unnecessarily." The term "razor" refers to the act of shaving away everything that stands in the way of the simplest explanation, making as few assumptions as possible, and eliminating those that make no difference. All things being equal, the simplest solution is best.

Thomas Aquinas recognized the value of simplicity a century earlier when he offered, "If a thing can be done adequately by means of one, it is superfluous to do it by means of several; for we observe that nature does not employ two instruments where one suffices." Albert Einstein added his brilliance to the discussion with his observation that "Theories should be as simple as possible, *but no simpler.*"

The idea that more is better and activity justifies existence is pervasive in many companies. Creating stacks of papers and millions of details do not prove competence; they show an inability to appreciate Occam's razor. Those who have the capacity to answer a question in a sentence frequently don't seem as dedicated as those who produce a volume of words. More isn't better, but those in power often reward it as though it were. Not allowing yourself to jump on that bandwagon can help you and others move ahead more quickly on critical issues, instead of squandering time on activity that keeps people busy but doesn't affect the strategy. Where complexity goes unfettered, bureaucracy, the triumph of means over ends, will surely follow.

In a business situation, the simplest explanation that covers all the facts will usually offer the best solution, but uncovering it may not be quite so easy. People complicate decisions because they can't separate the critical elements from the unimportant ones. They lump together the "must haves" with the "wants" and even throw in some "nice to haves." They introduce ways to execute a decision before the goal of the decision is clear, muddy the waters by trying to make all aspects of the situation a top priority, and skirt around the periphery of the problem instead of cutting to the core of it. As the senior leader, you can help your team evade these enemies by shaving away all but the simplest representation of the issue and by reducing labor intensity to concentrate on the problem. Occam's razor can be a much-needed addition to your leadership toolkit.

The Status Quo Trap

Fear of failure, rejection, change, or loss of control—these often unfounded fears cause decision makers to consider the wrong kinds of information or to rely too heavily on the status quo. According to psychologists, the reason so many cling to the status quo lies deep within our psyches. In a desire to protect our egos, we resist taking action that may also involve responsibility, blame, and regret. Doing nothing and sticking with the status quo represents a safer course of action. Certainly, the status quo should always be considered a viable option. But adhering to it out of fear will limit your options and compromise effective decision-making.

Confusing the risks of a decision with its seriousness also encourages us to stick with the status quo. True risk relates to the likelihood of an outcome, while seriousness defines the consequences of that outcome. For instance, the risks associated with flying are statistically infinitesimal. Yet, because the consequences of a plane crash are gargantuan, fear of flying tops the list of prevalent phobias. Similarly, your executive team may adhere to the status quo because of illogical fears. They dread the dire consequences of change, when in reality, the likelihood of those consequences remains quite small.

When considering the status quo, make sure it represents one and only one option. Then ask yourself the key question: If this weren't the status quo, would we choose this alternative? Often we exaggerate the effort that selecting something else would entail, or we magnify the desirability of staying the course over time, forgetting that the future may well present something different. Finally, when we face a multitude of various options, rather than carefully evaluating each, we give into the temptation to stick with the traditional approach.

The Anchoring Trap

A pernicious mental phenomenon related to over-reliance on the status quo is known as anchoring. This cognitive bias describes the common human tendency to rely too heavily, or to "anchor," on one piece of information when making decisions. It occurs when people place too much importance on one aspect of an event, causing an error in accurately predicting the feasibility of other options.

According to research, the mind gives disproportionate weight to the first information it receives, to initial impressions and preliminary value judgments. Then, as we adjust our thinking to account for other elements of the circumstance, we tend to defer to these original reactions. Once someone sets the anchor, we will usually have a bias toward that perception.

Because most people are better at *relative* than absolute or creative thinking, we tend to base estimates and decisions on our known anchors or familiar positions, then adjust decisions relative to this starting point. If I were to ask you if you think the population of a city is more than 100,000, instead of coming up with a number of your own, your mind will tempt you to use 100,000 as a relative frame of reference.

Another problem associated with anchoring involves decision maker's focusing on notable differences and excluding those that are less conspicuous but often critical. When making predictions about achievability or convenience, past events, trends, and numbers become anchors for forecasting the future. Sometimes these data offer an accurate starting point for making predictions, but too often they lead to misguided conclusions.

To avoid falling into the anchoring trap, don't reveal too much information. Once you give your opinion and shape information, others will tend to defer to your senior leadership position and echo your values and ideas. When this happens, you lose the opportunity to think about the problem from a variety of perspectives.

But be careful that you don't fall into the trap yourself. Think about the problem before you present it to others and possibly become anchored by their ideas. It's a tricky balance. Effective framing will improve decision-making; anchoring will worsen it. Here's the difference. To frame a decision, you might ask your team the following: "What, if any, marketing efforts should we initiate this year?" Anchoring will occur when you influence the answer: "Should we increase marketing in our Eastern regions by more than 20 percent?" Once you introduce the figure of 20 percent you have indicated your bias that marketing *should* increase by at least that much, and team members will adjust their thinking to consider that. What if the figure should be much higher? You would have given your direct reports implied permission to under perform, and if the company should reduce or eliminate marketing in the Eastern regions, you've just influenced your team to dismiss those ideas.

To dodge the anchoring trap, you'll want to remain open-minded and seek the opinions of others, and you won't want to color their reactions with your own. Frame the issue in a non-evaluative way, refrain from giving your opinion too soon, and be alert to language or perspectives that tend to anchor thinking in one arena. Awareness of how anchoring influences each of us defines the first step in sidestepping its effects.

The Sunk-Cost Trap

Adherence to the status quo and anchoring closely align with another decision-making trap: the predisposition not to recognize sunk costs. The sunk-cost fallacy describes the tendency to throw good money after bad. Just because you've already spent money or other resources on something doesn't mean you should *continue* spending resources on it. Sometimes the opposite is true, yet because of an illogical attachment to our previous decisions, the more we spend on something, the less we're willing to let it go, and the more we magnify its merits.

Sunk costs represent unrecoverable past expenditures that should not normally be taken into account when determining whether to continue a project or abandon it, because you cannot recover the costs either way. However, in an attempt to justify past choices, we want to stay the course we once set. Rationally we may realize the sunk costs aren't relevant to current decision-making, but they prey on our logic and lead us to inappropriate choices.

As a senior leader, you can steer your team away from the sunk-cost rationale by creating a safe haven for discussion and admission of mistakes. Sometimes senior leaders inadvertently reinforce the sunk cost trap by penalizing those who made decisions that didn't work. Instead of admitting the mistake and trying to move on, often the decision maker will prolong a project in a vain attempt to buy time, improve the situation, or avoid detection. Obviously, you will need to hold your team members accountable, but if others consider you draconian or severe, they will hide the truth from you and soldier on, making more mistakes instead of cutting their losses.

The Inference and Judgment Trap

Facts are your friends. When you face an unfamiliar or complicated decision, verifiable evidence is your most trusted ally, but also the one many senior leaders reject. Instead of steadfastly pushing for definitive information, they settle for the data others choose to present, seek information that corroborates what they already think, and dismiss information that contradicts their biases or previous experience. When guesswork or probabilities guide your decisions, or you allow them to influence the decisions of others, you fall into the trap of too little information or the wrong kind of information.

Facts are your friend, but they are scarce allies. Inferences and judgments, which can be more influential and pervasive, tend to dominate discussions and drive decisions. To the untrained ear, the inference can present itself convincingly as a fact. Inferences represent the conclusion one deduces, sometimes based on observed information, sometimes not. Often inferences have their origin in fact, but a willingness to go beyond definitive data into the sphere of supposition and conjecture separates the fact from the inference.

Similarly, judgments go beyond what one can observe and prove and add an evaluation of the information. Judgments offer a perspective—a good/bad coloring of the data. For example, if you were to walk into a room and notice a moose head above the fireplace, you might infer that the owner of the house is a hunter. You may or may not be correct. If you have strong positive or negative feelings about hunting or decorating with animal heads, you might then attach a judgment to your observation. Only one fact is true, however. Either the owner of the house is a hunter or not. Perhaps the owner purchased the house with the moose in it. Maybe the owner's former husband left it there instead of making it part of the divorce settlement. Several possibilities could explain the evidence.

Personal reactions, or judgments, will vary too. As the senior leader, you will subconsciously be drawn to the information that supports your own values and experience. However, if you discipline yourself and your team to gather more data, to check for reliability, and to examine all information with equal rigor, you will have taken important steps to improving your decision-making and taking off the leadership blinders that afflict so many.

How to Make Decisions Without Blinders

Executives tend to be unaware of the feelings—both positive and negative—that their direct reports have about them. Knowledge of the positive emotions feels good, but ignorance of the negative emotions can create blinders that engender other problems. Unwittingly, executives condition their people to tell them what they want to hear, even when that differs from what they need to know. Shoot just one messenger, and the other messengers get wind of it. The chances of your hearing bad news, much less conflicting points of view, diminish in direct proportion to the number of messengers in your wake.

"Bounded awareness" describes a phenomenon that occurs when cognitive blinders prevent a person from seeing, seeking, using, or sharing highly relevant, easily accessible, and readily perceivable information during a decision-making process. Bounded awareness can happen at various points in the decision-making process when decision-makers don't gather relevant data, consider critical facts, or understand the significance of the information they have. It can also happen later when these decision makers don't share information with others, thereby limiting general knowledge. Often decision-makers fail to notice the specific ways in which they reduce their own understanding, and their failure to recognize those limitations can have grave consequences.[5]

Systems thinkers have given us a useful metaphor for a certain kind of blinding behavior in the phenomenon of the boiled frog. The phenomenon is this. If you drop a frog into a pot of boiling water, it will frantically try to leap out. But if you place it gently in a pot of tepid water and turn the heat on low, it will float there quite placidly. As the water gradually heats up, the frog will sink into a tranquil stupor, and before long it will unresistingly allow itself to be boiled to death. When we fail to notice the gradual changes happening around us, we resemble the unfortunate frog.

That's what happened when experts overlooked the threatening changes in Mount Pinatubo. In June of 1991, Sister Emma, a nun who worked with the Aeta tribesmen living on the flanks of Mount Pinatubo, visited the offices of the Philippine Institute of Volcanology and Seismology to let them know there had been a large explosion near the mountain's summit. In previous months, scientists had noticed some activity in the mountain but had not thought it definitive enough to consider seriously. After more than four centuries of slumber, Pinatubo Volcano erupted violently and unexpectedly, pouring more than five billion cubic meters of ash and pyroclastic debris onto the island. It left in its wake hundreds dead, injured, or missing, and more than one million people displaced. Hundreds of millions of dollars in private property and infrastructure lay in ruins. For months the ejected volcanic materials remained suspended in the atmosphere where the winds dispersed them to envelop the earth, reaching as far as Russia and North America. Pinatubo's eruption signaled the world's second-most violent and destructive volcanic event of the 20th century, yet it took many by surprise.[6]

Executives put on their decision-making blinders when they become insensitive to changing environments too, much as the boiled frog failed to notice the gradual increase in water temperature and the scientists in the Philippines failed to detect Pinatubo's warnings. The dot-com boom-bust offers another perfect example. Bloated dot-com companies failed to discern shrinking markets, just as the gradual changes in the water's temperature failed to alert the frog to its impending doom.

People can learn to be more observant of changes in their environment, but only when leaders cultivate an awareness of the kinds of information that could directly affect their organizations. Tiltmeter measurements and seismic activity alerted volcanologists to convince those near the volcano to evacuate in time to save millions of lives that would have otherwise been lost. These scientists had accurate measuring tools and knew what to look for, and yet they still experienced shock and disbelief when they realized the magnitude of the explosion.

Will your team be similarly surprised with environmental changes? Or as fortunate as the inhabitants of the Philippines who had Sister Emma to alert the scientists? What gauges does your team use to foresee the future? What data would help them predict strategic changes for your organization? If you and they don't know what you're looking for, you run the risk that your blinders will lead to your being blindsided. The authors of "Decisions Without Blinders" suggest these steps to help you increase your awareness:

◊   Know what you are looking for and train your eyes to see it. Just as Secret Service agents scan a crowd to recognize risks, executives can prepare themselves and others to recognize threats and opportunities.

◊   Develop or pay for an outsider's perspective that gives you a new or different slant. Make sure you seek and hear disconfirming evidence.

◊   Think about the full context of the situation, without overemphasizing one focal event.

◊   Ask for information explicitly.

◊   Create a culture that makes information sharing the default position.

In general, executives must rely on others to streamline the data flow to them, but with preparation and a clear understanding of what those data should be, your direct reports can help you avoid the perils of bounded awareness. Learning to expand the limits of your knowledge before you make an important choice will save you from asking, "How did we miss that?" or "What volcano?"

Conclusion

Effective decision-making does not happen by accident. In most cases, executives have made a conscious, well-thought-out effort to make an effective decision. They have gained information to understand the problem that necessitates the decision; they have examined and evaluated numerous choices; and they have settled for nothing less than stellar data. Then, they did the courageous thing. They opted for the best, not the safest or most popular, course of action.

Chapter 3

Build Magnets to Attract Top Talent

Example is not the main thing in influencing others.
It is the only thing.

—Albert Schweitzer

When executives master the art of coaching, those in their organizations develop fierce loyalty, exhibit infectious enthusiasm for the work they do, and want to spend their careers growing along with their organizations. When high potentials *don't* receive attention from senior leaders, retention, productivity, and morale suffer. Coaching, however, is a misunderstood and much-underdeveloped skill among senior leaders, chiefly because they received so little of it themselves. They simply don't know what they should do to mentor the next generation of star performers.

Coaching involves more than patting people on the back. It's a powerful tool executives can use to help their best talent realize their personal aspirations, but it also provides a way to ensure the continuity of leadership and build the future of the company. Like the great athletic coaches of history, executives who commit to coaching the next generation know their people's strengths and limitations, understand the challenges they face, and recognize where they want to go with their careers. Armed with this information, great coaches structure jobs and opportunities so that high-potential candidates can excel and meet their potential; they provide resources and training; they continually monitor progress; and most importantly, they provide feedback.

None of this happens automatically, however. You need to know how to recognize top talent, how to move that talent through the pipeline, what it takes to be a coach, the techniques for mentoring, and how to coach the best and brightest to keep them within your doors.

A New Model of Talent Assessment

One of the most critical responsibilities of senior leaders involves assessing talent—something you've probably never been trained to do. Of all the leadership and managerial duties you'll face, this is probably the least intuitive, the most complicated, and the least familiar. If you're typical, you will tend to attract and be attracted to those who reflect your own work style, personality, and approach to decision-making. Often, attracting those like you will be the smartest move you can make, but at other times, you'll need to act as a magnet for those who represent a different skill set or approach to work. For example, if you're a gregarious CEO who finds discussion and conversation stimulating and fun, you might not immediately experience a sense of connection with a reserved finance person who prefers working alone. On the other hand, you might find yourself enormously impressed with a person who possesses some of your more salient behaviors, like a self-assured, executive demeanor, but who lacks some of your less obvious aptitudes such as advanced numerical reasoning. A person's behaviors and experience usually present themselves in the most obvious way—the aptitude appearing much later in the game. This very problem defines the reason so many of my clients rely on me to uncover aptitude in the pre-employment screening—it saves time and much angst.

Whether you're assessing the talent for hire or promotion, you'll need to weigh carefully the three constructs of talent. In all cases, you'll want to make sure the candidate for hire, coaching, or promotion demonstrates three key things: the aptitude to do the job, the behaviors that will ensure success in the job, and the requisite experience for success.

Aptitude involves a natural disposition or tendency toward a particular action, the readiness to learn, and the raw talent to function in the role. It involves three major capacities: verbal ability, quantitative skills, and strategic thinking. When people evince strong control of language through use of advanced vocabulary, well-developed writing and speaking skills, and a quickness at learning new skills from verbally presented data, you can infer robust verbal ability.

At the most basic level, quantitative skills involve the capacity to handle a budget successfully. More advanced evidence will be tied to stellar performance with profit and loss responsibilities. Engineers and accountants usually come in the door with well-developed quantitative skill—otherwise they could have never made it through school. But often those in operational roles will have these abilities too; they'll just need some help in honing them and applying them successfully to your organization's strategy.

In Chapter 4, I offer a complete explanation for identifying strategists, but in a nutshell, you'll want to see people who understand how to separate the critical few considerations from the vast number of nonessential ones. They maintain a global perspective as they quickly get to the core of complex problems, even when they haven't encountered the problem before. They typically multi-task effectively and keep the priorities clearly in focus. Most see the future as open and malleable, so they paint credible pictures of the future for others to understand. They usually handle change well, even when they didn't welcome it.

You can often infer aptitude from candidates' track records. How quickly have they learned new, unfamiliar tasks in the past? Handled unexpected, unpleasant change?

Aptitude implies that, with training and experience, this person can master the skills required to do the next job. If a person doesn't have the requisite aptitude for the job, nothing else matters. Without it, no amount of coaching, training, wishing, or hoping will make this person able to advance.

Behavior involves people's conduct—the way they present themselves, and it tends to be consistent. Although some behaviors change in radically differing situations—say, the home and the office—most are "comfort zone" behaviors, and therefore, highly repetitive. Behavior encompasses morals, deportment, carriage, and demeanor.

Experience, the most easily observed and objective aspect of talent assessment addresses the skills the person has displayed so far. In other words, they already know how to perform specific tasks and have demonstrated this in the past. To use a baseball metaphor, these batters have an impressive "at bat" record that demonstrates how they will likely perform in the future. However, to continue the metaphor, while behavior draws on past demonstrations of ability; it offers no guarantee of future performance. Many college star baseball players never make it to the minors, much less the majors. So, although important, experience offers limited prophetic value. In the assessing game, however, I find that companies give it unfair advantage. Here's a model that may help you see the differences:

Talent Assessment Model

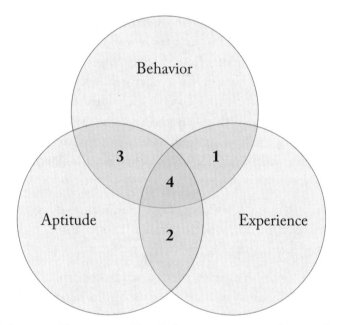

1   **Behavior + Experience:** Don't hire or promote these individuals if you need them to progress in the organization. They lack aptitude so can never be a high potential candidate.

2   **Experience + Aptitude:** Hire and promote these people cautiously. They lack the behaviors that will help them move up. With coaching, however, they can often learn to change behaviors and become 4s.

3   **Aptitude + Behavior:** A viable candidate for hire or promotion. With enough time and the right kinds of experience, these people can become 4s.

4 Behavior + Experience + Aptitude: The ideal candidate for hire or promotion. These people have all the essentials to be the top talent in your organization.

As you assess people, ask yourself into which section you would typically put this direct report. Obviously, you'll want all "4s," but you usually can't achieve that. Instead, you'll need to determine which of the "2s" and "3s" you can help.

At this juncture, you might find yourself distracted by questions about a person's attitude, which the model doesn't seem to represent. People display their attitudes through their mental states, emotions, or moods. Attitude influences the way they act, feel, and think. It has to do with the *desire* to do the job. When you face a situation in which you're not sure if a person lacks aptitude, requisite behaviors, or experience, or just has an attitude problem, ask yourself this question: "If this person's life depended on it, could he or she do the job?" If they have ever done it before but have quit doing it, you face an attitude problem. If they have never done anything at this level but have shown competence in similar kinds of situations, the person may just need training. But if you conclude the person would suffer dire consequences if his or her life depended on successfully completing the task, it's an aptitude problem, and there's nothing you can do to help. (There's not much you can do about a bad attitude either, but at least there's hope of an attitude change, especially if the person senses the dismal consequences.)

Generally speaking, you can't coach someone to demonstrate a better attitude as evidenced by a strong achievement drive, reliability, or ethics. Similarly, you can't coach people to have more aptitude, raw talent, or intelligence. People come through the door with these on their first day, so if you notice a scarcity of any one of these, realize you'll have to live with what you see or replace the person. No amount of coaching will help.

On the other hand, if you notice your direct reports simply lack skills, your coaching can make all the difference. For example, if they have trouble with people skills, presentation and writing skills, management abilities, or technical skills, you can help them develop these. Sometimes you can provide the guidance yourself, other times you can assign someone in the organization to train them, and sometimes you'll need to use outside coaching or training to aid in the development. But in each of these cases, you have every reason to be optimistic that the person will improve with the right training and experience, provided the talent to learn is there to start with. So, the first step in becoming a stellar coach is to know your people—their improvement opportunities, certainly, but more importantly their strengths. Then you're ready to select the methods that will move them to the next level of success.

How to Transform Solo Contributors Into Magnetic Bosses

As I mention in Chapter 6, not everyone shows the desire or skills to move up the management ladder. A few of these key people will choose to stay in solo contributing roles, but most of your high potentials will need a way to move up the pipeline, through the various turns, to the upper echelons of the organization. In many cases, the first step in the process—helping the solo contributor take on direct report responsibility—won't involve you directly. However, as with all important initiatives, it will need your oversight and direction. As the senior leader, you'll want to address the following to ensure that your organization does what it takes to attract and retain the future leaders:

◊   Identify the high potentials early. Unless you're desperate, hire with promotion in mind. When I do pre-employment assessments for clients, I will often determine that candidates can do the job for which they are being tested, but they offer no bench strength for advancement. Usually the hiring company just wants to fill the chair and doesn't think three to five years down the road. Although necessary in some cases, I don't advise doing this. With a little more searching, you can often find a better candidate that can do the current job and offer the potential to move forward.

◊   Begin to develop solo contributors for management positions as soon as they walk in the door or can be identified from your internal people. Test them out on small-project leadership, or give them one direct report. Actually managing something will give you the most reliable data about whether this person can take on more managerial responsibilities.

◊ Assign to the new hires, or the newly identified solo contributors, mentors who are outside their silos. Peer mentors also offer a great deal of value, especially for on-boarding new people.

◊ Develop a routine for offering management training once or twice a year. If you identify candidates early, you can send them through the training months before they assume responsibilities associated with a new position. When I offered this suggestion to one business owner, he asked, "Linda, what if I spend all this money on development and people leave?" I asked, "What if you don't, and they stay?" You can't afford not to develop your people for two main reasons: first, they represent the future of your organization's performance and profit. Second, if they don't get the opportunities in your organization, they will go elsewhere.

◊ Be sure the managerial training, whether in-house or external, addresses the core competencies of management:

   ♦ Sending and receiving messages.

   ♦ Setting goals with and for others.

   ♦ Giving balanced feedback.

   ♦ Building cohesive efforts and strong rapport.

   ♦ Delegating effectively.

   ♦ Holding people accountable.

Obviously, in the case of transitioning your high potential solo contributors to managers, you won't be the coach or mentor. Those in your chain of command will assume these responsibilities. However, whether you're offering the coaching to your own direct reports or overseeing it in your organization, you'll want to know what it looks like if you stumble across it. In addition to mentoring your direct reports, have the following:

◊ A policy that encourages stars to develop outside their business units.

◊   A formal mechanism that allows managers to see high poten-
    tials from other areas.

◊   A process of rewarding leaders for sending stars to other areas
    of the organization or for accepting stars outside their silos.

You need to prepare your best talent to take on broader roles, to develop
their capacity to manage the tensions between individual business units
and enterprise considerations without getting trapped in silos. They won't
have a reason to venture outside their silos, and indeed maybe not even
permission to do so, unless you implement a system that not only allows
but demands this sort of development.

But, to make this work, you'll probably need to examine your entire
reward platform. Typically, organizations tie rewards to unit performance,
regardless of overall strategy. Theoretically, companies reward cross-
boundary results, but too often this simply doesn't happen. A manager will
have authority over a budget that must be split among the stars in a particular silo. What then, provides the motivation, on the part of the star or
the manager, to venture outside the unit for performance or growth if the
economic reward doesn't exist? In short, to be successful in developing talent, senior leaders need to create both economic and non-economic incen-
tives to manage the tensions between unit and enterprise priorities.

When people feel trapped in business units, functions, or areas that
don't allow them to play their best games, they become disillusioned. The
responsibility for coaching the next generations, therefore, rests squarely on
the shoulders of senior executives. Only they have their hands on the controls of the ship; only they can break down the silos and forge imaginative
career paths for their high-potentials. Only they can create the venues for
managers to cooperate and discuss the tensions that characterize a complex
system of developing talent, and only they can realign reward systems to
motivate their team to lead according to the realities of today's competitive
environment. To do otherwise is to sail dangerously close to the winds of
failure. Avoiding this fate will require that you and others in the organization dedicate yourselves to more and better coaching. Here's how to make
sure that happens.

What It Takes to Be a Coach

First, let's define our terms. Depending on whom you ask, you will receive vastly different definitions of what a coach or mentor is and should be. You can be an expert who offers effective prescriptions or a leader who tries actively to involve others to get their commitments. You can be a traditional coach of the Knute Rockne ilk, who watches every play and directs necessary changes, or more a Yoda-like mentor, who gives the deserving Jedi Knights access to insights without actually telling them what to do. As you ascended the ladder to your current position as executive, you probably developed more of the Rockne approach than the Yoda style of mentoring, so in pressure situations, you will likely defer to the default position that feels most natural. (In addition to offering the fastest route to a solution.) Depending on the circumstances, you might be a little of both. In either case, trust and credibility will provide the framework for your coaching, just as it does for your leadership. In your role as a senior leader, however, you now need to develop others who will be developing still others, so modeling the best possible coaching and mentoring behaviors takes on a new level of seriousness. Now you have the responsibility of developing generations of leaders to come.

In the war for talent, senior leaders need to think of themselves as the generals; your VPs are colonels, and HR the junior officers. In a true war, what general would delegate critical decisions to junior officers? Yet this happens in almost every organization I work with. If senior leaders don't commit to developing the next generation of stars, no initiative HR drives will work. Mentoring programs can be successful, but not unless they are personal rather than generic. So, what does it take? Keen powers of observations, sensible judgment, and the willingness to take appropriate action. The effective coach must adopt the approach of teacher, not competitor; of helpful guide, not judge. The goal is simple. know your people and make the most of your most valuable resources: your high potentials.

Know the People Who Report to You

Years ago, I worked with Barb, the president of a small privately-owned company. Barb explained to me that one of the major problems she faced was her relationship with Kristy, one of her direct reports. Apparently, Kristy had been an above average performer for more than a year, but in the last six months her performance had slipped. I asked Barb what had changed. Did Kristy experience some sort of problem with someone at work? Was her family okay? Was she having trouble with her children? Barb repeated, "I don't know. I don't know," and then finally, "I don't know if Kristy even has children." I still don't know what triggered the change in Kristy, but from decades of experience, I can tell you there's very little doubt in my mind why Kristy's drive and loyalty had waned. She had come to the conclusion that Barb didn't know her and apparently didn't want to know her. Can you imagine working with someone for 18 months and still not knowing whether she had children?

In any leadership situation, your direct reports will ask three questions about you:

1. Do you care about me? Me? A person, not just a cog in the wheel or someone who accomplishes the task you hired me to do?

2. Can I trust you? Trust you to tell me the truth when you can and to do the honorable thing at all times? To behave in consistent, predictable ways that won't leave me second-guessing your mood, motive, or next move?

3. Are you committed to outstanding performance? Do you demand the best from yourself and all of us? Will your efforts and commitment to superior performance ensure we all have a place to work in the future?

Kristy asked these questions herself and received a resounding "no" to the first two. Because Barb had never taken the time to get to know Kristy as anything other than an undervalued part of the mechanism, Kristy knew it. Of course, you could make the argument that stars would perform well under any circumstances, as their motivation comes from within and doesn't rely on external reward. Fair enough. But given a choice, stars usually choose a better setting in which to perform, and that's exactly what Kristy did. Barb still doesn't know what changed in Kristy's life or why her performance changed. But it no longer matters, because Kristy took her talent elsewhere, and Barb has experienced several more turnovers because she never gives direct reports a reason to answer "yes" to those first two questions. In some form or another, people in all industries and all levels ask these same three questions. Kristy ended up leaving Barb, even though she enjoyed the work and had done it well.

As Barb never learned, no short cuts exist for knowing your people. You have to put in the time and effort to understand who they are and what they need from you and the organization. You can buy copious numbers of books that will advise you about how to adjust your management style to meet the needs of your people, but these exist primarily to showcase the author's research, speaking topics, or other revenue streams, not to offer cutting-edge insights about how to lead more effectively

For example, in your chain of command, you may have "Baby Boomers," some "Gen Xers," some members of "Generation Y," and probably some from "Why Nots?" or whatever names have made their way into the books since I started writing this one. These books are filled with advice about how you must manage and lead the people in your organization based solely on the year their birth happened. Apparently you will automatically understand all those who share your generation but remain flummoxed by those who don't.

A new, pervasive, insidious "ism" is sweeping the country, if not the world. People who would never dream of engaging in sexism or racism don't hesitate to jump on what I call the "generationalism" bandwagon. Consider this: Bill Gates, Bill Clinton—Baby Boomers. Tom Hanks, Michael Jordan, and Jay Leno—also Baby Boomers. Osama Bin Laden—Baby Boomer. Can somebody tell me what these men have in common with each other? If this much diversity can exist in this short list of Baby Boomers, doesn't it make sense that uniqueness and variety exist within each generation in your organization too?

Generationalism is the lazy executive's excuse not to appreciate the unique contributions of each person. Aside from wasting your time study-ing this never-proven theory, you will engage in biases that will certain-ly stand in the way of your identifying your stars. Top performers know no generational, gender, racial, or religious lines. But they do share three traits: yhey are smart enough to do the job, they are driven to do it well, and they have integrity. Throughout history, all the great leaders who positively influenced the course of humankind embodied all these traits. Certainly each came from a different generation—often separated by hundreds, if not thousands, of years.

Instead of investing time and money on books that won't really help you lead your stars anyway, try an easier method: listen to them. Theorists, researchers, and authors of every stripe have filled the bookstores with volumes about how to motivate, but the simplest and easiest way to motivate, or at least to avoid de-motivating already motivated people, is to ask them about their preferences and then to consider their responses. You can and should do this routinely throughout the year, but at least a couple of times a year you can also invite your direct reports to give you more focused feedback about what they need. These conversations should not occur at the same time that performance appraisals occur, however, because this does not involve you giving your direct reports feedback; it's the other way around. It's your opportunity to really listen to what they need from you.

I recommend a simple, 10-question format with a 10-point rating scale to identify their preferences. This scale allows you to debrief in percentages and makes things pretty clear to both the direct report and you. Once you put this process in place, your direct reports will start to expect the e-mail that asks them to fill out the questionnaire and then schedule an appointment to debrief it. Filling out the questionnaire takes about five minutes, and the debrief takes about an hour. Both you and your direct report will quickly learn that this is a painless, important process that pays huge dividends. (See Appendix.)

These 10 questions don't hold any magical power. Rather, they provide the vehicles that will drive the discussions that you need to have with your team to get to know them better. When you have the answers to these 10 questions, you will know what you need to do to help each person feel valued and appreciated—a process that will help you improve your coaching of average employees and keep your top talent from walking out the door. Once you understand your direct reports' preferences and work styles, you'll want to determine the traits you can develop and separate them from those you can't.

Make the Most of Your Most Valuable Resource

Companies have only to look inside their four walls to find the wealth of unrealized capacity that resides in every employee. But this takes time, a commitment to the process, listening, and a way for discovering strengths. Quite frankly, leaders more often operate under the flawed assumption that they should constantly address problems. Most executives take their direct reports' assets and skills for granted and focus performance reviews, feedback, and training on minimizing weaknesses. No successful company that I know of, however, has driven its strategy through corrective action. Truly successful companies learn to focus on leveraging strengths—those of the people and those of the organization.

Knowing more about your direct reports and their strengths is the first step to helping them to leverage those strengths. Giving people the opportunity to do what they do best is the second most critical action for keeping them productive and engaged. You need to know the answer to the question, At work do your people have the opportunity to do what they do best every day?

When people can do what they're best at and what they like most, they are far more likely to stay—and to stay engaged. In short, learning ways to help your direct reports leverage their strengths more effectively just makes good business sense. Yet many don't feel that their strengths come into play every day. And the longer employees stay with an organization and the higher they climb, the less likely they are to feel that they are playing to their strengths. Instead, responsibilities for running a department, overseeing tactics, and handling day-to-day business can overshadow the employee's forte.

When senior leaders don't understand their direct reports' strengths and preferences, they can make mistakes by legislating *work style*. Determined to uphold standards, leaders often concentrate on *how* their direct reports are doing a task rather than on that fact that they are doing it well in their own way. Policies and procedures are often critical factors to consider, but more often, allowing people the freedom to choose how they will be productive will ensure that they are.

Finally, leaders frequently make the mistake of giving the squeaky wheel all the grease. Troublemakers, average or below average performers, and malcontents siphon a disproportionate amount of the leader's energy and attention. When you allow this, in essence, you reward bad behavior by giving your attention to those who do things that you don't want, and you deny your attention to the ones who deserve it. You could better spend your energies on the high potentials in your group who will get the job done and take the organization to the next level of success. If you can help these people discover their assets and talents, and, working together, can coach them to their next level, you will build a boss/direct report relationship that anyone would hate to leave.

Commit to High Potentials

The military, better than many civilian organizations I've worked with, understands the value of committing to high potentials—a commitment that turns those who may not have reached their potential into top performers. Many senior military officers begin mentoring future candidates when those would-be generals are still captains.

For example, retired four-star General Bruce Carlson unknowingly began his journey to four-star rank when he was an Air Force captain stationed at Myrtle Beach, South Carolina. He served as an A-10 pilot but had no Air Force leadership experience to speak of.

He received a call to wear his dress uniform and report for an interview with General Bill Creech, the Commander of the then Tactical Air Command (TAC). General Creech, whose name Carlson didn't recognize at the time, went on to write *The Five Pillars of TQM* and to be hailed as "The father of the modern Air Force."

Having only his dress blues from ROTC, Carlson went to the appointed meeting with Gen. Creech with little idea what lay ahead. When then-Captain Carlson arrived for the interview, he was informed that he was one of three finalists—one was a Thunderbird pilot, the other an instructor at the Weapons School, the Air Force's equivalent to Top Gun—and both outranked him. With this kind of competition, Carlson realized he stood no chance of becoming the next Aide to the Commander of TAC.

Carlson had graduated from a land-grant college and had no "it's who you know" connections, yet Gen. Creech saw something that made him choose Carlson over the two more qualified men. Perhaps Gen. Creech perceived Carlson's innate abilities, his sense of integrity, his humility—we can only guess at this juncture. But the point is, aside from raw talent and integrity—which Gen. Creech could only infer from an initial meeting—Carlson had no special advantage over anybody else. Stellar mentoring, according to Gen. Carlson, made all the difference.[1]

According to General Carlson, he learned four main lessons from Gen. Creech's mentoring:

1. How to communicate. Gen. Carlson recounted examples of Creech working with others to reduce a 100-slide presentation to 10 slides. Creech was a superb speaker who knew how to get his point across.

2. The value of leadership succession. Gen. Creech had the ability to see strengths in people and to place them in situations that provided them the opportunity to leverage those strengths to get promoted. Creech's mentoring influenced every Chief of Staff for the Air Force for 20 years after his retirement.

3. The importance of getting into the details of things that matter while letting others handle the things that don't.

4. The critical nature of building relationships, putting others at ease, and reaching out to others.

Years after working for Gen. Creech, Gen. Carlson found himself in another situation for which he felt under-qualified. When he was a colonel, Carlson interviewed with John Deutch, the Under Secretary of Defense and Acquisition. Carlson anticipated his own retirement but nonetheless interviewed with Deutch. Once again, in spite of not having most of the experience one typically has had in the pipeline, Carlson secured the position and acquired another excellent mentor in the bargain. In this job, he worked around and with the senior leadership in the Pentagon and other thought-leaders and decision-makers.

Gen. Carlson commented that he might have been able to learn the leadership lessons his respective mentors offered, but it would have been tantamount to "learning math but never being able to do calculus." Gen.

Carlson retired after 37 and a half years of active duty in the Air Force and currently serves as the Director of the National Reconnaissance Office, reporting directly to both the Secretary of Defense and the Director of National Intelligence.

Dr. James Dennis, the president of McKendree University, offers another success story with strong mentoring as the hero. Dr. Dennis came to McKendree in 1994 after spending most of his professional life at the University of Southern California. While at USC, Dr. Dennis worked for the vice president of student affairs, Jim Appleton, and several other mentors who taught him the significance of "knowing when to fall on the sword," when to fight a battle, and when to walk away from the fray.

Dr. Dennis must have been an apt student. In the years since he has taken the helm, McKendree has grown its student body by more than 400 percent; he has transformed it from a college to a university, and in 2009 *The Chronicle of Higher Education* named McKendree as one of the Great Colleges to Work For and included it on its honor roll of only 39 institutions. In addition to knowing when to fall on the sword, Dr. Dennis's mentors taught him these lessons:

◊   Maintain life balance—work hard but wisely.

◊   Energy and activity don't equal leadership.

◊   The key to putting together a team with vision is to hire those not like you.

◊   Don't hire "yes" people. Surround yourself with people with different experiences who will mitigate your weaknesses.

◊   Hire well, and then get out of the way.[2]

Senior leaders recognized the potential in Bruce Carlson and James Dennis. They hand-picked them, gave them preferential treatment, and made sure they learned what they needed to know—that which was not set down in texts and training. Senior leaders modeled behaviors that Carlson and Dennis went on to emulate, one in the Air Force and federal government, the other in a small town in Illinois. These offer but two examples of the power of mentoring.

Proven Techniques for Coaching and Mentoring

What helps to motivate people? Unfortunately, for many companies, their senior leaders would give the wrong answer. Their motivation technique of choice involves frightening people until they are immobilized, or rewarding everybody with a worthless gift that bears the company logo. In these kinds of organizations, employees learn to spend an inordinate number of hours of "face time" at work, being burnt-out and practically useless. Ideas don't become actions with this kind of approach.

There are, however, techniques that do help. In the past decades, evidence suggests leaders can have a positive effect on moving ideas to action if they commit to mentoring. These findings revealed that leaders' expectations and their ability to communicate them determined performance outcomes. In other words, superior leaders who communicate high performance expectations often have direct reports who fulfill them. Here are some of the things they do.

Effective Delegation

Accountability is at the heart of motivation. We are motivated to put our best efforts into projects that we consider our "babies." When we babysit someone else's baby, we only worry about managing safety until the parents return. We don't worry about equipping the child for the future— piano lessons, education, braces, moral development, or the host of other things parents think and worry about. Instead, we try to bide our time and make it as pleasant as possible.

Some people, unfortunately, see their work the same way. They don't feel responsible for outcomes, largely because their boss is in the middle of things, often micromanaging. The antidote? Effective delegation. Delegation will trump motivation—every time. To keep your people focused, engaged, and motivated, consider the following:

⬥ Communicate, set timeframes, establish goals, and get out of the way. Talk to others about *what* needs to be done, but let them decide *how* they will go about it. Unless their way is wrong—that is, best practices, common sense, or the law indicates it shouldn't be done—let them experiment with their own methods. Be crystal clear about "what," "when," and more open to " how."

◇ Be aware that direct reports will not be motivated to reach high levels of productivity unless they consider your expectations realistic and achievable. When the goals aren't realistic, people become disheartened. Stretch them; don't snap them. Dangling the carrot just beyond the donkey's reach will just make for a very angry donkey.

◇ Help people formulate personal goals that support organizational and departmental priorities. Take care of your people, and they will take care of their jobs.

◇ Working with your direct report, break large projects into several smaller steps with deadlines for each step. Track completion and give balanced feedback on the success of the plan.

◇ Give each person whole projects instead of pieces or parts of a project.

◇ Grant authority and freedom to get the job done. Let people sign their names to their work, making them personally responsible for its quality and accuracy.

◇ Assign specialized tasks that enable people to become experts.

◇ Remove controls, but retain accountability.

◇ On a regular basis, introduce new and more difficult tasks not previously handled.

Delegation sounds simple—which it is—but it's not easy. If you fail to delegate, you rob yourself of precious time, deny your direct reports the opportunity to grow, and deprive the organization of the chance to have more highly skilled people on its bench.

To begin the process, ask your direct reports to list the major decisions they currently make. Then, using the assigned code of the following accountability chart, indicate what level of involvement the direct report thinks appropriate: making the decision alone, notifying you but proceeding without further authorization, or consulting with you before going forward. You can retain as much control as you think appropriate. You will encourage the development of your people if you not only allow them to make their own decisions but also insist on it.

When I suggested this process to Mike, a promising future company president, he was amazed at the immediate and profound payoff. People were doing their own work, they didn't come to him with problems they should be solving, and he left the office at a decent time each day, the first time that had happened in years. Mike also noticed he was growing in his own development, because he now had time to devote to learning about his next level of responsibility. (And his golf game got better!)

Here's the accountability chart Mike used, a variation of models that have been used in the worlds of project management and national defense:

Directions: Identify the major decisions that you make on a somewhat routine basis. Then, using the letters at the top, identify, not necessarily what you're currently doing, but the level of accountability that you think is appropriate.

If you are responsible for the outcome but don't have the authority to make the decision alone, put an R under your name and the appropriate letter under your boss's name or the name of the person who needs to be involved.

Accountability Chart

A = Authority to make decisions alone.

R = Responsibility for completing the task.

N = Notification: Person is notified of decision.

C = Consultation: This person must okay the decision before you proceed.

Major Decision/ Task	Direct Report	Boss	Other's Name	Other's Name

This is a fluid document that should change periodically. In fact, many leaders think it helps to put timelines on each decision. Others find that putting parameters around certain decisions helps too. For instance, working together, you and your direct reports may decide that up to a certain dollar amount, they will make the call; at another level, they will notify you; at a higher one they will consult with you before moving ahead. When you start to notice direct reports making good decisions at one level of difficulty or complexity, give them more rein. If you don't see progress, that's critical data too. Even though this process takes time initially (usually about an hour with each direct report) you will reap the reward of hours a week that you'll get back. You won't face the problem of direct reports not wanting more challenges and freedom to make decisions, but you may encounter your own fears of giving up control. What if they don't do the job as well as you do? That's a likely scenario, but with your coaching and feedback, they can learn to do things reasonably well—maybe not perfectly, but at least successfully. Remember, the goal is success, not perfection. Effective feedback holds the key to this success.

An ABC Approach to Feedback

The ABC approach to feedback is simple—feedback should be Achievable, Balanced, and Candid. Giving feedback to people about things they can't change just frustrates you and annoys them. Unbalanced feedback tends to engender the same sort of reaction—annoyance, with a touch of defensiveness. Candor certainly must play a role in the coaching relationship. This approach to feedback, though universal, does not involve a cookie-cutter methodology. Rather, it requires the discipline to develop a unique approach for each of your direct reports—a way of reaching that person based on what he or she *needs* rather than *wants*. It demands that you abandon the principles of the Golden Rule—which is neither golden nor a rule—and to treat people as *they need to be treated*, not necessarily as they want to be treated, or even as you would want to be treated. But candor also calls for you to give feedback that builds, not destroys.

The trick to balanced feedback involves giving both positive and negative, but not in the formerly popular One Minute Manager sandwich form—a positive, a negative, and then another positive. Most people resent this approach. When I give feedback, I address four major areas: decision-making and problem-solving, approach to work, people skills, and leadership style. I give the pros and cons in each area. In your own coaching, you can identify the major areas that you need to address. Perhaps you will want to use these four, but you may want to substitute productivity measures for approach to work or some other measure of performance.

Whatever criteria you decide to use, let the accountability chart serve as a starting point for defining action items. Inundate direct reports with enough quantifiable data to convince them of the facts but also enough to move them to action. Engage curiosity and competitive instincts, but point out defensive reactions when you see them. If you structure your conversations, you'll offer better coaching, and you and they will be glad of it.

The GLAD Communication Model

GLAD is an acronym I developed to explain for the four-step communication method that enables leaders and direct reports to have routine conversations, difficult discussions, and feedback sessions. Leaders who learn and practice this method discover that their modeling this behavior eventually causes others to adopt it too. The effort promises an environment in which employees are GLAD to be there, and so are their leaders. Here's how it works:

1. Get to the core of the performance issues.
2. Listen to the other first.
3. Add your own ideas.
4. Develop an action plan.

Getting to the core of the issue means focusing the discussion on one specific issue. It also means focusing the discussion on *actions or behaviors*, things the person can control and change. If personality issues or decision-making capacities interfere with the person's performance, the problem may involve an inability, rather than an unwillingness, to do the job. In that case, you will need to consider alternatives—either to give the direct report additional help, or to move him or her to an area better suited for that person's talents and strengths. When giving feedback or holding a difficult discussion, focus on *one* concern that can be expressed in *one* sentence. If it won't fit into one sentence, it requires more than one discussion. If you try to lump too many things together, the direct report will leave confused and frustrated.

Be sure to express the problem in *concrete, observable, descriptive* terms.

To help you determine if you have clear language, ask yourself these questions:

◊　If I were following the person around, what would I see? Hear?

◊　What does the direct report need to start doing? Stop doing? Do differently?

◊　If this were fixed, how would you know?

Too often leaders center the discussion on the *symptoms* of the problem instead of on the actual problem. For example, a grocery store manager told me his direct report just "didn't communicate with his own direct reports enough." I asked how he knew. In other words, where was the pain? He said turnover; shrink; and costs were high. I pointed out that he had just described three problems that may or may not have anything to do with the man communicating with his direct reports. When forced to separate the causes from effects, and unrelated issues from each other, he got his hands around exactly how he needed to coach his employee. Once this became apparent, the leader clearly articulated the most pressing problem: "The problem is that turnover costs the store X dollars per year, an increase in X dollars from this time last year." The direct report then knew exactly what the issue entailed and was able to address strategies for improvement.

Contrast this scenario to a leader's beginning with the statement, "You don't communicate with your people enough." The direct report would reasonably think or say, "I communicate plenty." If the boss and the direct report don't even agree on the nature of the problem, there's very little chance that they will be able to solve it. On the other hand, if you make a statement of *fact* that plainly describes the tangible consequences, there can be little room for disagreement, at least during this step. Often this statement of fact will describe the pain or consequences of an action, usually in their simplest terms. If you discipline yourself to talk about facts and further commit to listening first to the other's ideas, the likelihood of actually solving problems skyrockets.

If, however, you're like most leaders, when someone comes to you with a problem, you try to jump in to fix things. Solving problems, after all, got you where you are today, so it comes easily and naturally—plus, it just feels like the right thing to do, and it saves time. But however well-intended you might be, when you fix others' problems, you inadvertently pass up a chance to develop rapport with and abilities in the direct reports.

Listening first, before you offer a solution, has many advantages. First, you will *show* your concern and responsiveness by patiently allowing the other to explain the issue. Second, you will operate from a basis of knowledge, not guesswork or probability. Third, you will have more of a chance of understanding the whole picture, not just a segment of it.

Effective leaders understand that seeking to understand others comes *before* seeking to be understood. People will understand *you* better if you show them that you have taken the time to understand *them* first. But this scenario often doesn't play out in the in-the-trenches world of everyday business. Often caring, compassionate leaders register dismay when their 360 multi-rater feedback data indicate that their direct reports don't always know that their bosses care about them. More often than not, in fact, these 360 data show that direct reports don't feel that their leaders listen to them, much less understand them.

Leaders who are otherwise effective often need to develop or hone their listening skills. Taking the time to listen patiently to others, however, does not always have immediate payoffs. Therefore, in an attempt to move projects ahead more efficiently, leaders overlook opportunities to hear what their direct reports have to say. Listening to the other person first shows a willingness to consider new information, and if necessary, to change the nature of the discussion. Similarly, hearing the other person sets the tone for the give-and-take that will be necessary to create understanding and commitment between the two.

To improve listening, consider these four steps:

1. Listen first before you give your own ideas. Listen to understand, not judge.

2. Don't interrupt. When people are on a roll, just listen without saying a word.

3. Summarize and paraphrase—restate facts and reflect emotions that may interfere with the rest of the conversation. Paraphrasing is not parroting—it is a restatement of what you heard. The trick is to concentrate on responding non-defensively when people express viewpoints that contradict your own. Then, you're ready to move to the next step in the process.

4. Ask at least two open-ended "how?" and "what?" questions. Take advantage of the opportunity to address as many issues as possible with open questions.

You may be thinking "This will take so long! I don't have time to ask a lot of questions. It's so much faster to just tell people the problem and tell them how to fix it," True. The most economical use of time, at least in the short run, involves to telling people what to do to fix things. But that sort of behavior leads to other problems: sometimes people resist being told what to do, you don't give direct reports the chance to discover solutions, and they become reliant on you for decisions they should be making themselves. One way or the other, if you persist in jumping in to fix things for others, *you* will end up annoyed.

The behaviors outlined in this chapter will help you *show* you are a better listener, but to truly be one, you will need to adjust your listening habits and attitudes. Opening your mind to really *hear* the message is key. Listening for facts and ideas, though important, paints only part of the picture. You can't ignore emotions. I have often said, only partially facetiously, that if every boss in America would follow these simple four steps to better listening, the economy would improve overnight. (So far no one from the Oval Office has called to explore this idea, hence the ongoing economic problems!)

We know that listening is not the absence of talking; it is the presence of attention. It does not mean simply maintaining a polite silence while you rehearse in your mind what you will say the next time the slightest lull in the discussion presents itself, nor does it mean patiently waiting for flaws to appear in others' arguments so that you can annihilate them later. Listening is not simply hearing; it's comprehension, and it is the art of total involvement. It requires participation, action, and effort. It is the glue that holds conversations together and the foundation of understanding. Effective listening skills can be learned; like all communication skills, however, listening requires practice and technique. As the leader, you are going to encounter many opportunities to keep your mouth shut. Take advantage of at least some of them.

Listening to the other first doesn't mean you should not give direction. On the contrary, the third step, to add your own ideas, is the time to do just that. Ideally the discussion to this point should have implied a course of action for the direct report. If, in spite of your best efforts, that hasn't happened, the third step is the time to give that direction.

Once again, clearly defining the specific behaviors that the direct report should address will help to keep the discussion focused. If you disagree with the direct report's assessment of the situation, if there has been a shift in priorities, or if the two of you disagree on action steps, this is the time for you to express ideas and concerns and to begin a discussion about how to resolve differences.

Direct reports need to have a clear understanding of what you expect, those things that they need to do more of or less of to improve. Be sure to communicate the "why" behind the "what." Compliment efforts people have made to move projects forward, and offer suggestions when people seem stuck. Communicate clearly that *results* matter. Effective feedback concentrates on what the direct report has *accomplished*, not what he or she spent time *attempting* to accomplish.

After clearly defining the problem, listening to the other person first, and adding your own ideas, you and your direct report face the all-important question: "So what?" What needs to happen now to rectify the problem and move ideas to fruition? An action plan—the agreement you reach with your direct reports—provides a way to ensure that you and they agree to the next steps. It captures the essence of the conversation and holds people accountable to deliver on their commitments. The action plan should be a fluid document that changes with new information, accomplishments, unexpected events, and learning. To make the most of the action-planning step, you and your direct reports, working together, need to prioritize goals and objectives to identify the two current most important action items. More than two will jeopardize the direct report's efforts to accomplish anything. (There can be an unlimited number of "hows" to the two "whats," however.)

Timelines for goals help this process. Sometimes the timeline will be obvious. At other times, you will need to create them, often in response to new initiatives or demands. Some people have the capacity to break large projects into manageable parts; others need direction to do so. The main payoff of the action plan is neither the form nor the document, but the *discussion*. Once your direct report and you know what you need and expect, each has identified roadblocks, and you have set the timeline, the action plan becomes apparent.

This does not imply, however, that you should overlook *writing* the action plan. A written action plan provides the tangible agreement between the stakeholders. It serves as a kind of report card for tracking results and re-directing efforts. Both you and the direct report, therefore, should keep a copy of the original agreement and the subsequent notes and changes.

Appreciative Inquiry

"Appreciative inquiry" is another coaching technique that augments the GLAD Communication Model. The theory behind this technique surfaced during the 1980s and refers to both a search for knowledge and a conscious evolution of positive imagery. By asking questions about what has worked in the past for a person, you begin a search for the best examples of what might work in the future. Traditionally, however, coaching has been rooted in viewing problems that need to be solved, instead of on leveraging the strengths that the person has previously displayed. Appreciative inquiry, therefore, is the antithesis to "What the hell were you thinking?" questioning. By analyzing *positive* factors instead of focusing on problems, causes, and gaps, appreciative inquiry concentrates on achievement of the best possible outcomes.

This technique involves an attempt to generate an image of a new and better future by exploring the best of what is and has been. By looking at the finest part of a track record, you can help your direct reports discover the best of what might be, what should be, and what can be. The desired and likely outcome of this approach is stimulation of the direct report's personal drive and motivation. Once you *discover* what has worked, you'll be able to help your direct report *design* a future that will be even better.

Here's how it works. If a direct report had an 85 percent approval rating score from her customers, you might be tempted to try to discover why 15 percent were not happy, overlooking the fact that the vast majority of customers like what's happening. Why not find out what made the 85 percent approve instead of the 15 percent disapprove? What did this person do right? What made the customers value her? The answers to these questions will help you discover the positive attributes that led to this person's success and to visualize what should happen in the future. Something works. What is it, and how can people leverage it?

The goal of this method is to cause people to have a new insight—to realize what it took for them to succeed in the past. What we focus on becomes our reality, and the language we use creates this reality. The act of asking questions influences the way people respond to coaching and ultimately changes their behavior. You'll find that people will have more confidence about journeying into the unknown future when they carry forward positive parts of their known pasts. If you're their tour guide, in addition to leading the way, you will engender the loyalty that will give you a talent advantage over your competitors.

How to Coach Your High Potentials

In the discussion of General Carlson and President Dennis, I mentioned that both men had received preferential treatment—someone had singled them out and played favorites. Audiences almost always ask me about the fairness of this approach. How can I justify giving one direct report special attention over the others? Easy. Level the playing field. People who show you they deserve special treatment receive it.

If you played sports in college, did the coach play everyone equally? Create an egalitarian form of governance in which each person had a say? Or did the star, the one who had the innate athletic ability and drive to put it into action, receive a disproportionate amount of playing time and the coach's attention? If you won many games, I suspect the second scenario. Fairness demands each person receive an equal opportunity to succeed, not equal treatment along the way. If your high potentials show a willingness to work the extra hours, take the additional training, and attend night school for advanced education, why shouldn't you reward them differently than those who don't? As your athletic coaches understood, so you need to understand. Only by grooming the top 20 percent of your talent will you ultimately win the war for talent. Certainly, compensate them monetarily, but also reward them with the best and cheapest prize of all—your mentoring.

In organizations, however, we tend to resist this reality. We address non-productive behavior and underachievers. When we do this, our stars vote with their feet by walking out our doors. "A" players want to play on winning teams, and they don't suffer "C" and "D" players too long or too much. "A" players demand your attention, but giving it to them won't always prove easy.

One of the most challenging issues you'll face as an executive, in fact, will be coaching high potentials, because as people near peak performance, tasks become mundane, problems less interesting, and opportunities less fascinating. The adrenaline wanes. They start to experience discontent and to wonder what happened to the excitement. You may see less enthusiasm and a subtle loss of edge.

I have spent my career selecting "A" players during the pre-employment process and coaching them later for promotion. They embody the aptitude, behaviors, and attitude of stars. Sometimes they lack experience, but because they are so clever and learn so quickly, gaining requisite experience seldom stands in their way. I have found, however, that most senior leaders don't know how to coach them, even if they themselves would be counted as stars. Through the years, I have learned the following things about attracting and nurturing "A" players, stars, high-potentials—whatever term you choose to use:

⋄ Clever people learn quickly, so they bore easily. About the time they master a skill set, they itch to move on, and start to take the recruiters' calls.

⋄ You can't fool them with titles, even though they appreciate ones that mean something. They want ever-changing, challenging work and real authority to make a difference.

⋄ They require other "A" players on their team. Make your organization a place where the clever choose to work, and your stars will become your best magnets for other top performers.

⋄ Allow them to celebrate innovation and engage in experimentation, even when that means the occasional failure. Talented people like to create. You have to give them that chance.

⋄ They know their worth and expect to be recognized for it and compensated adequately for it. Even though star performers don't usually count compensation among their reasons for taking or leaving a job, they do have a sense of fair play and want to be rewarded for who and what they are.

⋄ Top performers don't respond well to autocratic leadership. Nor do they appreciate laissez-fair leadership. They want direction but in the form of democratic guidance, not an absence of direction.

⋄ Try to micromanage a star just a little, and you will lose that person.

⋄ "A" players want access—to you, your top clients, investors, and anyone else who is important to the organization. They have little patience with hierarchy or red tape. They want the fastest route to task completion without organizational roadblocks.

⋄ Star performers require praise, but unless you offer it sincerely and specifically, they will dismiss it.

◊   The best and brightest lead with strategy, not tactics. Often, in fact, they lack strong detail orientation and need others to keep them on track.

Learning to lead "A" players will be its own reward. When you can attract and retain the best in your industry, you can't help but realize success. They bring their own challenges, however. When they burn out, which happens frequently, they will need your benevolent guidance. They frequently set unrealistic expectations for themselves and then mercilessly punish themselves when they don't achieve them. Winston Churchill is said to have ended each day with this harsh ritual: "I try myself by court martial to see if I have done anything effective during the day." Like other top performers, Churchill pushed himself to extremes in an effort to achieve more. Your top performers may do the same. If you see troubling behavior—cynicism, anger, substance abuse, sexual indiscretions—speak up. But more importantly, listen. The world offers a limited number of clever people. If you have some, try not to let them self-destruct.[3]

Conclusion

No age group or time in history has ever cornered the market on talent. Certainly, circumstances coalesce in such a way to provide unique experiences for each generation, but true talent knows no age bracket. Companies have always wanted those who are honest, smart enough to do the job, and driven to do it well. As the senior leader, if you learn to assess aptitude, behavior, and experience—not generations—you'll take a critical step toward attracting and retaining the best in your industry and ensuring your success and that of those who depend on you.

In my work with numerous organizations and executives, I've discovered that senior leaders, not HR, are the point people for this talent search. Magnetic leaders hold the keys to the decisions, structures, and processes. They serve as the *personal examples* that attract, secure, nurture, and retain talent. Leading meetings, setting strategy, determining markets, ensuring profit goals, coordinating with the board, and all the rest of the traditional leadership roles will remain. But nothing will be as important as winning the war for talent. Mentoring your "A" players is one of the surest ways to do so.

Chapter 4

Strategize to Leverage Your Competitive Advantage

It is not enough to be busy—the question is, what are we busy about?

—Henry David Thoreau

In most organizations, you'll find more people who understand how to run fast than there are people who can decide which race they should enter...more people with well-honed skills for producing results in the short run than visionary strategists. Certainly, you need both to succeed, but most organizations are replete with those who can plug ahead and lacking on those who can *plan* ahead; the competition, however, is more likely to outmaneuver you strategically than to outperform you tactically. Your tactical to-do list (plugging away) will often keep you in the game today, but only a clear strategy can ensure your success tomorrow. Therefore, as the executive, you must understand the nature of strategy, embrace the changes it brings, set priorities for achieving what your competition can't match, and choose the right people to drive your vision. Only then will you outwit your rivals and claim your unique position.

The Foundations of Strategy

What is strategy? The definitions vary slightly, but the common elements and their effects on the realities of organizational life remain constant. According to three long-standing experts in the field, strategy is:

◊ "a framework of choices that determine the nature and direction of an organization."[1]

◊ "those policies and key decisions adopted by management that have *major* impacts on financial performance. These policies and decisions usually involve significant resource commitments and are not easily reversible."[2]

◊ "the *key* factors that dictate the...direction of an organization together with the *process* that the CEO...uses to set direction."[3]

Every organization is headed somewhere. Too often, however, that direction is not the result of a conscious choice. Instead, leaders engage in *perceived* potential, reactive decision-making, or short-term gains designed to placate shareholders and analysts.

Conversely, an effective business strategy provides a way to create and capture value while serving the customer. It offers the winning formula for an organization's purpose, direction, goals, and standards: the organization's mission, vision, and values. People often talk about mission, vision, and values as if they were all the same thing, but we should think of them distinctly; each plays a complementary but separate role in the success of any strategy.

Mission

In 2001, I was working with the leaders of a family-owned business to help them set their strategies for the next year. In our first meeting, they told me they were eager to have a discussion of execution because they wanted to set up a two-day seminar during which each officer of the company could identify a clearly articulated goal and timeline, both of which would be used to evaluate his performance at the end of the year. I assured them we would have that discussion, but first I asked to see a copy of their mission and vision statements. Looking confused and more than a little annoyed, the father said he thought they were somewhere around there in a framed picture, and the son was pretty sure they had hired a company to put them on some mouse pads that they had used a year or so ago. But neither father nor son could tell me what the mission and vision were! At one time, they had written and wordsmithed a mission and vision statement, but clearly these were no longer serving as the foundation for their strategy formulation, nor, apparently, even for their desk accessories. These owners, unfortunately, represent the mindset I frequently encounter. Too often leaders assume that simply creating (or having a consultant create) and distributing a mission statement will accomplish something important.

As I explained to them, before taking any steps to formulate a strategy, they should have a clear understanding of the mission and of their organization. A mission statement should play the same role in your organization that the Holy Grail did in the Crusades. Your mission defines your reason for being, the touchstone against which you evaluate your strategy, activities, and expectations for overcoming the competition. Without one, you will diffuse resources, enable individual units of the organization to operate in silos, create conflicting tactics, and confuse customers, suppliers, financiers, and employees. Conversely, when you have a well-articulated sense of purpose, you will build a firm foundation that provides clear guidance for all significant decisions and establishes a point of reference for setting strategy and planning its execution. A mission statement answers these questions:

◊   Why do we exist?

◊   What is our business?

◊   Who are our customers?

◊   What do our customers value?

In addition to defining the organization's identity, the mission guides its development through time. Although it should be resistant to capriciousness, as the external landscape changes, leaders must tweak the mission statement as they recognize how to translate purpose into practice.

For example, in 1979 Americans experienced long lines at the gas pumps. Gas prices soared (or at least we thought so then) to 86 cents a gallon while supply dwindled. The writing had been on the wall years earlier, but not everyone at the Ford Motor Company read it. Henry Ford II was the chairman of Ford. Lee Iacocca headed Ford US, and Hal Sperlich served as Iacocca's deputy of product design.

In 1976, recognizing the American car buyer's need to respond to gas shortages, and certain that the American market would demand smaller cars, Hal Sperlich recommended that Ford downsize its automobiles, advocating smaller, more fuel-efficient cars to compete with foreign imports. Even though the Mustang had enjoyed great success in the 1960s, Henry Ford disagreed. He pontificated from the outset that he did not want a small, new, front-wheel-drive car because he didn't think the market would change too much. He advocated taking an existing middle-level Ford car, stripping it down, and making it lighter. That car became known in the dustup as the "Panther," Henry's favorite.

Even before this debate, in late 1975, after hearing the arguments about how costly a new small line would be, Iacocca offered what he considered an inspirational idea: use a Honda engine.

Honda had impressed Iacocca with its engineering and front-wheel-drive technology, so after a surreptitious trip to Japan to discuss a joint venture, Iacocca presented his idea to Henry: build the Fiesta within 18 months with a Honda engine and transmission in it. Henry was indignant, "No Jap engine is going under the hood of a car with my name on it," he announced. "Small cars mean small profits" became his mantra. For years, key leaders at Ford disagreed about the fundamentals of strategy, including a shared purpose that responds to change. Iacocca and Sperlich agreed with each other about what they wanted the mission to be—to respond to customer demands—but Henry disagreed. He wanted to stick with the status quo. The stalemate led to dire consequences. Ford fired Sperlich, and the American car buyer punished Ford Motor Company.[4] Iacocca went on to write a bestseller entitled, *Iacocca,* but he could have just as easily called it *I Told You So!* As Iacocca foresaw, failure to make decisions based on the mission of the organization would cost Ford dearly in the late 1970s, yet more than 30 years later, organizations still mistake the writing on the wall for graffiti when it comes to putting purpose into practice.

During a recent speech, when I asked an audience of 200 people from different companies to recite their mission statements, I saw bewilderment and discomfiture. Three of the 200 hands proudly shot up to proclaim the executive of that company could remember the mission statement, but the other 197 sat stoically. Yet, when I asked these same people to tell me what's on a Big Mac, the entire audience recited, "Two all beef patties, special sauce...." In other words, a commercial that has not been on TV for more than 20 years stayed in their memories more prominently than their own mission statements! If you're like the majority of that audience, you are missing a basic element of your strategic direction. How can your mission serve as the foundation of your strategy and help you know where you're going if you and your people don't know what it is and how it can help you define your vision?

Vision

Once you have established your mission, a vision statement paints a clear picture of what you intend to do and what you will commit to do. This concise statement defines what success will look like in one, three, and five years, sometimes beyond that. A well-crafted vision statement should include a stretch goal that challenges even well-performing organizations to become better. (Jack Welch issued the classic version of this kind of stretch goal when he challenged every GE business unit to become one or two in its industry.) Other components of a vision statement should be a definition of focus and a timeline for execution.

For example, in 1961, everyone understood the vision of NASA to "land a man on the moon and return him safely to earth" within the decade. In the summer of 1969, Americans glued themselves to televisions as Neil Armstrong took his famous one small step for man and giant leap for mankind. Because of the clarity of this vision, legend suggests that during NASA's Apollo initiative a reporter couldn't find anyone else to interview about the upcoming launch, so he decided to talk to the man vacuuming the floor. The reporter asked the janitor about his job, to which the janitor responded, "My job is to put a man on the moon," clearly communicating his understanding that he played a vital role in accomplishing NASA's vision.

Even when the leadership responds to change or customer demands, the mission of a company tends to remain constant, even when the vision changes. For example, Nike's vision in the 1980s was to annihilate Adidas and then in the 1990s to annihilate Reebok. The mission of annihilation of the competition remained a constant; only the object of the obliteration changed.

During World War II Churchill had a bold, unwavering vision that England would not just survive the war but that it would prevail as a great nation. In spite of the grim reality that the Nazis controlled much of Europe and North Africa and the United States had not entered the fray, Churchill held to his vision, which he shared with his countrymen:

We are resolved to destroy Hitler and every vestige of the Nazi regime. From this, nothing will turn us. Nothing! We will never parley. We will never negotiate with Hitler or any of his gang. We shall fight him by land. We shall fight him by sea. We shall fight him in the air. Until, with God's help, we have rid the earth of his shadow. [5]

Prior to the war, Britain had never had a mission to destroy Hitler, but with the stark realities facing him, Churchill knew he needed to unite the country to support this difficult vision. To this end, he created a department outside the normal chain of command, the Statistical Office, that had the primary function of providing him continuous, updated, unfiltered information.

As Churchill illustrated, and Ford failed to illustrate, a simple but clear vision statement helps you decide where you're going, a critical first step in formulating strategy. It defines something significant you want to do in the future; it inspires, motivates, and challenges. When used in conjunction with your corporate values, it also helps you take a stand on ethical issues.

Values

Corporate values describe the principles and standards that will guide an organization's ethical and business decisions. Organizations typically list things such as leadership, integrity, quality, customer satisfaction, people working together, a diverse and involved team, good corporate citizenship, and enhancing shareholder value. Though all of these are laudable, which would a successful company *not* value? A list of ideals that *any* organization would promote doesn't really distinguish your company from any other, and you're not likely to have any arguments about the importance of embracing these ideals. But how? How do you translate value on paper into value in practice?

Corporate values should address the thorny issues and provide a compass for navigating uncharted seas, even when the price of doing so is significant. For example, in 1987 CEO Robert Haas, the great-great-nephew of founder Levi Strauss implemented corporate values that have helped the clothing company produce loyal employees and customers, but not without a cost. Because the company values included a stated desire to be a "company that our people are proud of and committed to," the leadership at

Levi Strauss decided not to do business in countries that have unsatisfactory labor conditions. Therefore, they decided not to use suppliers in mainland China—an expensive decision for a company that needed to reduce manufacturing costs but one that remained true to its values.[6] For the Levi Strauss Company, their values on paper became their values in practice.

In 1992, the United States Navy faced a similar test of its values when the Kuwaiti government purchased F/A18s and contracted to have them ferried to Egypt. The Navy named then-Lieutenant Commander Trish Beckman, who performed acceptance and operational testing at McDonnell Douglas, to fly in the back seat to deliver one of the planes. In spite of fears that the Kuwaiti government would object to accepting a plane a woman had operated, Beckman, who had more than 3,000 flying hours in 66 different types of aircraft, flew the mission. Even though decision makers knew the customer was likely to protest Beckman's involvement, based solely on the fact that she was a woman, the Navy leadership decided to put Beckman in the rotation. The decision makers insisted she fly the mission but indicated a willingness to compromise with the customer, to address their concerns that a woman would have sat on the ejection seat that one of their Kuwaiti male pilots would eventually have to use. As each crew before them had done, the pilot and Beckman flew the F/A18 into Egypt, but on this delivery mission, an additional procedure seems to have been added to the acceptance checklist: changing the cushions on the ejection seat. (This change to the checklist was never officially verified.)[7]

Like Strauss and the US Navy, your organization needs to live its principles, not just write them. Your values should mean something and serve as criteria for making business decisions. Will you fire your company's most valued, high potential person for a violation of these values? Will you do business in countries that engage in unacceptable labor practices? Will your people accept bribes in countries that otherwise make doing business very difficult? What will you do to protect the environment? When you grapple with these kinds of questions, you will be able to develop a list of standards that will become more than a nice poster in your foyer; these values will serve as the bedrock of your strategy.

The Nature of Strategy

As the leader, you are the architect, steward, and guardian of the strategy. It is a job that cannot be outsourced, completed, or scheduled. It is the most uncertain thing leaders do, because it involves speculation about unknowns and requires a journey into murky waters. Coupled with hiring and developing talent, however, it ranks as the most important thing you do—and makes success more certain. Effective strategy formulation concentrates actions and resources on critical issues, gains commitment, provides a rationale for allocation of resources, enhances communication, and increases your chances of not just surviving but of thriving in your industry. I typically encounter a three-fold problem among my clients relative to strategy: they confuse strategy with tactics; they don't hire enough strategic thinkers who can handle the situational and episodic nature of strategy; and they make strategy an annual event, not an ongoing process.

Strategy is *what* you are trying to do, not *how* you'll do it. It involves setting the destination for the organization, not planning the way to get there. In fact, premature tactical planning often kills strategy development because planning, by its nature, works bottom up; strategy functions top down. Planning relies on facts, operations, and budgets, whereas strategy demands the synthesis of these data and creative thinking about how to gain a competitive edge. Obviously, both strategy and execution are important, but too many organizations mistakenly concentrate on the tactics before they have a clear strategy. Strategies are few; tactics are many. Strategy comes first, tactics second.

In the past decade, however, many companies have confused operational effectiveness and its merits with strategy. The importance of operational effectiveness became apparent in the 1980s when it formed the core of the Japanese challenge to Western companies. The Japanese were so far ahead of their rivals that they could offer lower cost and superior quality at the same time. Therefore, the success of operational effectiveness and its tools unwittingly drew organizations toward imitation, homogeneity, and benchmarking. Operations, tactics, and execution are crucial to success, but only when leaders lose their preoccupation with improving operations can they focus on a competitive strategy that means deliberately choosing to deliver a unique mix of value.

Generic solutions, best practices, and benchmarking cannot succeed in the long run because your competition can easily replicate them, and using them overlooks the reality that each organization is a unique system. A system is a collection of parts that interact with each other to function as a whole. Systems thinking is a discipline for seeing wholes rather than parts. It is the framework for noticing *interrelationships* rather than things, for seeing *patterns of change* rather than static snapshots. If something is made up of a number of parts that do not interact, and the arrangement of these parts is irrelevant, this is a pile of materials rather than a system. For example, a pile of bricks is a pile of bricks whether we add to it or subtract from it. Cutting it in half gives two piles of bricks and adding to it yields a bigger pile of bricks, but essentially the mound of material remains unchanged. Cutting a car, which is a system, in half does not produce two smaller cars nor does adding additional parts to it make a bigger car. Instead, the entire altered system, the car, would cease to perform.

If experts could determine the best parts of each type of automobile, could they manufacture a preeminent automobile by taking disparate parts and putting them together? Taking an engine from one type of car, a transmission from another model, and a carburetor from yet another would not combine to create a system that works. The parts would not be compatible, nor would they create a functioning machine, much less a superlative mode of transportation. Therefore, competitors that want to match your activities and operations gain little by imitating some tactics but not incorporating your entire system, provided that system is based on a sustainable strategy.

Companies that embrace systems thinking tend to be more strategy-driven. They separate themselves from the herd behavior that drives organizations to imitate one another in an attempt to be all things to all customers. Continuous improvement in activities is not the enemy of strategy. In fact, it is essential for achieving superior performance, but it isn't enough. As a leader, you need to go beyond the orchestration of operations to define your organization's matchless position and make the tough calls about trade-offs. You can't import your strategy from another organization because your system is inimitable. Instead, you must define your uniqueness and leverage it in new ways—the only path to a competitive strategy.

Distraction occurs easily, however. In a recent strategy setting session with a client in the technology business, the business leaders were eager to jump to the tactics before any discussion of strategy. When they reviewed the data from the customer surveys and discussed the various metrics, they immediately started to talk about how they could fix those problems. They had no clear direction about where they wanted to go, yet they were certain of the modes of transportation to get them there. Making good time in a vehicle that you enjoy driving on a highway that offers numerous amenities is still non-productive if you haven't established your destination. Yet organizations decide daily to do the equivalent of that.

In working with this particular client, I began to write down their suggestions and simply ask, "Is this a 'what' or a 'how'?" They quickly realized they were concentrating on the tactics and did not have a clear strategy. As they learned, strategies are few; tactics are many, and discussing tactics too soon encourages people to keep the argumentative shuttlecock in the air. To illustrate the differences in approach, consider this model, an adaptation of the Tregoe Model:[8]

Strong Strategy

	Future at Expense of Today	**Competitive Advantage**	
Unclear Tactics	◊ Clear vision of future ◊ Weak plans for execution ◊ No assigned accountabilities	◊ Proven track record of success ◊ Clear direction ◊ Strong plans for execution	**Clear Tactics**
	Laurel Resting	**Instant Gratification**	
	◊ Past success but no commitment to future ◊ Failure to ask, "Is this still worth doing?"	◊ Strong short-term goals ◊ Well-planned implementation ◊ No clear vision of future	

Weak Strategy

Each quadrant represents desirable or undesirable ways for companies to operate.

The Competitive Advantage quadrant represents an organization that has established a competitive advantage that includes a strong strategy and the clear tactics to support it. Based on a proven track record, this company has identified those decisions that have led to success in the past and that promise success in the future. By responding to customer needs, developing talent, implementing effective operations, and defining sound financial objectives, this organization has acknowledged what it must do to beat the competition and has identified ways to implement this strategy. A company that has clarified its competitive advantage commits itself to excellence, the foundation of strategy. High-performance organizations who have stood the test of time and promise to continue productivity in the future provide examples of this. When a commitment to excellence exists, passion and profitability often follow.

Organizations operating in the Instant Gratification quadrant often succeed in the short term. Despite current profitability, they lack a strong strategy. They engage in effective operations that have accounted for their success in the past, but success is doubtful in the future. Often hospitals and manufacturers operate in this quadrant. In the long run, rivals take over, but for a period of time, these companies can stay afloat with hard work. Companies like this frequently offer good products or services and are passionate about what they do, but they lack excellence or profitability.

Members of these organizations frequently resist discussions of strategy because what they're doing seems to be working. In these situations, I often encounter a significant commitment to lean processes, Six Sigma, or Total Quality Management, all tactics for driving a strategy. The leadership makes solving immediate problems their primary focus, and strategy formulation seems like a distraction from that priority. Investing the time to engage in a strategy formulation process will lead them to fewer wasted hours and distracted efforts in the future, but for an organization accustomed to instant gratification, the future seems too far off and too abstract. Yet most failed companies get buried strategically, not tactically. They may have been making the best horse-drawn buggy in the world when they went under. They may have had strong day-to-day tactics, but they picked the wrong direction or chose too many directions simultaneously. In other words, the problem usually isn't an inability to produce a quality product or service; it's knowing what customers will want more of in the future.

The Future at the Expense of Today quadrant depicts a company that has invested the time and energy to write and develop a strong, clear strategy. However, they have failed to formulate the ways they will execute. Some of the high-tech companies and pharmaceutical manufacturers offer examples of how a company might operate in this quadrant. This kind of situation most often occurs when leaders have left the strategy setting session with no accountabilities for each initiative. When no one has a vested, personal interest in the outcome, you put tactics, execution, and implementation at risk, not to mention your overall success.

Laurel Resting organizations struggle tremendously. Most of the major airlines fall into this quadrant. At one time they may have had some clear direction, perhaps some strong leadership and committed employees who developed the processes and systems for driving the business. But, for whatever reason, these best practices have eroded. Apparently no one has asked recently, "Is this still worth doing?" Usually companies that operate in this quadrant for very long don't stay companies for very long.

If your organization is operating in quadrants other than the Competitive Advantage one, you must first rid yourself of the strategies and tactics that no longer produce results, sloughing off the decisions of yesterday in order to make the pivotal ones for tomorrow.

To limit your servitude to the past, try asking the critical question: "If we did not already do this, based on what we know today, would we start doing it?" If the answer is "no," stopping the initiative, curtailing it sharply, or limiting resource allocation to it can alert you to opportunities to respond to today's demands and to commit today's resources to the future. Deciding what you will *not* do often becomes as important as deciding what you *will* do. Sometimes this means a change in strategy; often it requires a change in tactics. Occasionally, it even demands an entirely different strategy, because, in fact, there may not always be a market for the world's best horse-drawn buggy or even an effective buggy-whip.

The key to a successful strategy is to make enough good decisions—not to avoid mistakes. Strategy looks to the future, which by its nature is unpredictable. Your most successful strategies will align commitments that you have to make *now* with future uncertain, unpredictable circumstances. No one knows what those circumstances will be, and the future is fickle. Successful companies *do* make mistakes, often significant mistakes, but they keep a strategic perspective. Therefore, the most successful leaders are curious about tomorrow. They leverage their company's competitive advantage and build on a position in the market that competitors cannot readily replicate. These give them their strategic focus and help them take the first step toward improving their strategy formulation.

Forces That Drive the Business

The strategic forces of a given organization decisively affect its nature and direction. The categories of strategy components are numerous, but the first question an executive team would want to ask goes back to the basic "What are we about?" For example, Walmart, Nordstroms, and Neiman Marcus are all successful retail chains, but each defines itself differently, based on the strategy they have set. Walmart is the price leader. They offer a large number of products at the least expensive price, under one roof, which makes shopping convenient for customers, but their customer service is almost non-existent once you're in the store. Nordstrom, on the other hand, defines itself by good customer service. They offer a variety of high-end products, but their sales force focuses on responding better than other retailers to the needs of the customer. Neiman Marcus has a strong customer focus too, but they distinguish themselves by offering products that are not available in most other stores. Each chain is successful because of a different strategy that has remained constant through time. So the first question to ask is, Which of the three distinguishes your company from the competition?

1. The lowest prices.
2. The best customer service.
3. The best product/service.

Once you clarify this, you are ready to examine more closely the fundamental forces that drive your company.

The overarching strategic force of any organization occurs at the intersection of its distinction, passion, and profitability (or unique contribution if you operate a non-profit or military organization). This strategic force explains why customers choose your products or service, why you make money at what you do, and why people want to work for your organization. The strategic force forms the foundation of your competitive advantage, the area that exerts the greatest influence on your business. Clarifying what it is and leveraging it to its fullest allow you to do something your rivals can't match.

Another way to think about the intersection of your distinction, excellence, and profitability is to consider the world with your organization versus without it. The difference defines your unique added value—what would be lost to the world if your organization disappeared. To discover this unique added value, ask yourself the following:

◇ If we stopped doing what we're doing, to whom would it matter?

◇ Who would miss us most?

◇ How long would it take another organization to step into the void?

The answers to these questions will help you understand and recognize the unique contribution your organization makes.

In their classic 1980 work, *Top Management Strategy*, Tregoe and Zimmerman discussed driving forces, which exist by default, even if you have not deliberately chosen them.[9] After nearly 30 years, the wisdom of identifying your strategic forces before making strategic forecasts has not changed, even if the alternatives and examples have. As you look at this list, you might determine that all play a role, at least in part, but if you can identify the most salient, the one that explains your success, you will have taken a significant step to defining how you will allocate resources:

1. Products/Services—*What* will you sell?

  ♦ Products or services play a key role in the future of the company.

  ♦ Company will continue to deliver products similar to those it has.

  ♦ New products will be very similar to current ones.

  ♦ Leaders will look for ways to improve products.

Example: Automotive companies, Coca-Cola, the former Anheuser Busch (now InBev).

Question strategist will need to ask: "What is engineering doing to improve next year's model?"

Anheuser Busch was a product-driven company. They specialized in adult beverages, so they continued to develop and market drinks that addressed the needs of their customers. For example, in response to low-carbohydrate diets, Anheuser Busch developed Budweiser Select. Similarly, Coca-Cola specializes in soft drinks and develops new products to respond to demands for new flavors or diet alternatives.

Sometimes the product or service will be related to technology, the learned body of knowledge your company can sell. In this case, your organization offers primarily products and services that capitalize on your technological capabilities, and technology determines the scope of products and services. This type of company typically seeks a variety of applications for its technology and converts breakthroughs made elsewhere to a variety of applications.

2. Customer/Market Needs—To *whom* do you sell?

- ◆ Focus is on filling current and emerging customer needs within a defined demographic.

- ◆ Company constantly looks for alternative ways to fill customer needs.

- ◆ Needs analysis and market research determine use of current resources.

Example: Gillette, Fisher Price Toys, Mayo Clinic, and Alpha Wire.

Questions strategists will need to ask: "What other needs do our customers have?" and "What market do we want to serve?"

Even though making men's toiletry items, manufacturing toys, providing health care, and manufacturing wire may not have obvious things in common, they share the same strategic force—they exist to respond to a specific demographic and the needs of that group. For example, Alpha Wire responds to customers' needs by providing wire and cable in smaller quantities with a faster response time than their competitors can match. This, therefore, clarifies the strategic force for the company.

3. Production Capability

   ♦ Capability includes the production processes, systems, and equipment to make and improve specific products.

   ♦ New products can be different from previous products while still utilizing existing production systems and equipment.

   ♦ The organization may make products for another organization.

   Example: A cream cheese company and Boeing.

   Question strategists will need to ask: "Who will lease or buy our capability?"

A company that specializes in making cream cheese has to make few adjustments to respond to current trends in using cream cheese. For example, using its current processes and equipment, a company that already makes cream cheese can easily add flavors or offer an option that is low fat. Similarly, the leadership can decide to offer products that are similar to cream cheese.

An aircraft company that already has the processes, systems, and equipment to make planes and equipment for planes can readily adjust to a new type of plane or products for planes. Boeing is an example of a company that also makes products for other companies.

4. Method of Sale or of Distribution—*How* will you sell your products or services?

   ♦ Method of sale determines the products it provides, the markets it enters, and its geographic scope.

   ♦ Relationships are key to the organization's success.

♦ Organization may sell products from another organization to fully maximize the method (catalogue sales, for example).

♦ The way products reach the customer and the systems and equipment to support the method drive this kind of company.

♦ Products, customers, and geographic scope that the company can handle through its established distribution channels drive this organization.

Example: Avon (previously), Book-of-the-Month Club, Pampered Chef, Tupperware (previously), Girl Scout cookies, Amway, time shares, McDonalds, Amazon, and Dell.

Questions strategist will need to ask: "Using our existing sales force and method, what products can we offer?" or "What can we sell and where can we sell it, using our existing method?"

Perhaps Avon taught us the most about the importance of the method of sale and distribution. A team of women sold the product, door to door, to people they already knew. The only way to buy Avon was to form a relationship with an Avon Lady. Today, however, Avon has a new method of sale—their products are in some of the department stores. Similarly, Tupperware relied on home parties but is now available in some malls. Girl Scout cookies, however, rely exclusively on their junior sales force to sell their products to people they know.

No one goes to a fast food restaurant to window shop. The buyer has made the decision to buy before driving into the drive through lane. Browsing seldom happens in that line. (In fact, failing to go as quickly as possible through the lines often engenders honking and other angry responses.) Chains have begun to offer lower fat, healthier choices, which indicate they are customer responsive, but their distinguishing feature continues to be the method of distribution.

Amazon sells books and related products via the Internet. They don't have stores or a sales force that visits stores, but they have expanded their product offerings to include CDs and other items that can be sold and distributed with their current systems support distribution.

5. Growth and Profit

     ♦   Desire to become larger determines the scope of the products, markets, and geographic area.

     ♦   Desire to grow leads to a change in products and market scope.

     ♦   This does not typically remain a driving force during a long period of time.

     ♦   The company makes a change in the product or market *only* to achieve return /profit requirements.

     ♦   Company often seeks a variety of unrelated products.

     Example: Cell phone companies and The University of Phoenix.

     Question strategist will want to ask: "What will make us the biggest in the industry and meet our profit targets?"

     Rapid growth organizations rely on more than existing products and services; they push for new, unrelated products or markets.

     Cell phone companies concentrated on acquiring as many customers and contracts as they could. Once they had locked up the market, they were able to copy what the other companies were doing.

     In order to have a presence in most metropolitan areas and ensure swift expansion, The University of Phoenix abandoned the single campus concept that traditionally defined institutions of higher learning. Online courses have further expanded its presence. Once enrolled, students don't tend to transfer, so like the cell phone user who has an existing contract, the student is locked in and a factor in the organization's growth.

     Identification of your organization's strategic force is fundamental to your strategy formulation. It establishes, or should establish, the unifying concept and the strategic framework that guides you in your decisions. When you need to make strategic decisions, agreement about the strategic forces provides the starting point for generating and evaluating future alternatives. Without a clear understanding of these insights, you run the risk that you will not have a mechanism for developing, specifying, and understanding the different alternatives that are available, and you will lack an invaluable tool for resolving differences.

The Role of Growth in Strategy Formulation

Usually a growth strategy exists for a limited period of time until another driving force makes more sense, but sometimes an organization identifies expansion as a long-term objective. Among all other influences, the desire to grow has one of the most dramatic, often hazardous effects on strategy. Limits and trade-offs take a back seat to the desire to escalate, increase, or expand. In the short run, passionately committing to one or two driving forces constrains opportunities and excludes customers and revenue generators. The low-hanging fruit of growth opportunity is truly tempting. Therefore, perceived opportunities for growth tempt leaders to go in new directions—paths that can blur uniqueness, trigger compromises, and undermine competitive advantage. Adding new products, features, services, or markets is both alluring and appealing, but doing so without screening these opportunities or adapting them to your strategy also invites trouble.

The challenge of the leader is to offer a disciplined approach—an intellectual framework to guide decisions and serve as a counterweight to the quick and easy fix of unfettered growth. This requires an examination of which industry changes and customer needs the organization will respond to and which ones it will reject. Penetrating existing markets and reinforcing the company's position help to maintain distinctiveness and competitive advantage, while squelching their enemies, distraction and ill-advised compromise. Of course, major changes in the industry may require an organization to change its strategy, but taking a new position must be driven by the ability to find new trade-offs and leverage a new system of complementary activities.

Managers at lower levels lack the perspective, confidence, and authority to decide on, much less oversee, a growth strategy. Constant pressure for results will entice them to compromise, emulate rivals, and relax trade-offs.

Your job, as the executive, is to teach others in the organization about strategy and to choose what *not* to do as often as what to do.

The Role of Competitive Intelligence in Strategy Formulation

Once you understand who you are and where you want to go as a company, the next step is to understand how you stack up against the competition. Knowing what the competition is up to and what their winning move might be, however, presents another layer of complexity to your strategy formulation. But finding this information is not impossible, either. Competitive intelligence is a field of strategic research that specializes in the collection and analysis of information about rivals. It involves aggregating information to compare and contrast your company with your competitor's.

Start with the critical list of questions you need to have answered, the most significant being, How do we maximize our strengths at the expense of our rivals' weaknesses? But also consider questions similar to these:

◊ What should you know about the competitor to avoid being blindsided by their best move (new products, geographical expansion, mergers, acquisitions)?

◊ What comparable products do your competitors offer, and what are the benefits of these products?

◊ How do they represent their missions, visions, goals, and guarantees?

◊ What kinds of people do they want to hire?

Most of the answers to these questions are online, so go to the Internet first. Find out through Websites, trading information, annual reports, advertisements, and blogs what the competition has been up to. Google the company name, the names of their major talent, and the names of their best customers. Set up a Google Alert that will notify you when any of the aforementioned appears in the news or on the Web. (Be sure to put quotation marks around the name to avoid irrelevant hits.)

Much of what you will need to research a U.S.-based company, especially a publicly traded one, is available publicly, in the form of regulatory filings or legal documents. (Go to *www.sec.gov* and click on the EDGAR database, which offers free and paid search options.) You can also check a company's annual filing with the SEC (called a 10-K) to see if it identifies potential moves. The "Use of Proceeds" section explains how the company has used money and whether the company is saving cash for a specific goal.

Private companies are more difficult to research, but Hoover's and Dun & Bradstreet offer services that disclose headquarters locations, names of principals, number of employees, and revenue. Each company generates a paper trail that becomes part of a public legal record. If you visit the town where a competitor is headquartered, you may find other sources of data, even if it's a family-owned or privately held company.

The following are some of the databases you might find useful:

◊   United States Securities and Exchange Commission.

◊   Dun & Bradstreet.

◊   Standard & Poor's.

◊   Hoover's.

◊   LexisNexis.

◊   Patent Application Information Retrieval.

◊   Newsalert.com.

◊   Industry Watch.

◊   NewsPage.

◊   PrNewsire.

Depending on the nature of your competition, another simple way to gain intelligence is to shop them. Either in person or on the phone, find out what it's like to buy from this company. How do they connect you with a decision maker? How do their prices compare to yours? What value do they offer customers? What about their process is superior to yours? Inferior?

Attending industry conferences and reading industry journals provide other easy and inexpensive ways to gather competitive research and stay on top of changes. Through casual conversations at networking events, find out who the major players are and get to know people who know your competitors. Who is the top talent in your competitor's company? Who has the largest sales volume? Who is the most respected in the industry because of particular expertise? What do customers value about the people who work for the competition? Six degrees of separation refers to the idea that everyone is an average of six "steps" away from each person on Earth. In a particular industry, you are probably separated by two or three relationships and maybe by only one conversation.

Finally, if you can't find what you need on your own, hire a research firm that specializes in competitive intelligence in your industry. You can start by going to *www.scip.org* to read about the Society of Competitive Intelligence Professionals.

Ways to Improve Strategy

Today's uncompromising, competitive environment leaves you little choice other than to develop a disciplined approach to improving strategic performance. How?

◊ Determine your strategic forces, those dimensions of your organization that define your excellence, profitability, and passion. Realize that some activities are incompatible; therefore, gain in one area of your organization can often be achieved only at the expense of another. The failure to make difficult trade-offs leads to failure in general. Once your driving forces are clear, decide what you want to do with the information you have. With your products, services, or production, are you trying to maintain competitiveness? Gain a competitive edge? Or attempting to achieve dominance?

◊ Consider four main perspectives:

1. Financial: How do we generate value for our shareholders or stakeholders? How do we make money with this strategy? What should we be doing to ensure our continued success? Which of our products or services is most profitable? Distinctive? What are customers willing to pay a premium for?

2. Customer: How do customers perceive our value? How do we build our customer base? Which of our customers is most satisfied? What are our customers' most important

priorities and how do we address them? How do we differentiate ourselves from our competition, and do customers care about that differentiation?

3. Internal business processes: In what internal processes and technologies do we need to excel to satisfy customers? What must we improve to maintain our competitive advantage?

4. Innovation and growth: What knowledge and talent must we have to sustain our ability to change and improve? What are our growth objectives? What do we need to learn?[10]

◊ Separate *what* you're trying to do from *how* you'll do it. Concentrate on *what*. *How* comes later.

◊ Gather and analyze data to determine your strategic vision. Consider the voice of the customer, examine driving forces, consider SWOT (strengths, weaknesses, opportunities, threats) *relative to your top three competitors*, garner competitive intelligence, and take into account any other source that gives you salient information about what you should and should not do.

◊ Compare and contrast your strategy with those of your top three competitors. How are these competitors, and potentially new competitors, likely to affect customers' purchases?

◊ Predict how long this strategy will be sustainable. What changes would require a change to the current strategy?

◊ Know that strategy should focus on change, not corrective action. Strategy allows you to exploit the unexpected, make the most of opportunities, and innovate your way to success, but it doesn't allow for stagnation, scapegoating, or excuse making.

◊ Encourage prudent risks. Strategy exists not to minimize possibilities but to encourage sensible risk taking. Changes to the status quo demand clear direction and deliberate choices that you base on the driving forces of your organization.

◊ Look at strategy constantly, not annually or sequentially.

◊ Embrace ambiguity. It is the norm, and only by living in harmony with it can you lead others through it. Although many appreciate certainty, executives are paid to make sense of ambiguity. But they must hold others to concrete accountabilities. Based on the information you have, explore the "what ifs."

◊ Assign accountability. Strategy works best when each person on the team has a stake in the ground and when each initiative is related to one of those stakes.

◊ Understand, and help others understand, that strategy hurts. It's about creative destruction of the status quo.

◊ The CEO and executive team should set the strategy for the company. The board of directors then gives approval and input. Leaders who have profit and loss responsibilities should conduct separate but aligned strategy formulation sessions.

Identifying these critical aspects of strategy formulation allows you to take the first step; having the right people to do them allows you to take the second.

How to Identify Top Strategists

Aardvarks are really good at one thing: eating bugs—sometimes 50,000 in one night! No other creature on the planet can match their appetites. Star performers in their own corner of the jungle, when they tuck a napkin under their aardvark chins, they produce impressive results, just like your hard-working employees can in their jobs. Too often, however, in an attempt to do the aardvark and the organization a favor, a decision maker will insist the aardvark fly. There are no flying aardvarks. You can certainly throw an aardvark out of an airplane midair, but you won't end up with a flying aardvark; you will just have a very unhappy aardvark. The damage to the splattered aardvark cannot be underrepresented, but destruction to the organization can be notable too. Being splattered doesn't motivate your employees, not the one who just failed or those who witnessed the crash. Pretty soon you have neither productive aardvarks nor soaring eagles.

But how do you know the difference? Psychologists continue to rage about the role of the nature/nurture relationship in the development of cognitive talents. Are we born with the ability to think analytically, for example, or do we learn it? Can you develop it through time with experience?

(For the purpose of this discussion, the words *strategic, analytical,* and *critical* are synonymous.)

My work with thousands of individuals suggests that by the time you retire, you will have the same strategic abilities you brought with you on your first day. Education and experience can polish them up, provide some new and useful information, and bring previously unused talent to the fore, but nothing can create what isn't there. Aardvarks cannot fly, just as some employees cannot soar beyond certain capabilities. However, many leaders with fervent hope fail to grasp this reality. Decision makers often conclude that coaching, mentoring, and experience can recast an aardvark into an eagle's mold. It doesn't happen. What you see is what you get. Your job as the decision maker is to ensure that the newly-vaulted has the wings to venture into unknown realms.

What does it take to be an eagle in the organization? Strategy work is not for the fainthearted or the tactical thinker. It demands courage, experience, innate abilities, and discipline. Only those who possess these traits can ensure aspirations are not guillotined by limitations.

But how can you recognize those who can and will engage in this critical but difficult work? Whether making a hiring or promotion decision, based on the individual's proven record of success, ask yourself the following:

◊ Does this person understand how to separate strategy from tactics, the "what" from the "how"? Can he or she keep the strategy clearly in focus while executing only those tactics that are relevant?

◊ Can this person keep a global perspective? Or does she or he become mired in the details and tactics? "Analysis paralysis" has caused more than one otherwise top performer to allow opportunity to slip away.

◊ Do obstacles stop this person? Or do they represent challenges, not threats? The ability to bounce back from setbacks and disappointments frequently separates the strong strategist from the effective tactician.

◊ Can he or she create order during chaos? Top strategists don't manufacture catastrophes. Instead they keep problems in perspective and realize that very few things are truly as dire as they first seem.

◊ Does this person have the ability to see patterns, make logical connections, resolve contradictions, and anticipate consequences? Or is she or he unaware of trends?

◊ What success has this person had with multi-tasking? Often the ability to handle a number of things at once implies good prioritizing and flexibility. You're looking for the human equivalent to a Swiss Army Knife, a person who has the capacity to use the knowledge, skill, and talent required to address unfamiliar problems. Because this person has more than a hammer in the tool kit, problems seldom look like nails.

◊ Can this person think on his or her feet? Or does this person miss opportunities because of an inability to respond? Quickness, however, does not guarantee effective critical thinking skills. Some people rush to make mistakes; others take their time and then err. Look at the overall track record. What caliber of decisions prevails? And how much time did the person take in making the good ones. After all, there is some merit in having the ability to make effective decisions fast.

◊ Can this person prioritize seemingly conflicting goals? Is this person able to zero in on the critical few and put aside the trivial many when allocating time and resources?

◊ When facing a complicated or unfamiliar problem, can this individual get to the core of the issue and immediately begin to formulate possible solutions? Or is he or she distracted by inconsequential factors or ones that are immaterial to your mission and vision?

◊ Is this person future oriented and able to paint credible pictures of possibilities and likelihoods? Can he or she interpret past experiences from new vantage points? Creativity and analytical reasoning don't always go hand in hand, but when they do, a top strategist is often at the controls. Strong strategic thinkers are concrete and practical, but agile. The key question remains, "Can this person solve complicated, unfamiliar problems?"

⬥ How do unexpected and unpleasant changes affect this person's performance? If their analytical reasoning is well-honed, organized, systematic decision makers can respond favorably to change, even if they don't like to.

⬥ When in a position of leadership, does this person serve as a source of advice and wisdom? Can she or he act as an effective sounding board to others who struggle with complex issues?

The core competencies that drive a particular organization may differ, but the ability to think analytically and dispassionately remains constant. The overarching question is this: When acting in a strategic role, has this person typically performed as needed? If the answer is yes, the person probably has the innate talent to be a strategic thinker and will just need to improve requisite skills to support the talent. If the answer is no, don't gamble by putting this person in a more demanding position. As valuable as the aardvarks of the organization can be, virtually all organizations need more eagles, strong critical thinkers who can learn from mistakes and make bold decisions. Only then can you succeed and be ready to launch a strategy initiative.

Ten Steps for Launching a Strategy Initiative

Understanding your organizational direction and the innovative nature of strategy, accepting the risks associated with making future-based decisions, and identifying and developing talent are all essential for ensuring you have a strong enough strategy to drive operations. But you also need to take the time to engage in a strategy-setting process. As Dwight Eisenhower pointed out, "Our plans may be useless, but the process is indispensable." The *process* of walking your team through a strategy session will create focus and discipline, two of the hallmarks of successful organizations. Follow these 10 steps:

1. Have the right people in the room. In general, only the senior leadership team of the company or division should be involved in a strategy session.

2. Create or revisit the company's mission, vision, and values. Based on what we set as our foundation, what does success look like?

3. Analyze the current situation, critical issues, and allocation of resources. Do a SWOT analysis and examine how your tactics support the current strategy. Identify those issues that can jeopardize implementation of the strategy and throw the organization off course.

4. Discuss the driving forces of the organization, customer feedback, and other information relevant to setting goals.

5. Based on the analysis of the current situation and all relevant data, set the year's strategic objectives and make sure they align with the three- and five-year plans. Look for cause/effect relationships among the data. What patterns emerge?

6. Prioritize the objectives.

7. Identify the core competencies you will need to support the strategy. Ask yourself what talent is not currently in the organization.

8. Define performance measures. How will you know when you have succeeded?

9. Set timelines and deadlines for each initiative.

10. Assign areas of accountability for strategy deployment. Each member of the leadership team should "own" one of the objectives and be responsible for its execution. Divide major strategic objectives into sub-goals with a 30-, 60-, 90-, 180-day deadline for each. An Excel spreadsheet can help detail this process, and you and the team can use it for each follow-up meeting to see whether people are completing goals on time.

Conclusion

"Strategic" is probably one of the most overused and misrepresented words in today's organizations. Executives use it to denote anything they consider important, yet true strategy is limited to those situations that are likely to affect critical outcomes. Strategy identifies your competitive advantage—something you can do that rivals cannot match. It defines the nature of your organization, impacts financial performance, and guides your choices. Done well, it allows you to survive in a jungle where others perish, not only to endure but to prosper in the fickle future that lies ahead.

Chapter 5

Turn Great Strategy Into Great Execution

Freedom is only part of the story and half the truth....
That is why I recommend that the Statue of Liberty on the
East Coast be supplanted by a Statue of Responsibility on
the West Coast.
    —Victor Frankel, *Man's Search for Meaning*

A breakthrough product, dazzling service, or cutting-edge technology can put you in the game, but only rock-solid execution of a well-developed strategy can keep you there. You have to be able to deliver—to translate your brilliant strategy and operational decisions into action. If you're like many executives, however, in an effort to improve performance, too frequently you address the *symptoms* of dysfunction, not the root causes of it. You focus your attention and that of others on what's going wrong instead of why it doesn't work.

Of course it all starts with a strong strategic principle—a shared objective about what the organization wants to accomplish. Clear strategy leads the process; great performance completes it. However, the two should not be confused. *Strategy* is an over- and misused term to describe anything important, and *strategic planning* is an oxymoron. Leaders *formulate* the strategy; they *plan* the execution—or at least the successful ones do. Execution involves discipline; it requires senior leader involvement; and it should be central to the organization's culture. Done well, execution pushes you to decipher your broad-brush theoretical understanding of the strategy into intimate familiarity with how it will work, who will take charge of it, how long it will take, how much it will cost, and how it will affect the organization overall.

Effective tactics form the foundation of execution, but the two differ. Tactics are the activities that lead to execution, but by themselves, they aren't enough. Execution shapes strategy, and strategy defines execution. Strategy formulation involves asking "what?" Execution is a systematic process of rigorously discussing "how?" questioning, tenaciously following through, and ensuring accountability. It includes linking the organization's mission, vision, and strategy to implementation, creating an action-oriented culture of accountability, connecting the strategy to operations, and robust communication. When you execute effectively, you get smart answers to these questions:

◊   How do we position products, compared to our competitors?

◊   How can we translate our plan into specific results?

◊   How can we attract the right kinds of people to execute our plan?

◊   How do we make sure our activities deliver the outcomes to which we've committed?

In other words, the heart of execution lies in three core constructs: strategy, people, and operations. To implement the strategy successfully and get answers to the above questions, you'll need to address all three.

Tie the Mission and Vision to Execution

Failure to link all elements of strategy to its execution explains why so many companies crash in the implementation stage. If your mission is only a plaque in your foyer, your vision remains firmly planted in the CEO's head, and the strategy, if memory serves, somehow involved those two days the senior team spent at the resort shortly before the golf tournament, your organization might be on the road to perdition. As I mentioned before, every organization is headed somewhere, but too often decision-makers don't consider all the constructs of success when planning the path. Instead, leaders engage in reactive decision-making or short-term gains designed to placate shareholders and analysts. The successful ones know they have to do better.

So let's look at mission again. As I stated in Chapter 4, a mission statement should answer these questions:

◊   Why do we exist?

◊   What is our business?

◊   Who are our customers?

◊   What do our customers value?

In addition to defining the organization's identity, the mission guides its development through time. Building on the foundation of the mission, the vision statement paints a clear picture of what you intend to do and what you will commit to do. Vision defines what success will look like in the future and often includes a strategic principle that challenges the organization to become better. Both should also distill an organization's strategy and serve as a beacon throughout the company. A clear mission and vision help companies maintain strategic focus while fostering flexibility among employees that permits them to be innovative and respond rapidly to opportunities.

Instead of attempting to mimic its rivals' unsuccessful strategies, Southwest Airlines, for example, decided to go a different direction. With their mission of "dedication to the highest quality of Customer Service delivered with a sense of warmth, friendliness, individual pride, and Company Spirit" in mind, they were ready to set their course. They created a vision to "Meet customers' short-haul travel needs at fares competitive with the cost of automobile travel." Southwest Airlines, the only successful US carrier of recent decades, can summarize its raison d'être in these two pithy statements—two declarations that leave little doubt about what they are, what they want to become, and what their customers can expect.[1]

Other airlines weren't so fortunate. Impressed with Southwest's success, Continental Airlines, a full-service carrier, decided to create a new service called Continental Lite. Because Continental remained a full-service airline, however, and could not reduce costs though the types of activities conducted by Southwest, Continental lost hundreds of millions of dollars and Continental Lite ultimately failed. The low-fare service it heavily promoted and trumpeted as an industry-leading innovation became a $140 million mistake.

What went wrong? Continental Lite was a short-lived "airline within an airline" that began in 1993 and folded in 1995. It had no mission or vision of its own—only a dedication to chase the lead. This offers yet another reason why it's never a good idea to play leapfrog with a unicorn. It was an extremely expensive experiment that started as a pilot project—no pun intended; it should have been proven before it was expanded.

The identity crisis at Continental and the $1.5-million mistake (*Time Magazine* put the number closer to $300 million) don't remain a mystery when, with 20/20 hindsight, one looks back at their ties among mission, vision, and execution.[2] Continental Airlines' Mission Statement reads more like an action plan or balanced score card than a mission statement: "The Go Forward Plan; Fly to Win; Fund the Future; Make Reliability a Reality; Working Together." Disjointed as this is, it doesn't address a commitment to low-cost service. It does focus on flying and winning, which sounds more like a mission for the Air Force than a commercial carrier.

United didn't fare much better than Continental did. Its mission, "To be recognized worldwide as the airline of choice" is succinct, but it doesn't reflect a strategic principle. Following closely in Continental's failed footsteps, in 1994 United launched Shuttle by United, which company decision-makers hoped would compete successfully against the new wave of low-cost, no-frills carriers. It didn't. Shuttle existed from 1994 to 2001. United declared bankruptcy in 2002. Not quick to learn from its mistakes or those of its fellow airlines, United then created Ted Airlines in 2004 but ceased operations in 2009.

The failure of Continental Lite, United's alternate airlines, and other similar ventures suggest that strategic positioning requires that organizations make trade-offs in competing. Furthermore, as volatile markets create questions along with opportunities, organizations must choose what *not* to do as often as they choose what to do. Only then will they be able to link execution of the strategy to the basic components of it.

Link the Strategy to Execution

Too many examples exist for us to argue with the fact that more companies fail at execution than at strategy formulation. Corralling the senior team to spend a day or two hashing out the objectives for the year is the easy part. The hard work involves implementing the ideas. As many business leaders have observed, you're better off with a strategy that is 80-percent right and 100-percent implemented, than with one that is 100-percent right but doesn't drive consistent results.

The mission defines what the company is; the vision, where it will go; the strategy, what it will do; and the succession plan, who will do it. The operating plan provides the *path* for those people. It breaks long-term strategic goals into short-term targets. Meeting those targets forces decisions that need to be integrated across the organization, both in response to internal and external business conditions.

You don't want your operating plan to concentrate on the past—to focus on the reflection in the rearview mirror. You also don't want it to be a distortion of future possibilities—like an image in a fun-house mirror. Instead, your operating plan should be a kaleidoscope that exhibits various symmetrical patterns that reflect the loose bits of information you have aggregated. As you rotate it with new information and contingencies, new patterns and answers will appear. It is a look forward to the "hows." It includes the programs your organization will complete within a year to reach your strategic objectives in four major areas: finance, customers, processes, and people. It specifies how you will synchronize these four moving parts to achieve the objectives, negotiate the trade-offs, seize opportunities, and plan for contingencies.

The operating plan goes beyond last year's budget to include challenges and opportunities that didn't exist in last year's reality. Too often the budget becomes number and gaming exercises designed to help silo mangers protect their own best interest. Frequently budgets represent little more than an increase based on the previous year's results and don't engender the requisite tough analysis and dialogue to determine what the financial goals really should be for the year. Budgets also limit growth and innovation if a new opportunity "isn't in the budget."

Decentralization, rapid growth, and turmoil have become common in many companies. Therefore, a corresponding need for a mechanism to ensure coherent strategic action has emerged. The operating plan gives continuity to the strategy, even if the leadership changes. A new CEO may bring a new approach, but if the organization's mission remains the same, so does stability of execution. Strategy and execution portend success when they do these things:

⬥ Force trade-offs among competing resource demands. As I mentioned, Southwest Airlines, one of the industry's true success stories, offers an example of what it means to make trade-offs. When decision-makers at Southwest faced the problem of continuing service to Denver, they measured the higher costs associated with weather and on-ground delays against their strategy. They realized they could not maintain low-cost fares in the face of the costs of doing business in Denver. Instead of sacrificing their consistency, image, or reputation, they forced the trade-off and pulled out of Stapleton three years after inaugurating service there.

⬥ Test the soundness of a particular action or initiative. Trade-offs arise from activities and initiatives themselves. In other words, when employees face a decision about what to do, they need to test the soundness of that activity against the company's strategy. For instance, St. Louis-based Weekends Only Furniture focuses on meeting the home furnishing needs of young furniture buyers who want style at low cost. As the name implies, they open only on weekends. They don't attempt to try to satisfy customers who require higher levels of service, more flexible shopping times, or designer labels. Their activities and initiatives, instead, concentrate on advertising for weekend shopping and bargain pricing.

This started in 1997 when Tom Phillips owned Phillips Furniture, a high-end store that catered to affluent customers. Tom noticed that customer trends had been changing. Though competition remained for the brand-named furniture, no competition existed for "extreme value," which included reducing overhead to save the customer money. Tom decided to force the trade-off. He realized his new company couldn't offer all the amenities of his former furniture store, but it could give customers something they needed—extreme value. To test the soundness of his idea, he began asking himself and others, "How low can we go?" not "How much can we get?"

For instance, customers frequently buy furniture that requires some assembly. Delivery charges aren't built into the cost of furniture, and rather than keeping their doors open during the week, they use that time to locate the strongest deals from some of the world's most reputable manufacturers. When they do open every Friday, they offer a new selection of quality items, new displays, and a store full of savings. Their philosophy of gauging their activity to match their strategy has kept Weekends Only in business while many other more famous chain stores have closed. In fact, in an independent 2008 survey, researchers found that Weekends Only has the largest share of the St. Louis furniture-buying market and has grown by nearly 50 percent during the worst economy since the Great Depression.[3]

◊   Set clear boundaries within which decision-makers must operate as they experiment with innovative and traditional tactics. Companies that try to be all things to all customers will confuse employees who will be forced to make day-to-day operating decisions without a clear framework. It will also puzzle customers and endanger your brand. No better examples exist than those in retail.

On February 28, 2005, Federated acquired The May Department Stores Company for $11 billion in stock, creating the nation's second-largest department store chain, with $30 billion in annual sales and more than 1,000 stores. On July 28, 2005, Federated announced its plans to similarly convert 330 regional department stores owned by the May Company to the Macy's name.

Because many considered these department stores beloved local institutions in the regions surrounding them, the conversion of the May brands met with negative reaction. The strongest opposition occurred with the loss of Filene's, Marshall Field's, and Kaufmann's, which were all well known for their flagship downtown stores and local traditions. Kaufmann's, for example, established itself as an icon, in part by operating the "Kaufmann's Celebrates the Season Parade," which was traditionally broadcast live throughout Pennsylvania.

Many customers publicly vowed never to shop at the May stores that were converted and to switch their loyalty to other major department store chains beyond Federated's control. Prominent film critic Roger Ebert voiced the grief of many Chicagoans at the loss of Field's when he wrote in his column on September 21, 2005, "I thought the day would never come. I am looking at my Field's charge card, which I have cut up into tiny pieces. They look like little tears the color of money."

A Website for Field's Fans surfaced, demanding not only a return to the name "Marshall Field's" but also a commitment to the high-quality merchandise that Field's offered. In a time of economic turmoil that has hit virtually every industry, but disproportionately the retail industry, one has to wonder why this retail giant has not responded better to the boundaries of its most ardent fans.

According to the 2009 Annual Report from Macy's, they had $23.5 billion in sales and 810 stores—that's a loss of $6.5 billion in annual sales and 190 stores in four years. Lest the argument surface that the entire economy has suffered, let's do an apples to apples comparison: Based on online financial reports, Macy's ratio of debt to revenue looks out of proportion compared to its competitors. Macy's had almost twice the comparable debt load of JC Penney and five times the debt of Sears. Clearly, decision-makers in at-risk industries need to experiment with novel approaches and innovative ideas, but sometimes traditions remain traditions because they work.

Formulate your strategy and then set boundaries for executing it. Sometimes that will mean change, but in the case of Macy's, it should have meant status quo.

◊   Seize opportunities. Organizations achieve results by exploiting opportunities and strengths, not by solving problems. Solving problems does one thing: it restores the status quo. The status quo may explain where you are, but it won't serve as a roadmap to where you want to go. Growth requires you to allocate your resources to opportunities, not to problem solving. Maximizing opportunity requires effective execution of the strategy, not efficiency. You'll want to ask yourself: How do we find the right things to do? How do we concentrate our energy and resources on them?

Change and opportunities exist outside the organization. *Activities* that can lead to both occur inside the business, but results depend on those outside—your customers. They will demand that you surpass competence and strive for excellence. They will require value—a driving force that separates you from your competition and, perhaps, creative destruction.

Austrian economist Joseph Schumpeter popularized the economic theory of radical change known as "creative destruction." It occurs when something new kills something older—a process of industrial mutation that incessantly revolutionizes the economic structure from within, incessantly destroying the old one, ceaselessly creating a new one.[4] The revolution in personal computers offers a perfect example. Microsoft and Intel destroyed many mainframe computer companies, but in doing so, they created some of the most important inventions in recent history.

Schumpeter viewed the economy as a living organism that constantly grows and changes to maintain its health. When once revolutionary organizations, such as Xerox and Polaroid, failed to grow, their profits fell, and their dominance vanished. Rivals launched improved designs and cut manufacturing costs, thereby destroying the old and creating the new—creative destruction in action.

Just as nimbler competitors challenged older behemoths such as Montgomery Ward and Woolworths, Walmart now faces a similar threat. If it doesn't find ways to seize opportunities, the dominant Walmart may well find itself an antiquated company of the past. Progress refuses to stand still or to lope along at a leisurely pace. The cassette tape replaced the 8-track; the compact disc took the place of the cassette, which MP3 players undercut. This is the process of creative destruction. Organizations that fail to understand this phenomenon doom themselves to exemplify it. Those who seize opportunities, however, take the first steps to creating a culture committed to change and improvement.

Create an Action-Oriented Culture

After senior leaders have given their attention to linking the organization's strategy to its execution, they need to ensure that they have a culture that supports their ambitious hopes. Often, however, a strategy-to-performance gap encourages a culture of underperformance—not an action orientation. Why? Bottlenecks. Bottlenecks can take on several forms, many of which stay hidden from or invisible to senior leaders: bureaucracy, lack of accountability, and flawed performance review and reward systems.

Bureaucracy

Hierarchy and bureaucracy stand at cross purposes with discipline, which in turn compromises productivity and the action orientation you want to create. Bureaucracy exists to compensate for incompetence and lack of discipline. Many companies build the bureaucratic rules to justify the existence of those who influence rule-making and to manage the small percentage of people who simply can't or won't do their jobs. When you tie a culture of discipline to a commitment to attract and retain the best and brightest in your industry, a magical alchemy of action and results occurs.

But discipline by itself won't produce results. Numerous organizations throughout history have exhibited tremendous discipline as they marched in lockstep precision to ruin. You need a *system* of discipline—an action-oriented culture. That means people understand that implementation of the strategy holds the key to everyone's success. Interdependence coexists symbiotically with rugged self-reliance. People depend on others when task completion requires teamwork, but they also know how and when to make and carry out decisions independently. They understand the structure for getting work done.

Decide Who Owns the Work and the Decisions That Drive It

In companies that know how to implement strategy, people have a good idea of the tasks for which they are responsible. Most companies demand some sort of goal-setting session that managers tie to the end-of-the-year post-mortem appraisal system, but what happens to make people truly own these goals? They may hold themselves accountable for performing certain tactics or tasks, but do they truly feel responsible for profitability? Often not. If they can prove they "met expectations" on their stated goal, they feel satisfied and entitled to the bonus that comes from this. They fail to ask themselves, and their bosses fail to ask them, if they made the company any money in the process of carrying out the goals.

The problem doesn't usually center around people not knowing what objectives they should address—more often it is related to confusion about who makes the final decisions, especially when these involve changes to the plan. In smaller companies people tend to know what everyone else is doing. Not true of larger organizations, however. Sometimes as companies grow and expand, so does the confusion. Once the strategy is in place, people erroneously assume "they" will handle the decisions or solve the problems as they arise. Some of this might be laziness, but confusion offers a more apt explanation. People simply don't know what objectives they should "own" or what decisions they should make to drive results related to these objectives.

In Chapter 2, I explained in detail the nuances of decision-making, but at this juncture I'd like to focus on the critical role decision-making plays in execution of the strategy. Decisions are the coin of the realm in all organizations. Research suggests, and my anecdotal evidence confirms, that when a company fails to implement the strategy, leaders should look first to clarifying decision right. Not restructuring or employee morale: decision-making ownership. Simply put, in order to turn great strategy into great performance, managers must have crystal clarity about the decisions and actions for which they are responsible.

In Chapter 3, I discussed the use of accountability charting as a coaching tool. In addition, this tool should be used to ensure execution, because quality and speed of decisions lead to results. Ambiguity over who should make the decision or who is accountable for carrying it out cause the company the bottleneck. In these scenarios, people often look to the top of the organization for decisions that line managers should make. The rule has always been the same: delegate entire tasks, along with the decisions to carry them out, to the lowest possible level of the organization. Anything else clogs the pipeline, engenders bitterness, and slows productivity.

The Role of Promises in Execution

Every company is a dynamic network of promises—at least those companies that execute their strategies are. In these organizations, employees up and down the corporate ladder make pledges to one another—often in the form of stated objectives—but also through the act of articulated commitment. People make commitments to colleagues in other divisions, to customers, partners, and other stakeholders. The very act of making a promise moves the conversation from casual interaction to guarantees that the work will be accomplished. Promises foster a sense of personal obligation to deliver and create a sense of community among employees. That is, people promise to do things because they buy in to the company's overall mission and see their part in making things happen. The act of making a promise gives the individuals a sense of ownership and pride, especially when they can deliver on them. This latitude in managing negotiations around individual promises dramatically increases employees' engagement, thereby boosting overall performance. Here are the things you can do to encourage people to define not only their areas of accountability but also to commit to their role in the execution of objectives. Well-made promises share these traits:

- ◇ They are public. Ask people to state them in a group and then write them down so everyone will remember what was said.
- ◇ They go beyond a passive nod. They involve active, sometimes robust negotiation.
- ◇ They are voluntary, not obligatory or forced.
- ◇ They involve specific language so that everyone can agree on the metrics for accomplishing them.
- ◇ They address something of value, not just day-to-day operations.

In their research of companies that encourage promise-making, Sull and Spinosa found that many of the vexing challenges leaders face related to executing the strategy—a lack of organization agility, disengaged people, poor communication—stem from broken or poorly crafted commitments. So, the answer lies in encouraging more promise-making.[5]

Promises offer many rewards: they coordinate activities, foster collaborative efforts, and stoke the passions of employees and customers. As the senior leader, you will do well to weave and manage the webs of promises and encourage fulfillment of commitments. If you do this, you will build the agility required to seize new opportunities and tap employees' entrepreneurial energies. But before you exact promises from others, you'll need to make and keep some of your own, the most significant of which involves giving your people the feedback they need and the rewards they deserve to keep them motivated to execute their promises.

The Role of Appraisals in Execution

Too often senior leaders haven't received the training that would help them stretch the performance of their team. Consequently, instead of hearing balanced feedback that would help them understand what they need to do to execute the strategy, direct reports endure appraisals that can be confrontational and judgmental; goals remain unclear; and the discussion occurs when it's too late to do anything about the problem.

The first step in linking appraisals to results involves the points I just mentioned: clearly define specific objectives and responsibilities for each person and the decisions that person is entitled to make. These will set the criteria against which each person will be rated.

My best clients have performance evaluation systems that start the year with goal setting, continue with ongoing feedback, and conclude with the end-of-the-year evaluation that is often tied to raises and bonuses. In general, four meetings per year work well. The first sets goals; the second addressees progress on the goals; the third brings to light any problems that might interfere with the end-of-the-year appraisal; and the final one serves as a formality that ties the progress to rewards. This does not imply that ongoing feedback should not take place between meetings. On the contrary, the four-meeting format is the *minimum* number of meetings that should occur. Even though managers often resist adding to the number of formal meetings per year, they soon learn that the increase in productivity and morale among their direct reports more than compensates for the extra time they commit to the process.

This sort of schedule avoids surprises and the once-a-year mentality that dooms most performance appraisal systems. Also, the periodic reviews give your team members a chance to take corrective action when there are still opportunities to make a difference.

Many companies discuss compensation, raises, and bonuses in one end-of-the-year discussion—the same discussion that addresses goal setting, feedback, evaluation, and action planning. When all this is lumped together in one meeting, the session becomes a type of post-mortem. Even though it's now too late to do anything that will make a difference, employees are somehow supposed to be motivated and enthusiastic to charge into the upcoming year more focused and productive. It doesn't work that way. On the contrary, they are angry and resentful, especially if they have had no warning that their performance was sub-standard.

The Importance of Rewards and Promotions to Execution

The simple truth about rewards and bonuses is that you have to deliver what you promise. Even if you have a bad year, if you've promised bonuses to divisions that have had a good year, you need to follow through. Nothing compromises morale more dramatically than people not receiving what they thought they had coming and had rightfully deserved. The more transparent you are about how bonus decisions will be made—the formula you will use to decide on rewards—the more people will perceive fairness.

You also need to make sure managers feel empowered to hold others accountable and to reward them with compensation, advancement, or both. Organizations that have learned the secrets to successful strategy execution understand that these circumstances must exist for the action-oriented culture to thrive:

- ◊ People have a crystal clear idea of the decisions they are entitled to make and are responsible for delivering on.

- ◊ They expect that once made, these decisions will not be second-guessed.

- ◊ They understand what objectives they will take responsibility for.

- ◊ They recognize that their ability to deliver on these objectives will influence both their compensation and their career advancement.

- ◊ Everyone knows that leaders will differentiate among high, average, and low performers.

- ◊ High potential performers appreciate that they will advance more quickly than others, often involving a lateral move that will give them valuable experience in another part of the company.

- ◊ When an objective demands teamwork, each member of the team understands the interdependent nature of their success. They will succeed or fail as one.

Companies that create tight links among their strategies, execution, and ultimately, performance often experience a *cultural multiplier effect*.

Through time, as they turn their strategies into great performance, leaders in these organizations become more confident of their own capabilities and much more willing to make the stretch commitments that inspire and transform organizations. In turn, individual contributors who keep their commitments receive rewards—faster promotions and fatter paychecks—reinforcing the behaviors needed to drive profits. Eventually, an action-oriented culture emerges and thrives. Boards and investors start giving management more support when it comes to bold decisions. Soon, the leaders' reputations attract star candidates for hire, and the organization creates a vibrant cycle in which talent causes performance, performance leads to rewards, and rewards draw more talent.

Inexorably Connect Execution and Operations

Despite the enormous time the CEO and members of the leadership team spend developing the strategy and planning for its execution, many senior leaders feel the frustration of having little to show for their efforts. Some research suggests that companies, on average, deliver only 63 percent of the financial performance their strategies promise, and only 15 percent of companies create systems to know why.[6] Even more frustrating, often the causes of the strategy-to-performance gap remain hidden from senior leaders. Then, in their attempts to turn things around, senior leaders pull the wrong levers or push the wrong buttons, further exacerbating the problem. Without question, a strong strategy leads the way, but effective tactics must support it. The only way you'll know if you have the right combination is to keep track of key indicators.

Develop Tracking Systems

In the 1920s researchers conducted a series of scientific management studies at the Hawthorne plant of the Western Electric Company outside Chicago. The initial purpose of the research was to determine the impact of level of illumination on worker productivity. By modern research standards, the classic Hawthorne Studies were seriously flawed. Researchers did not attempt to assure the participants were representative of all the workers, research facilities differed, and researchers conducted the tests in different ways. Yet, nearly a century later, the lessons remain relevant.

Several groups of employees took part in these studies. The control group worked in a room where the level of lighting remained constant; another worked in a test room where the lighting varied. Productivity increased in *both* locations. In fact, outputs remained high in the test room even when illumination was reduced to that of moonlight.

Baffled by the results, researchers went on to test 13 changes in work conditions, including length of breaks, length of work day and week, method of payment, and place of work. Productivity increased with almost every change in work conditions. Even when subjects returned to the initial standard conditions, productivity continued.

Conversely, when Elton Mayo, the leading expert in these experiments turned his attention to an existing work group to observe their productivity with no changes to the environment, the results differed. In what he called the *Bank Wiring Room*, productivity did not rise continuously. Instead, researchers soon inferred that workers deliberately restricted their output.

Why did these workers restrict their output while those in the previous study had increased theirs? Mayo and his colleagues arrived at the following answer: Work settings involve complex social systems. In order to comprehend them fully, one must understand worker attitudes, communication among workers, and a host of other factors. The researchers concluded that productivity increases when people feel as though they are receiving special attention. In contrast, output decreased when participants feared that high productivity would lead to an increase in the amount they were expected to produce and might even cost some of them their jobs.[7]

Modern research confirms that the strategy-to-performance gap can occur for a variety of reasons, such as poorly formulated strategy, weak tactics, misallocation of resources, breakdowns in communication, and fuzzy accountability. We have understood for decades the importance of giving attention instead of issuing threats, yet many senior leaders remain in the dark about the reasons for ineffective execution of their well-planned strategies. Because they haven't developed "early warning systems," often by the time a decision maker learns of a problem, it's too late to take appropriate corrective action. Inadvertently, these leaders foster a culture of underperformance.

Tracking performance provides one of the surest ways to understand what your business currently produces and to make the necessary adjustments.

⬦ Do you make it a regular practice to compare results with the performance forecasts?

⬦ Do you analyze several years' performance to uncover outliers, those things that change for a specific reason or season?

If you do, you can easily know whether your projections predict actual performance. Two things happen when you take the time to do this. First, you don't risk causing disconnects between results and forecasts in your future investment decision. Second you won't develop sunk cost tendencies—ongoing commitments to continue funding losing strategies rather than searching for new and better ones.

Depending on the nature of your business, you may need highly sophisticated tracking systems or fairly uncomplicated ones. The specific tool that will work best will depend on the size, complexity, nature, and culture of your organization. The main benefit of any tracking system is the understanding of where the resources are going and how much ROI you are receiving. None of this should stay a secret. Your line managers need to know what metrics you will use to measure their productivity. They should be involved in determining the criteria for the tracking system and agree to the frequency of formal reviews. As the Hawthorne Studies taught us, they will appreciate the attention but resent a threat.

High-performing organizations use real-time tracking. They continuously monitor resources, patterns, and results. They compare productivity to forecasts and adjust as needed. Real-time information allows decision-makers to spot and remedy flaws in both the strategy and the execution—and to avoid confusing the two. When selecting a tracking tool, remember the principle of Occam's razor: "Entities should not be multiplied unnecessarily." All things being equal, the simplest solution is best. The tracking system should be as simple as possible but *not simpler.*

Set Up Formal Reviews

Most companies use measures to evaluate their strategies. The *best* companies differentiate themselves by developing tracking tools that they use for formal reviews. The purpose of the formal review is to address implementation obstacles. Too many reviews, however, turn into a giant data dump that puts myriad details on the table but falls short in finding answers for *why* the obstructions actually reared their ugly heads in the first place. Ironically, an over-emphasis on uncovering all the pertinent information can actually serve as an avoidance mechanism, enabling those accountable to shy away from discussing *why* things haven't worked. The purpose of the formal review is not to audit; it's to give support. If, as the senior leader, you act as a passive listener, your run the risk that the review will become the former.

In Chapter 2, I mentioned that Taiichi Ohno described the "5 Whys" method as the basis of Toyota's scientific approach. According to Ohno, by asking "why?" five times, the nature of the problem and its solution become clear. Manufacturing organizations have embraced this practice more enthusiastically than some other industries have, but it can serve nearly any organization well. During the formal review, when someone presents an impediment to implementation, simply ask "why?"

Executing a strategy without formal reviews dooms the process from the start. On the other hand, if you agree to specific metrics, meeting structures, and agendas, you take significant steps in the direction of success. Often a sense of urgency will cause decision-makers to put aside the formal review process, arguing that the economy demands swifter action and fewer meetings. Big mistake. Lean times demand better processes. If you don't have the right people in place, the right processes or allocation of resources, then the sooner you uncover the problem, the sooner you can spur the execution process to success. As with most improvement initiatives, it all starts with better communication.

Engage in Robust Communication

Communicating every nuance of the strategic plan throughout a large corporation can prove difficult. Too often employees fail to see the connection between the organization's strategy and their own actions. Robust communication provides one of the surest ways to illuminate the way—to show concretely how each person plays a part in developing and carrying out day-to-day activities that move the company toward its strategic objectives.

First, let's define our terms. "robust communication" means healthy, vigorous, tough, and forceful dialogue. It doesn't involve aggression, scolding, temper-driven exchanges, or one-way communication. It requires an exchange of ideas and opinions with little censoring or hidden agendas. Those who engage in robust communication understand that truth is more important than harmony and listening trumps talking. Here are some ways to encourage more robust communication:

⬧ Provide information to employees. Ensuring that most employees are clear about their roles in achieving the most critical 80 percent of the plan usually proves more important than communicating the remaining 20 percent to everyone. Robust communication is the way to do that. Make sure people have information they need to understand the bottom-line impact of their routine choices. When they lack this insight, they tend to veer off in directions that don't support either the strategy or the tactics to support it.

⬧ Encourage information exchange across silos. When information flows freely across organizational borders, execution of the strategy becomes more likely. When people hoard information or compete with others within the four walls of your company, it becomes less probable. As with any behavior, reward that which you want to continue. If people receive monetary rewards or non-monetary recognition for working with those in other parts of the organization, they will be more motivated to make sure they do so. In addition to driving results, this sort of exchange tends to develop managers who have a broad-based knowledge of the organization rather than ones with tunnel vision.

⬧ Make sure information gets to headquarters. In their work with organizations that understand the secrets of strategy execution, researchers found that 77 percent of individuals in strong-execution organizations agree with the statement "Important information about the competitive environment gets to headquarters quickly." Only 45 percent of those in weak-execution organizations do.[8] My experience echoes their findings. Among my best clients, those organizations that have clearly established areas of accountability and decision-making outperform those who suffer from ambiguity. Similarly, in these organizations, headquarters serves a powerful function by identifying patterns and promulgating best practices. By concentrating on strategic issues, senior leaders can coordinate efforts instead of serving as referees or "the final word." Headquarters can only serve this purpose, however, if high-caliber decisions have originated throughout the organizations by those who knew they had both the right and duty to make them.

Execution Assessment

As I mentioned before, the other keys to successful execution lie in strategy and operations—or more specifically your ability to tie your operations to the strategy. Neither can exist in a vacuum. To determine how well your organization applies the aforementioned critical actions to implement the strategy, take this simple test. For each of the following, give yourself a score of 1 to 10.

Assessing Execution

For each of the following, circle a score of 1 to 10.

Clear links between mission and execution.	1 2 3 4 5 6 7 8 9 10
Forced trade-offs and clear boundaries for decisions.	1 2 3 4 5 6 7 8 9 10
Clear areas of accountability and decision making.	1 2 3 4 5 6 7 8 9 10
Transparent and fair reward/bonus program.	1 2 3 4 5 6 7 8 9 10
Performance-based appraisal system.	1 2 3 4 5 6 7 8 9 10
Tracking system to measures results against objectives.	1 2 3 4 5 6 7 8 9 10
Formal reviews of implementation.	1 2 3 4 5 6 7 8 9 10
The ability to seize opportunities.	1 2 3 4 5 6 7 8 9 10
Involvement of line managers.	1 2 3 4 5 6 7 8 9 10
Robust communication across all levels of the organization.	1 2 3 4 5 6 7 8 9 10

More than 90

You have a superior plan for execution. Continue to do what you're doing. Leverage strengths and continue to look for improvement opportunities.

70–89

You have a strong implementation plan, but you have room for improvement. Look at the categories where you scored less than 3 points. These will need immediate attention.

Below 70

You need significant work on your execution plan. Start by evaluating each of the above 10 measures of success. Concentrate your efforts on improving the worst two and then move from there.

Conclusion

When people ask me about the role of creative problem solving in moving an organization forward, I point out that creativity by itself, like other cognitive skills, is intellectual firepower. *Innovation*, on the other hand, is *applied* creativity. Of course, only those with the intellectual firepower to think creatively will formulate innovative solutions, so as always, realize that talent is at the heart of all progress and productivity. Without it, nothing else matters.

When you have it, however, much more separates you from the competition. Instead of solving problems and repeatedly returning the organization to the status quo, your talent can use *innovative thinking* to formulate a successful strategy and then apply *advanced critical thinking* in developing the plan for execution. The formula may seem easy, but judging from the number of companies that allow the strategy to die before it's executed (pun intended), it's not easy. Only the select few can sort out what needs to be done to turn great strategy into great execution.

Chapter 6

Plan Succession and Ensure the Leadership Pipeline

If you want one year of prosperity, grow grain.
If you want ten years of prosperity, grow trees.
If you want one hundred years of prosperity, grow people.
—Chinese Proverb

Mergers, acquisitions, downsizing, and growth all require an unprecedented need for information about key executives and a framework for assessing the competencies required to lead people during extraordinary times. Much of the impetus for the current succession planning movement surfaced in the aftermath of September 11, 2001, when 172 corporate vice presidents lost their lives in the terrorist destruction of the World Trade Center. Many of the companies affected that day learned a hard lesson about the importance of accurately evaluating and preparing leaders for promotion *before* the company needs them to take the helm. Many more organizations have learned these hard lessons individually since 9/11.

Yet, even with the revolving doors at the top of many companies spinning faster than ever, organizations still overlook opportunities to develop talent from the bottom up, and they continue to allow the selection of top leadership to turn into messy melodramas. Instead of leaving the future of your firm to fate, as the senior decision-maker, you need a systematic, comprehensive course of action that takes the guesswork out of determining the future. You and your organization need a process that provides objective, indispensable data to help make succession decisions and avoid costly mistakes as the Baby Boomers leave the workplace and the next generation enters.

The previously perceived quiet crisis of succession is now sounding its siren, and smart companies are responding by creating disciplined approaches to managing their futures. When circumstances usher in change, you should be ready with a carefully tended pool of candidates. Unfortunately, most of these talent pools are not well tended, and too many could use a dose of the organizational equivalent of chlorine.

Decisions-makers at smart companies know they must do better. They must assess their group of candidates and their bench strength to determine which leaders are ready for promotion—to identify individuals' strengths and weaknesses before making promotion decisions. A well-designed talent strategy defines the critical moves that companies need to map out a clear succession plan and develop a timeline that allows individuals to develop skills and gain experience to move forward. Understanding the succession planning process is the first step. Building confidence among stakeholders that you are indeed promoting the most qualified candidates is the next. As Winston Churchill advised, "Let our advance worrying become advance thinking and planning."

What Is Succession Planning and Who Needs It?

In the past, leaders used the terms *replacement planning* and *succession planning* synonymously, but the two differ. Convincing decision-makers to have a disaster replacement plan in the event that key individuals die or depart unexpectedly is not too difficult; persuading them to prepare people for advancement years ahead of their actual promotions presents more challenges. Therefore, replacement planning is a start, but only a start.

Replacement planning harkens back to the 1960s, when managers at General Electric identified four backup candidates for their positions. GE has progressed past this approach, but many organizations have not. Three fundamental problems limit an organization that chooses this path. First, most small companies don't have one, much less four, possible replacements for key positions. Second, attempting to designate a replacement for a job that may change, in an organization that may change, is fraught with problems. Third, focusing on replacement encourages decision-makers to concentrate on immediate needs, not long-term requirements. Succession planning balances the short- and long-term needs and promotes the simultaneous analysis of each.

Talent inventory advocates propose another approach for fueling the leadership pipeline. They recommend gathering a group of talented individuals to serve as backup to those departing key positions. Though solid in fundamentals, this method has problems too. Equating *potential* with *performance* can be risky because not all high-potential individuals actually end up performing. Only by placing these people in ever-evolving leadership roles can you accurately observe how they perform. Successful succession planning requires a balanced evaluation of talent, potential, experience, and performance. A course of action for identifying talent throughout the organization, it involves the selection of talented employees to replace key managers who will leave the company because of personal preference, retirement, reassignment, or termination. Here is my own definition of succession planning: *Succession planning is a deliberate, systematic effort to guarantee leadership continuity, a process for ensuring a suitable supply of candidates for current and future key jobs so that the careers of individuals can be managed to optimize both the organization's needs and the individual's aspirations.*

Done well, succession planning maintains a balance between implementing business strategy and the achievement of organizational goals with keeping the disruptions that often accompany personnel changes to a minimum. In contrast to an automatic promotion system within the chain of command, succession planning prepares people for present and future work responsibilities so that high-potential individuals are preparing for promotion at all levels. A powerful way to maximize human capital both now and in the future, it creates an ongoing, continuous plan to focus attention on talent. It establishes a way to meet the organization's needs for talent during a long period of time, starting with the sometimes daunting plan to advance someone to the number one position, the Chief Executive Officer.

A variety of reasons can lead senior leaders to establish a succession planning program in their organizations: to support the company strategy, identify replacement needs, increase the talent pool, provide increased opportunities for high potentials, and improve retention. But how do you really know if your current processes sufficiently address your succession planning issues? Ask yourself the following:

⬥ Do managers complain that no one is ready when vacancies open up?

⬥ Are expenses for external searches increasing?

⬥ Will you compromise your strategy because you don't have the talent to support it?

⬥ Are possible successors for key positions leaving because they perceive no room for advancement?

A yes answer to any one of these questions implies that your company has not adequately established or communicated its plans for the future of its people, both for replacing people in key roles and for developing high potentials for advancement.

One has only to pick up the *Wall Street Journal* to understand the depth and breadth of the leadership crisis in corporate America and to learn of CEO failure. Clearly, whether they are being forced out or whether they are retiring, CEOs are leaving organizations, and too many companies have not developed a well-thought-out plan for replacing them with internal candidates.

Why should that matter? First, your company will have trouble holding on to the talent you have if those in key positions perceive that they have no hope of advancement. Also, the perception that no one is ready to fill vacancies fuels the insecurities of both employees and other stakeholders. Keeping talent in your organization depends on you having a deep pool of skilled candidates who have been part of a well-defined leadership initiative, stars who have been given every opportunity to realize their full potential.

Second, when organizations lack the culture or discipline to grow their own talent, they have no choice but to look to outsiders; however, companies are usually better off with internal contenders. One has only to look at the National Football League for examples of why companies gamble when they hire outsiders.

Harvard Business School professor Dr. Groysberg and his team of researchers studied trades of star NFL wide receivers and punters to determine what kinds of performance are portable, and what kinds are not. Not surprisingly, they determined that the more the new hire depends on teamwork, the longer he will take to acclimate to the new environment. The performance of wide receivers, who are governed by complex interactions among teammates, declined initially and did not stabilize for a year. Conversely, punters, who engage in the comparatively individualistic act of kicking a football, showed no significant differences in their performance when they changed teams.[1] When considering outside talent, decision-makers do well, therefore, to ask themselves how transferable the skills will be and how long people will need in order to produce in your organization as well as their résumés indicate they did in their last jobs.

Also, external candidates usually create greater risks because no one knows them well. According to Booz Allen reports, 55 percent of outside CEOs who departed in 2003 were forced to resign by their boards, compared with 34 percent of insiders.[2] Granted, the differences are not huge, but the numbers point to an indisputable conclusion: Both now and in the future, companies fare better when they grow their own talent. In organizations that stretch their abilities and expand the knowledge of their high potentials throughout a period of time, when replacement becomes necessary, decision-makers can select from internal candidates that they have spent time observing, evaluating, and developing.

A word of caution: When companies do not have a well-defined succession plan, the reliance on internal candidates can backfire. Known quantities may sail through the promotion process when board directors and senior leaders fail to engage in the rigorous and sometimes arduous task of evaluation. Instead of engaging in due-diligence, decision-makers can allow social and emotional ties to particular individuals to guide their choices. Outside candidates should always be an option, but they should not be your only option.

Getting Started

When is the right time to start succession planning? Now! If you start five or even 10 years before the estimated departure of the CEO or other key leaders, it may be too late. Unforeseen circumstances can interfere with your best-laid plans, and the company will be faced, not with the "quiet crisis of succession," but with a screaming one. Whatever your current situation, these steps describe how you can start a strategic succession plan:

1. Clarify expectations. What does the current CEO expect from each level of the organization? No initiative has a hope of succeeding if the CEO doesn't support it and require commitment to it. Certainly the human resource department will probably oversee the step-by-step process of implementing the plan, but the CEO must drive the process. Don't forget the board of directors. Particularly when it comes to future CEOs, board members will want to be involved and informed.

2. Review the current succession plan for the organization. Audit its architecture to reveal vulnerabilities. Determine if this leadership pipeline supports your mission, vision, and values of the organization. Analyze the one-, three-, and five-year strategies, and evaluate these strategic objectives vis-à-vis the current pool of talent.

3. Based on this information, forecast future talent needs. Examine current versus required performance, existing enhancement initiatives, projected turnover, anticipated retirements, talent growth projection, demographics, and changing business trends.

4. Working together, the members of the leadership team establish competencies for each key position. The reason for doing this is that key positions underscore and dramatize important work processes that must be carried out. Key positions warrant attention because they represent strategically vital leverage points affecting organizational success. When leaders leave them vacant, the organization cannot confront the competition

successfully. Key positions exert critical influence on both strategy and execution, and have traditionally been viewed as those at the pinnacle of the chain of command.

5. Identify excellence markers and critical success factors for each position on the leadership team. Ask yourselves, "What are the skills, experience, knowledge, and personality characteristics required for exemplary performance?" Competency models can be created for each job or each level in the organization, but there should be some commonality at the upper echelons of the company. In general, you will want to address decision-making and problem-solving, results orientation, leadership abilities, and people skills. For as many roles as possible, identify different levels of achievement and the criteria for moving from one level of achievement to the next. Start with your most important roles and scrutinize your top performers. Build a talent profile that encapsulates the best practices of these achievers. Any leadership pipeline demands a continuous flow of talent, so extend succession planning throughout the various levels of the organization. In other words, establish a systematic method for moving from the bottom to the top.

6. Next, as a team, agree on standards for high-potentials. Some organizations concentrate on the top 5 percent of their population. The criteria for determining a high-potential would include the following:

   ♦ The ability to advance two job levels in five years.

   ♦ A willingness to relocate or acquire requisite field experience.

   ♦ The potential for at least 10-15 years with the organization.

7. Identify the strengths and weaknesses for each individual you are considering for key positions. Assess "ready now" people, identify a timeline for "ready now" in the future, and examine each high-potential vis-à-vis this list.

8. Ask each member of the leadership team to identify high-potentials currently in the organization and one or two possible successors for each key position in the pipeline. For immediate decisions compare this list of high-potential candidates with the list of "ready now" candidates, or look at the timeline for projected readiness to determine when they will be able to take on new responsibilities.

9. Finally, assign members of the leadership team accountability for development plans for each high-potential.

Critical Leadership Competencies

Authors have filled the shelves with books about leadership personality, charisma, and emotional intelligence. Management schools offer classes that teach accounting, marketing, and finance. Arguably, leadership is a complicated concept and a somewhat abstract one. Yet, in order to define what your organization requires, you need an explicit list of criteria that you will need to consider in order to make high-caliber succession planning decisions at each juncture in the leadership pipeline. As previously mentioned, there are four major leadership competencies that you will want to evaluate at all levels: decision-making and problem-solving, task orientation, leadership skills, and people skills.

Even though all four of these are critical predictors of future leadership success, the most crucial forecaster of executive success is brainpower, or the specific cognitive abilities that equip us to make decisions and solve problems. Three main components define what I call leadership intelligence: critical thinking, learning ability, and quantitative abilities. Of these, *critical thinking* is the most important and the least understood.

Dispassionate scrutiny, strategic focus, and analytical reasoning form the foundation of critical thinking. These abilities equip a person to anticipate future consequences, to get to the core of complicated issues, and to zero in on the critical few while putting aside the trivial many. Lucent Technologies CEO Patricia Russo, who led the company's turnaround, described this ability as "clarity of thought." Avon CEO Andrea Jung made an analogous observation that "clear thinking" in senior leadership is one of the primary attributes they look for in hiring and promotion.[3] Former Chairman of the Joint Chiefs of Staff, General Richard Myers, described it similarly when he commented that "agility of thought" separated a good Air Force officer from a great one.[4] General Myers, Russo, and Jung described the same, very specific talent that forms the foundation of *leadership intelligence*. (See Chapter 4 for how to spot a strategic thinker.)

Sometimes the absence of critical thinking skills becomes obvious in a leader's ultimate downfall. Underdeveloped critical thinking skills may help to explain the demise of Carly Fiorina, the ousted CEO of Hewlett-Packard. Fiorina, whom *Fortune* named the most powerful woman in business in 1998, lost her job at Hewlett-Packard just two years later. The company's controversial deal to buy Compaq in the spring of 2002—after a bruising proxy fight led by one of the Hewlett family heirs—did not produce the shareholder returns or profits she had promised. Fiorina either failed to anticipate the implications of and obstacles to her decision to buy Compaq, or she simply didn't pursue feedback that may have revealed errors in her judgment or resistance to her plan. Had she explored multiple perspectives, particularly those of the Hewlett family, she may have been able to identify probable consequences and to avert the temporary plummet in HP stock, widespread job losses, and her own downfall. Both HP and Fiorina paid for her weak leadership intelligence.

General learning ability is the second most important aspect of leadership intelligence. When leaders can acquire new information quickly, they do not lose valuable time moving through the pipeline. They size up the new leadership situation, learn about their people, learn about products and processes, and then immediately act on this knowledge. When this happens, the organization responds by moving the new leader's idea to action. Reading ability, vocabulary, and fundamental math skills form the foundation of learning ability. Often, but not always, educational success is an accurate predictor of how quickly someone will learn in the organization. Certainly, ongoing learning teaches people about their own learning styles, so they become more proficient at acquiring new information and skills.

Not every turn in the leadership pipeline requires quantitative abilities, but they are critical at the top levels of most organizations. Knowing what the numbers mean and using them to make sophisticated business decisions equips an individual to make budget or profit and loss assessments. Superior development of these skills allows a person to evaluate the nuances of mergers, acquisitions, and risk-taking ventures as they analyze strategy. Numerical problem solving, critical thinking, and proficient learning define the basics of business acumen.

Leadership intelligence accounts for success at the upper echelons of any organization, but no one succeeds without also demonstrating a strong achievement drive. Certainly the talent to zero in on best uses of time helps prioritize what needs to be done and the critical nature of some tasks, but without a clear bias for action, longevity in the company, much less movement through the pipeline, cannot occur. Once a person has clearly defined a problem and differentiated between essential objectives and less relevant ones, his or her willingness to work hard and a high-energy, go-getter approach define task orientation. A competitive spirit, a "can do" attitude, self-discipline, reliability, and focus further augment it. Personality assessments can help identify achievement drive in new hires and internal high-potentials, but the surest way to know if a person has what it takes to get the job done is observation. Once again, performance reviews and feedback from multi-rater surveys or interviews will provide the insight to judge a candidate's commitment to realizing goals.

Even though succession planning concentrates on leadership development, realize not everyone in your organization is cut out to be a leader. Some can be strong solo contributors, perhaps throughout their careers. However, the most important leadership competency, integrity, is non-negotiable at every level. Warning flags usually begin to surface early in a person's career, but if the person performs well, productivity can serve as a cover for the lack of integrity. Phil Condit, the former Boeing CEO learned this the hard way.

Condit, who resigned December 1, 2003, as a result of the defense contracting scandals that led to two Boeing executives being sent to jail, seemingly ignored a series of warning flags and ethical violations. His resignation was forced during the fallout from the freezing of a tanker contract with the US Air Force. This occurred due to an investigation of a former procurement staffer, Darleen Druynun, over corruption charges. (Condit offered her work at Boeing while she was still a U.S. Government employee, a violation of Boeing ethics.) In addition to making this questionable decision, Condit apparently lacked the skill to evaluate honesty in others. Either that, or he chose to turn a blind eye as evidenced by him failing to recognize the culture that was developing around him.

Fifteen months after Condit's departure, Boeing forced its new chief executive to resign after an investigation uncovered that he had an affair with a female employee. Boeing has a Code of Conduct that states that Boeing employees "will not engage in conduct or activity that may raise questions as to the company's honesty, impartiality, reputation or otherwise cause embarrassment to the company." However, at Boeing, as in your organization, posting a code of conduct or an explanation of ethics is not enough. Leaders must constantly embody, discern, and demand integrity and ethical behavior.

The other skills and traits that create the foundation of successful leaders are *dominance, emotional maturity*, the knowledge *of how to build cohesion*, and an understanding of *how to structure work* for and with others. As an individual moves through the leadership pipeline, the list grows, but as soon as a person takes on direct report responsibilities, this list becomes essential.

People skills round out the list of leadership competencies. Once again, the list of requisite skills and characteristics grows as leadership responsibilities increase, but as soon as people move from solo contributors to managers of others, they need to spin up their responsiveness and fairness. A large part of their job will now involve understanding others, not necessarily making sure others understand them, so strong listening skills reign. Empathy and a commitment to building trust will also help them construct a team that focuses on collaborative efforts and strong rapport, and finally, a knack for spotting and developing talent.

Steps in the Leadership Pipeline

Because succession planning is a deliberate, systematic effort to guarantee leadership continuity, organizations need a clearly defined way to understand the steps in the leadership pipeline. Some authors offer five or six "turns" in the pipeline that represent significant passages that outline the challenges involved in making each leadership transition. Your organization, depending on your size and structure, may define the transition from solo contributor to CEO in as few as three or four steps. For the purpose of this discussion, however, I offer five stages of leadership development that can be applicable to both large and small organizations.

The following are the cognitive, task accomplishment, leadership, and interpersonal requirements for each stage in the leadership pipeline. Each stage encompasses the skills, talents, and abilities of the previous stage but defines the specific additions required for success at the next level in the pipeline. Here's what it looks like:

Leadership Pipeline

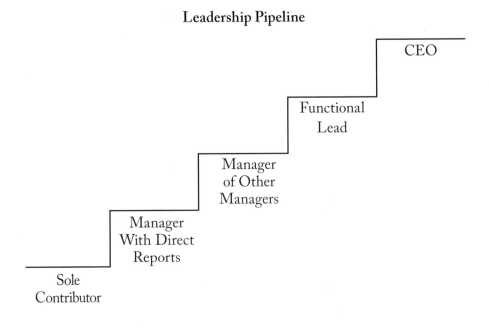

Solo Contributor

As I mentioned earlier, not everyone can or wants to be a leader. Some find fulfillment in working by themselves without the additional responsibility of direct reports. Although most organizations view the role of solo contributor as a stepping stone on the leadership path, others find ways to utilize the talents of those who want to remain in this role. For most, however, this needs to be only a step on the path and a proving ground for moving forward. The talent you select for these positions should reflect the qualities for what you want in a future functional leader or CEO. These are the basic requirements for success as an individual contributor (See Appendix for these in table format):

Decision-Making/Problem-Solving:

◊ Technical expertise.

◊ Capacity and desire to learn quickly.

Task Orientation:

◊ Strong achievement drive and bias for action.

◊ Systematic approach to work.

◊ Time mastery.

◊ High energy level.

◊ Strong commitment to meeting deadlines.

◊ Results focus, even when the work is hard or demands long hours.

Leadership Skills:

◊ Integrity.

◊ Reliability.

People Skills:

◊ Strong interpersonal skills.

◊ Teamwork orientation.

◊ Respect for peer group.

Manager With Direct Report Responsibilities

Perhaps the most difficult passage in the leadership pipeline is the first one, because it demands a transition from actually touching the work to managing others who do it. Clients tell me they miss that feeling of accomplishment that comes from a job well done. They also report that they feel an enormous vulnerability. No longer will their own efforts define their destinies; now they must rely on others, who may or may not do a good job, to determine their fates. Jumping in to fix problems instead of helping others develop their problem-solving skills saves time. Similarly, just doing the job yourself ensures quality and efficiency. Yet only those who overcome these tendencies stand to move further through the pipeline. A new manager must embody these are the additional traits and behaviors:

Decision-Making/Problem-Solving:

◊   Capability to separate tactics from strategy.

◊   Knack for zeroing in on critical issues.

Task Orientation:

◊   Capacity to satisfy achievement needs through work of others.

◊   Focus on short term objectives.

◊   Willingness to delegate.

◊   Knowledge of goal setting.

◊   Ability to define roles for and with others.

Leadership Skills:

◊   Dominance.

◊   Motivation to give candid, balanced, developmental feedback.

◊   Readiness to make unpopular decisions and influence firing decisions.

◊   Ability to discipline without destroying.

◊   Emotional maturity.

◊   Knowledge of how to build cohesion.

⬥ An understanding of how to structure work for and with direct reports.

People Skills:

⬥ Knowledge of how to build teamwork.

⬥ The ability to identify talent and influence hiring decisions.

⬥ Openness and tolerance, especially for people whose ideas, customs, and beliefs are different.

⬥ Insight into the underlying agendas and motivations of others.

⬥ Ability to get to the core of conflict.

⬥ Capacity to build trust.

⬥ Empathy.

Manager of Other Managers

Even though the first step in the leadership pipeline is usually the most difficult adjustment, the transition to managing other managers offers its own challenges. As a director, vice president, or division lead, this individual will not only be asked to manage those who were once peers, she or he will now oversee those who do most of the work within the organization. Therefore, the following will be essential at this juncture:

Decision-Making/Problem-Solving:

⬥ Strategic focus.

⬥ Well-developed critical thinking skills.

⬥ Talent for evaluating strategies of other managers.

⬥ Ability to anticipate consequences.

⬥ Talent for prioritizing seemingly conflicting goals.

⬥ Proven track record for solving unfamiliar problems.

⬥ Ease of multi-tasking.

⬥ Solid track record for making high-caliber decisions.

⬥ General business acumen.

◊   Facility with budget decisions.

◊   Ability to create order during chaos.

Task Orientation:

◊   More pronounced tendency to feel accomplishment through others' efforts.

◊   Capacity to overcome obstacles.

◊   Preference for working independently, neither wanting nor needing close supervision.

◊   Eagerness to bring about continuous improvement by questioning the status quo.

Leadership Skills:

◊   Emotional toughness, especially when making unpopular decisions.

◊   Ability to establish and articulate performance standards.

◊   Willingness to fire when necessary.

◊   Confidence and self-assurance.

◊   Coaching/mentoring orientation.

◊   Competence in serving as a sounding board for others.

◊   Resilience.

People Skills:

◊   Gift for spotting and developing talent.

◊   Insight about own strengths and weaknesses.

◊   Social poise and astuteness.

Multi-Business Leader or Functional Lead

The "C-Suite" of an organization's officers, general managers, and presidents of divisions defines those in the ranks of multi-business leaders and functional leads. These people enter the arena of significant autonomy, profit responsibilities, and tremendous ownership of the company's future. They can usually count on receiving much less guidance and mentoring than they did at other stages of their careers, and they are likely to experience, sometimes for the first time, the loneliness at the top that plagues many. Highly visible from both above and below, these leaders often serve as a buffer between the CEO and other areas of the organization, and must engage in the tough and sometimes frustrating business of allocating resources to competing entities. Those with thin skin need not apply. The following should also be apparent:

Decision-Making/Problem-Solving:

◊ Aptitude for making sophisticated financial decisions related to profit and loss.

◊ Skills for blending specific business strategy with overall enterprise strategy.

◊ Aptitude for critiquing strategy by asking questions and requiring support data.

◊ Complex thinking to manage more than one business.

◊ Three- to five-year vision.

◊ Decisiveness.

◊ Global perspective.

◊ Creative problem solving.

Task Orientation:

◊ Value of and responsibility for unfamiliar functions.

◊ Focus on both short- and long-term objectives.

◊ Risk orientation.

◊ Resourcefulness to be alert to opportunities.

◊ Talent for working under time constraints.

Leadership Skills:

◊ Ability to trust others in the chain of command to handle the day-to-day decisions related to running the businesses.

◊ Talent for asking the right questions to draw out the ideas of others.

◊ Obvious maturity in use of power.

People Skills:

◊ Succession planning—ability to select and develop leaders of leaders.

◊ Predisposition to be a source of advice and wisdom.

◊ Cross-cultural awareness

◊ Agility to balance the different needs of various stakeholders.

◊ Ability to put others at ease in social situations.

The CEO

The job of CEO is like no other. It requires managing the enterprise in its totality and responsibility for multiple constituencies: the board of directors, investors, shareholders, employees, and the community. Room for error becomes nonexistent, yet others hesitate to bring you bad news. Interacting with external groups and projecting a positive image of the organization appear on the radar screen, yet minding the store never ceases to be tantamount. For this unique position, only those who have successfully navigated the previous steps in the pipeline can hope to do well. But even that offers no guarantee. The following need to be added to a CEO's requisite competencies:

Decision-Making/Problem-Solving:

◊ Visionary thinking—five- to 10-year focus.

◊ Ability to handle ambiguity.

◊ Knowledge of how to grow the business organically and acquisitively.

◊ Insight to create policy that will affect everyone in the enterprise.

Task Orientation:

◊ Change orientation.

◊ Focus on stock price, shareholder value, financial solvency.

◊ Portfolio management.

Leadership Skills:

◊ Leadership of disparate entities, often geographically dispersed.

◊ Capacity to set the pace of change and to orchestrate it well.

◊ Capability of serving as a trusted exemplar.

◊ Skill for articulating vision.

◊ Crisis management skills.

◊ Commitment to ongoing learning.

◊ Management of top and bottom lines.

◊ Emotional fortitude.

◊ Courage.

◊ Ability to handle failure.

People Skills:

◊ Skills for managing board of director relations.

◊ Skills for managing investor relations.

◊ Community orientation.

How to Evaluate Leadership Readiness

Defining leadership competencies is the voice; evaluation for readiness is the echo. The two must exist in tandem, neither alone guaranteeing success, but together making it more likely. To evaluate your bench's leadership competencies, begin by collecting applicable data on existing employees, and discover where the gaps are. One of the advantages to starting the succession planning process early is that there will be time to assimilate these kinds of data. If there is an emergency push to fill a vacated position, this advantage is lost. Therefore, starting now to aggregate data can have enormous returns down the road. What kind of data? Gather information about each person's education, work history, performance reviews, aspirations, competency levels, problem solving abilities, learning potential, strengths, developmental imperatives, and leadership style.

Interviewing and testing are two ways to pull together information that would not ordinarily be in a person's personnel file. This will take time and will probably involve the company's hiring an outside consultant who has been trained to administer and interpret psychometrics and cognitive data. However, the inclusion of quantifiable, reliable data increases objectivity and fairness and facilitates more accurate comparisons and contrasts. In other words, this part of the plan creates a system for all participants to be evaluated impartially. Developing a succession planning tool will centralize all the significant information.

Performance appraisal rankings should be included in your evaluation of any discussion of succession planning. Cognitive scores and personality data offer invaluable information, but nothing trumps a high-performance track record. An individual may fit the profile of a leader, but if she or he either hasn't had ample opportunity to perform at a high level or simply hasn't performed, question that person's readiness for promotion.

Including multi-rater feedback results in this process is a controversial issue, but I advocate its inclusion. Even though occasionally results can be skewed in either positive or negative directions, knowing what others in the organization think of the candidate, and providing feedback to the person about these results, benefits both the decisions-makers and the candidate. Some consultants and experts advocate its inclusion, but others disagree.

Tyson Foods, the Sprindale, Arkansas, food giant, provides a good example of how to use data to make succession planning decisions. Despite its size after its 2001 acquisition of International Beef Products, the company had invested in very little leadership development and had no system to ensure a steady supply of qualified talent. Also, with the addition of another large company, there were redundant positions at the top. John Tyson, the grandson of the founder, decided to change that in the summer of 2002. When he realized his ad hoc approach to leadership development was not working, Tyson formed a task force that included succession-planning experts to look at the problem. I was a member of this team.[5] In 2006 Richard Bond replaced John Tyson as CEO of the company, but Tyson had laid the foundation for the company to move forward with its succession planning initiative, one that was based on reliable data and a plan for development of internal talent.

When you have all the available information, do two things. First, separate skills and abilities that can be developed from those that cannot. Then, determine if you need to "grow" or "buy" high-potentials at each level of the organization. Coaching skills, delegation skills, communication skills, interpersonal competencies, and performance management skills can all be developed or honed, provided the individual is willing to commit to the work of changing behaviors. Learning potential, decision making capabilities, problem solving skills, critical thinking, abstract thinking, creativity, and strategic planning are all difficult to develop. Generally speaking, if these aren't present in an adult, there's very little anyone can do to create them. People can certainly improve in these areas, and, with help, they can learn to develop coping behaviors for using what they have to their fullest potential, but improvement will be limited.

Once you have aggregated information on each person, define readiness for promotion. When you have completed the previous steps, readiness for promotion and the speed with which a person can progress should be apparent. A four-tiered scale works well to classify candidates:

- A Players are ready now for promotion and can advance two levels in five years.
- B Players can be ready to advance in one year.
- C Players can handle responsibilities at their present level or one level above.
- D player should be held in their current positions or cut.

Analyzing the readiness of internal candidates provides critical information about the gaps that are present now and the ones that are likely to surface in the future. If no one can be ready to fill vacancies when they occur, a search for outside replacements may be indicated. Bringing that person on sooner rather than later may cost in the short run, but in the long run, having someone ready for key positions can pay huge dividends.

Train and develop high-potential candidates. Gathering data to make promotion decisions begins the process of developing each participant to his or her greatest potential. This ongoing process can take many forms but should include the development of individual action plans, ongoing internal mentoring, and performance management from the boss. Training, external feedback and coaching, and educational opportunities are other options. (See Appendix for Development Plan.) One CEO recently asked me, "What if I spend all this money on development, and people leave?" I asked him, "What if you don't, and they stay?" Suddenly spending time, money, and effort on development made more sense.

Track the loss of high-potentials. If you ear mark an individual for rapid movement through the pipeline, and that person decides to leave, find out why. If more than one top performer mentions the same problem, you have a clog in the pipeline. More often than not, their reason for leaving will be bad leadership, either in their immediate boss or in the overall leadership of the organization. When you have a transparent, fair system for moving top performers through the pipeline, people feel in control of their own destinies, and they perceive opportunities to advance. The reason they leave is usually that they have not received what they consider just treatment or adequate mentoring.

Objective analysis is at the heart of success for this kind of process. Very often decision-makers focus on what people are like and ignore what they actually *do*. When they consider all available information about the pool of candidates, they can help the organization realize both future and present benefits.

Future Benefits of Succession Planning

Decision-makers at Colgate-Palmolive have developed a succession plan that positions the company to be ready for challenges and changes of the future. According to Bob Joy, the senior vice president of global human resources, they begin their leadership evaluations within a year of the person's joining the company. They believe that the earlier they start to identify talent, the earlier they can provide the job assignments and develop the broad business experience needed by a candidate for the company's highest positions. Then, throughout their careers, high potentials receive assignments that stretch their abilities and expand their knowledge, exposing them to a variety of markets, cultures, consumers, and business circumstances. Also, Colgate mandates that all senior managers retain their high potentials or risk their own compensation. Colgate sends an obvious message that the leadership is committed to attracting, developing, and retaining stars in their leadership pipeline.[6]

As the officers of Colgate have learned, not having to replace people puts the company in a position of strength; however, all companies are not so fortunate. Most organizations still need a procedure for identifying replacement needs *before* they occur, or they will not be able to respond to the sudden loss of key talent due to unexpected changes. Long-term planning for the company depends on its ability to see its bench strength, to clarify the direction they need to take, and to provide opportunities for star performers to play their role in making that happen. Not only does this ensure continuity of leadership for the future; it also helps to create current benefits for both the company and the individual.

Current Benefits

One of the most apparent advantages for starting a succession plan now is to develop talent *now*. By identifying a person's assets and liabilities *now*, bosses can work with both high potentials and struggling employees to help them do the best they can. A well-developed succession plan lets people know that they are being prepared for advancement, which not only builds their confidence that they will advance, but also lets them know that they will receive the needed help and guidance to make those advancements happen. Succession planning exists primarily for the good of the company, but when it is integrated with career-planning efforts, individual participants benefit too. When an organization's culture is characterized by honesty and openness and opportunities for advancement are clearly articulated, why wouldn't a star want to stay?

In addition to retaining top performers, a well-developed system helps the company recruit top talent. People want to know up front that they will have opportunities to grow and advance within the company. When recruiters and internal interviewers can articulate what a person can expect by way of development, it increases the likelihood that A players will want to join your team.

Preventing premature or ill-advised promotions is another compelling reason to institute a succession plan. Knowing if and when people will be ready for assignments helps to ensure that both they and the organization will benefit from their advancement. The benefits to the company are obvious—it will receive the best each person has to offer at the right time for that person to offer it. The benefit to the individual is a little less evident but not less real. People who are promoted too soon are often doomed to fail, something that no one wants to happen.

Conclusion

In short, successful succession management can lower employee turnover, improve morale, fuel the leadership pipeline, and place the most qualified candidates in key positions. Clearly, succession planning is critical, and efforts to put it in place should begin immediately, but it can't happen overnight. It will require considerable attention to design, commitment of top managers, the credibility of the planning staff, and resource allocation, but with CEO buy-in and a well-planned approach, you can begin to collect the data that will start the process. First, however, you might want to consider what you will call the initiative. Instead of calling it succession planning, I usually recommend that clients call it "leadership development" or "career advancement." Initially you can expect some resistance to any kind of change like this because people will worry that they won't pass the tests or that they will somehow jeopardize their chances of moving forward if anyone takes the time to notice them. With time, however, people will come to realize that they will benefit from the opportunities to advance. In fact, I often recommend that companies create the impression that being invited to be a part of this sort of initiative is a rite of passage or a badge of honor of sorts. Whether embraced by all or not, the future of any company is too important to let popular opinion deter that which is in the best interest of the organization. Leadership continuity and excellence is the paramount responsibility of the CEO and the board of directors, and nothing should stand in its way. It is truly no accident that the root of the word "succession" is "success."

Chapter 7

Lead a Team of Virtuosos

Coming together is a beginning. Keeping together is progress. Working together is success.

—Henry Ford

Up until now you've probably had numerous opportunities to coach teams—perhaps even very good teams. But usually leaders don't experience the rare delight of guiding a team of virtuosos until they reach the executive chair. Now, if you have followed my advice to hire and promote the best and brightest, you may have ended up with such a team. If that's the case, you're one lucky senior leader. But the news is not all good. Leading a team of virtuosos presents its own challenges. In order to leverage this opportunity, you'll need to be aware of the kind of person you're leading and understand how a team of them interrelates.

What Is a Virtuoso?

In previous chapters I addressed individual excellence by using terms such as "A player" and "high potential." Virtuosos certainly embody all the qualities and traits of these people, but they do more. They distinguish themselves and exemplify what I call E^5: excellence, expertise, experience, enterprise, and ethics.

They force people to take them seriously. They don't raise the bar—they set it for everyone else. They serve as gold standards of what people should strive to be and attain. If you were to scour the world, you'd be hard-pressed to find people who do their jobs better. You wouldn't hesitate to hire them again, and you'd be crushed if you found out they were leaving.

Because they are thought leaders, others look to virtuosos for guidance and example. Often they consider virtuosos edgy and contrarian, but they seldom ignore them. Virtuosos chafe at too much supervision or tight controls—fortunately they need neither. They constantly search for the new horizon and welcome the unforeseen challenge. No synonym for the word *virtuoso* exists. Some might substitute *artist*, *expert*, or *musician*, but these don't suffice. Many can lay claim to these titles and still fail to be virtuosos. By definition, few virtuosos exist. If you're fortunate to have a team of them, recognize them for who they are, and use your influence to help them make beautiful music.

You Can't Whistle a Symphony

No stranger to virtuosos, Maestro Antonio Pappano faces a stage full of them each time he takes baton in hand. As the music director of both the Royal Opera House, Covent Garden in London, and the Orchestra dell' Accademia di Santa Cecilia in Rome, and a guest conductor of many of the top orchestras in the United States and Europe, Pappano works with some of the best musicians in the world.

When I spoke with Pappano about what it takes to lead an orchestra at his level, he mentioned several things he has to consider simultaneously. He said he repeatedly urges the musicians to listen to each other. There is a constant swing in who and what the priority needs to be—with an ongoing shift in balance. His job involves guiding the harmony and tempo—all the time working with the individual musicians and sections so that little by little, element by element, a coherent message is developed—not unlike the work of executives who strive to do comparable things in their organizations.

Often Pappano doesn't meet his orchestra until three days before a concert, but he maintains he can detect the level of the group within a few minutes; similarly, he pointed out, an orchestra can size up a maestro in about the same length of time. As Pappano evaluates the maturity of the orchestra, he looks at three major areas: their seriousness of purpose, their sound quality, and their ability and willingness to listen to each other—the three things an executive would need to assess: purpose, quality, and willingness to work together.

Pappano pointed out that the individual talents of the musicians will vary, but the result often becomes more than the sum of its parts. Even though each member doesn't contribute in exactly the same way or even at the same level, the contributions combine to create the intricate network that is involved in the clear, focused, and distinctive performance of a symphony. Keep in mind, however, that the weakest members of the orchestras that Pappano conducts would still be considered exceptional. Similarly, the excellence and contribution of your team members may vary, but if you start with top performers, like Pappano, you will be able to guide them much more quickly to the point that they can make beautiful music together.[1]

Pointing out that no one person can whistle a symphony sums up conventional wisdom but also defines the frustration of using teams. When people can't do the job alone and must rely on others to produce the work, leaders face the tough decision of whether or not to assemble a team. The question of whether or not to assemble a virtuoso team causes even more angst. This avenue can be fraught with headache. Star performers can be elitist, fiercely independent, high-strung, egocentric, and volatile. And sometimes they don't "play well with others," so they resist identifying themselves with a team.

People use the word *team* to mean any group of people that works for the same company, shares a common purpose, or has any degree of interdependency. Most companies don't have teams; they have committees. Beautiful music requires more than a collection of people; it demands the collective efforts of people who devote themselves to creating an opus that no one of them working alone could achieve. True teams of every stripe share four common traits:

◊ Complimentary skills.

◊ Commitment to a common purpose.

◊ Shared goals.

◊ Mutual interdependency and accountability.

Even though teamwork often trumps individual contributions at the senior echelons of most organizations, it rarely happens, chiefly because people haven't been rewarded for it. Until they reach a critical point in their careers, people have excelled, for the most part, not because they have been good team players, but because they have been such strong solo contributors. To require these same people suddenly to develop esprit de corps can prove not only daunting but also intimidating and more than a little confusing.

Well-intended leaders, in an effort to speed along the transformation from a solo contributor mindset to one of team membership, often schedule expensive team experiences. These offer a variety of unpleasant situations, often in outdoor settings, that are designed specifically to advance cohesion. They don't. They just bother people, cost copious amounts of money, and keep people from doing what it takes to tackle the tough issues related to building collaboration among a group of people who have always been fiercely self-sufficient.

Before you invest in this sort of mistake, ask yourself this question: "Do we need a team?" If one person has the requisite resources, knowledge, and experiences, and buy in from others is not important, an individual should make the decision or carry out the task. On the other hand, when no one person can make the decision or accomplish the task, or when the outcome will affect others whose support is crucial, you need a team. But keep this in mind. Creating a team—even a team of virtuosos—is not your goal. It is a means for achieving an organizational goal that people working alone cannot accomplish.

The next question becomes: "Do we need a team or a collection of solo contributors?" If you need solo performers to operate as a team occasionally, you will have a different point of view than if you truly need a cohesive, high performing team that cannot function without the collaboration of the other members. The principles remain the same, but the standard to which participants will need to model them differs.

Teams as Living Systems

As I mentioned in Chapter 4, a team is a system of parts that interact with each other to function as a whole. When something is made up of a number of parts that do not interact, and the arrangement of these parts is irrelevant, this is a collection of materials rather than a system. For example, a stack of blank sheets of paper is merely a collection of material. You can cut it in half or quarters and still not alter anything important. Conversely, a book is a system of interrelated parts that combine to create the whole.

Teams are even more complicated; they are *living* systems. As Pappano pointed out, each person on the team is a separate part of the system, but the effect of the interactions among the members is more than the sum of the parts. The dynamic relationships members create by constantly defining and redefining themselves, their behavior, and the functions of the team causes *synergy*. Consequently, combined, the team members can do things—like play a symphony—that no one of them could do separately. A team of virtuosos can do even more than an ordinary team.

What Is a Team of Virtuosos?

Leading experts comprise a team of virtuosos. Independently, these people possess some of the most laudable skills, talents, and natural ability that anyone could offer. When they collaborate, they work together frenetically and energetically to bring about results that have never occurred before. They create what hasn't been. As a group, they set themselves apart in their ambition and intensity. Sometimes the individuals bring a superior attitude to the table; often they clash mightily when temperament and egos overshadow the goals.

Unlike traditional teams that leaders throw together from among those available, a team of virtuosos consists of top talent that the leader has handpicked. You'll find teams of virtuosos in almost every area: business, art, science, athletics, and politics. But let's start with some history lessons.

Apollo 13

On April 11, 1970, James Lovell commanded the third Apollo mission that was intended to land on the moon. Jack Swigert served as command module pilot, Fred Haise as lunar module pilot, and Gene Kranz as flight director at NASA. Ken Mattingly had originally been scheduled to make the flight, but because he had been exposed to German measles, Swigert took his place. Mattingly, however, did not develop measles but did help with the rescue.

NASA had established a rotation for the astronauts' crew assignment that allowed management to select from a sea of experts. However, some individuals caused themselves to be eliminated from the rotation because they didn't perform up to standards or they made choices in their personal lives that cast doubt on their suitability to represent the space program in the most positive light. In other words, not all the experts proved to be virtuosos. But the members of the Apollo 13 crew certainly met the criteria.

Apollo 13 launched successfully, but the crew had to abort the moon landing after an oxygen tank ruptured, severely damaging the spacecraft's electrical system. Despite great hardship caused by limited power, loss of cabin heat, shortage of water, illness, and the critical need to reengineer the carbon dioxide removal system, the crew returned safely to Earth on April 17. Even though the crew did not accomplish its mission of landing on the moon, the operation was termed a "successful failure" because the astronauts returned safely.[2]

In the 1995 movie by the same name, Tom Hanks made famous the line, "Houston, we have a problem." Actually, Tom Hanks' character, Jim Lovell, did not say the line initially. Jack Swigert did, and he said, "Houston, we've *had* a problem." Ground control responded, "Say again please." Lovell then repeated, "Houston, we've had a problem."[3] Filmmakers intentionally changed the line because the original quote made it seem as though the problem had already passed.

For the purpose of this discussion, however, the original and accurate line gives us more of an understanding about why we should count Lovell among those who have led a team of virtuosos. Even though he found himself in the throes of the consequences of the problem, he realized the problem existed in the past. The solution to the problem needed to occur in the present and future. Subtle difference? No, huge difference. Strong leaders shift from grieving the loss of what *was* to formulating solutions for what *is* in the blink of an eye. And they encourage their team to do the same. Lovell's comment immediately focused those in space and those on the ground on the need to creatively discover a way to save them. No time for gnashing of teeth or wringing of hands.

The Apollo 13 team worked around the clock to bring the crippled spacecraft to safety, in spite of the unprecedented and overwhelming odds against their success. The same team had launched the spacecraft, but their finest hour came when they faced the life-or-death situation. Here's what Jim Lovell teaches us about leading a team of virtuosos:

◊ Although face-to-face dialogue represents the ideal for team communication, it isn't critical. Lovell had team members with him in space and others on the ground. Exceptional individuals can work together to overcome adversity, regardless of whether they operate in the same time zone, or even the same planet.

◊ Lovell supported his team. Swigert originally told Houston that they had had a problem. Lovell echoed the response and used the same verb tense to describe the situation.

◊ Although others had gone to the moon, the Apollo 13 crew went where no man had gone before in terms of solving problems that hadn't existed before. They created solutions for unique problems that saved their lives in the short run, but that made space travel safer for those who would follow.

We can reach back to 1970 when Lovell and the leadership team at NASA teach us lessons, but a century before another leader led a team of virtuosos into uncharted seas.

Abraham Lincoln

On May 18, 1860, William Seward, Salmon Chase, and Edward Bates, all contenders for the presidential nomination, waited to hear the results from the Republican National Convention. When Lincoln emerged the victor, his rivals felt dismayed and angry. But Lincoln put that aside. He knew he had to assemble a cabinet that represented the best talent available, regardless of their previous differences. Lincoln also included Montgomery Blair, Gideon Welles, and Norman Judd, all former Democrats, and William Dayton, a former Whig. Lincoln could have made more predictable choices in establishing his cabinet, but he didn't. Instead he assembled a team of virtuosos.

Lincoln understood his rivals and respected them. Those feelings led him to bring his disgruntled opponents together, to create the most unusual cabinet in history. By marshalling the talents of these men, Lincoln was able to preserve the Union and win the war. Each day brought new conflicts and decisions. Cabinet meetings were contentious with members arguing for and against the blockade of Southern ports. On the one hand, the blockade would grant the Union the power to search and seize vessels. On the other hand, no one wanted to encourage foreign powers to extend belligerent rights to the Confederacy. Closing the ports was an option. The cabinet split down the middle on this complicated and unprecedented decision. Even though he had initially questioned the advisability of the blockade, Welles executed the blockade with great energy and skill.

The cabinet consisted of strong men—all virtuosos in their own right—but Lincoln teaches us something else. The leader of the team, in this case the prairie lawyer from Illinois, was the most notable virtuoso of them all. But it wasn't easy, and it ultimately cost him his life.[4] Here are Lincoln's other lessons:

◊ Lincoln showed remarkable courage and prescience. He succeeded in surrounding himself with the strongest men from every faction of the new Republican Party because he had a very clear goal. He never lost sight of the intricate task he faced in building a cabinet that would preserve the integrity of the Republican Party in the North while providing the fairest possible representation from the South.

◊ He put a premium on collaboration, but he wasn't reluctant to encourage confrontation to get it. The members of his cabinet clashed violently and continuously, but together they emerged victorious.

◊ Lincoln proved himself an extraordinary judge of talent. He didn't let his personal feelings for these men or his past experiences during the campaign cloud his judgment. Instead, he sought and obtained the best thinking available.

◊ Few leaders invite conflict, even when it could result in the best outcome. Lincoln put aside his own emotions and required his team to do the same. They may not have liked each other, and certainly they didn't share common opinions, but together they shaped history with their interactions.

Jimmy Doolittle

Immediately after the December 7, 1941 attack on Pearl Harbor, President Franklin Roosevelt sought to restore the honor of the United States with a dramatic retaliatory bombing raid on Tokyo. The very notion of an attempt by America—which was ill-prepared for any sort of warfare—to make a direct assault on Japan's superpower was almost inconceivable. But FDR would not be dissuaded.

On April 18, 1942, 80 men, most of them scarcely out of their teens—but one in the middle of middle age—took off from a navy carrier in the Pacific. Their 16 planes, B-25 bombers, successfully attacked Tokyo, Osaka, Yokohama, Nagoya, and Kobe. The action bolstered US morale, slowed the Japanese offensive, and won the leader of this team of virtuosos—Lt. Col. James Doolittle—the Medal of Honor.

Doolittle led the raid with men who had volunteered for the mission months before April. On January 21, 1942, just six weeks after the bombing of Pearl Harbor, the men of the 17th Bombardment Group received orders to transfer from Oregon to South Carolina. As members of the Army Air Corps, these men had grown accustomed to following orders, but this mission would not involve following orders; it would mean volunteering for something secret and unparalleled.

When the men arrived in South Carolina, Doolittle informed them that the mission would be highly secret, dangerous, important, and interesting—and some of them probably wouldn't return from it. In spite of his candor, Doolittle didn't lose a man. One airman reported, "Within five minutes, we were his...we'd have followed him anywhere....I don't think there was any doubt in anybody's mind that as long as he was with us, whatever he wanted to do, we'd go ahead and do it."

From the volunteers, the commanders selected 140—enough pilots, copilots, navigators, bombardiers, and gunners for 24 B-25 bombers. Navy Lt. Henry Miller took on the job of deciding which 16 of the 24 crews would actually go on the hush-hush operation, and which would be left behind. His selection further ensured only the best of the best would engage in the dangerous but ultimately important mission. We'd soon learn to call these volunteers of the Special Aviation Project # 1, The Doolittle Raiders, or the first American heroes of World War II.[5]

One of the volunteers, Richard Cole, served as the co-pilot on Jimmy Doolittle's plane. From that vantage point, he had the opportunity to observe what Doolittle said and did before, during, and after the raid. I had the rare and exciting opportunity to interview Lt. Colonel Cole about the days leading up to April 18, 1942 and his reaction to both the raid and Doolittle's leadership.[6]

According to Col. Cole, the crew members were not exceptional before working under the direction of Doolittle. Most of them were new graduates flying their first combat missions, but Doolittle set the example and developed the team. He put people at ease, invited questions, and patiently treated people with respect. He was, in Cole's words, "The ideal person to work with." Cole mentioned that Doolittle had earned the title "master of the calculated risk" far before FDR and others conceived of the raid. Doolittle had earned the reputation for pushing the edge of the envelope, but he had another trait that served him well. Cole described him as "very persuasive," which explains, at least in part, why this group of aviators didn't balk, even when they faced uncertain odds.

The plan called for the Raiders to bomb military targets in Japan and to continue westward to land in China because, at that time, landing a medium bomber on an aircraft carrier was impossible. The raiders faced several unforeseen challenges during their flight to China: night approached, the aircraft ran low on fuel, and the weather was rapidly deteriorating. None of the planes would have reached China except for a fortuitous tail wind that allowed them to increase their speed.

Even before takeoff, the crews realized they would probably not reach their intended bases in China, leaving them the option either to bail out over eastern China or to crash land along the Chinese coast. When I asked

Cole to describe the fear they all felt as they stood on the deck of the Hornet, realizing that they wouldn't have enough fuel to return, he said he didn't feel scared and didn't see signs that others did. Rather, they all focused on the objectives and the "job we had to do."

During the flight, Cole said he could look at Doolittle and see the wheels turning as Doolittle pondered what was happening and what he had to do. He continued to make and alter decisions as the mission progressed—nothing had gone as briefed.

Doolittle and his team bailed out over China and were picked up almost immediately, but that didn't end Doolittle's leadership. He located a phone, found an interpreter, and began the process of finding his lost crews. They were scattered but not forgotten—and never would be.

All of the aircraft involved in the bombing were lost, and 11 crewmen were either killed or captured. Most of the members of Doolittle's squadron ran out of gas and crash landed in enemy-occupied China. Japanese patrols captured eight of the men, confined them to years of solitary imprisonment, and subjected them to torture. The Japanese captors executed three by firing squad; they starved one to

Doolittle Raiders: Crew One. Left to right: Lt. Col. Jimmy Doolittle, Lt. Richard Cole, Lt. Hank Potter, Bombardier SSgt. Fred Braemer, Engineer Gunner SSgt. Paul Leonard

death. The Soviet Union interned other Raiders for more than a year as hostile aliens. Tom Casey, the manager for the Raiders, summed up Doolittle's devotion. "There never was a leader more devoted to his men and they to him."[7] Doolittle didn't rest until he knew the fate of each person on his team. The Raiders would not be in the same room again until 1945 when they had their first reunion. At that time, Doolittle expressed his interest in each man and communicated his concern for their well-being.

The raid caused negligible material damage to Japan, but it succeeded in its goal of helping American morale and casting doubt in Japan on the ability of the Japanese military leaders. Doolittle thought the raid a complete failure because the aircraft were lost, and he feared he would be court-martialed upon his return. Doolittle erred on both counts. The raid led directly to what many historians now believe defined the turning point in the war against Japan—something only a team of virtuosos could have accomplished. Doolittle's leadership teaches us these lessons:

◇ Fortune favors the bold. Mythology teaches us that the goddess Fortuna was a fickle, consummate risk-taker. She could bring good fortune or bad luck. Doolittle demonstrated the role of boldness and risk-taking in achieving greatness. Those who don't possess the wherewithal to discover unique solutions doom themselves to bad luck and mediocrity. But those like Doolittle and his team, who dare to face fear and overcome obstacles, hold the power to turn the tide of history. Doolittle may have earned the title "master of the calculated risk" before the war, but he cemented it with the raid.

◇ Role modeling holds the key. Doolittle didn't stay in the hangar and communicate with his men via radio. He flew alongside them. He risked his career, and indeed his own life, to fly into an uncertain situation that offered little chance, much less a guarantee, of complete success. As Cole put it, he wasn't a "I'll see you when you get back" kind of leader.

◇ Doolittle relied on the skills of his team members. As the group devised ways to lighten the weight of their aircraft so they could take off on the short runway of the aircraft carrier, Doolittle pushed them to discover their own best thinking. He created an environment for members to energize each other and formulate solutions.

◇ Doolittle responded favorably to unwelcome changes. The crew had planned an afternoon launch, but at 7:44 a.m. the *Hornet* lookouts spotted a Japanese reconnaissance ship 10,000 yards away. Admiral Halsey's subsequent message from aboard the *Enterprise* was "Launch Planes. To Col. Doolittle and Gallant

Crew: Good Luck and God bless you." Conditions were not optimal for a naval aircraft launch, let alone one that inexperienced land-based bomber crews would attempt. The flight crews would have to contend with heavy seas, a strong northwesterly wind, and broken clouds. They were too far from their Chinese destinations to ensure safe landings, yet they all responded to the order, "Army pilots, man your planes."[8]

◊ Doolittle didn't micromanage. Once the planes took off, the crew members had to depend on each other for success. Doolittle's communication with the crews ended shortly after the bombings. Team members relied on themselves and each other to survive the crashes, and in some cases, imprisonment.

As Lovell, Lincoln, and Doolittle show us, virtuoso teams are not without their problems. A collection of clever people will most certainly engender more challenges for a leader than any one clever person could alone. These people bore easily. Once they accomplish the goal and create the solution, they want to move on to the next mountain to climb. The mundane and predictable make them weary.

Leaders who choose to lead a team of clever people will witness more clashes of ego and unfettered ambition. They will have to work to create a plurality with mutual goals and a shared identity. Instead of emphasizing compromise and task completion, leaders of virtuoso teams know they must funnel the individual talents of each person toward a breakthrough solution. It's hard work. Many leaders would rather settle for a more traditional approach to team leadership that nearly guarantees consistent, predictable, acceptable results. That path, however, also most assuredly promises mediocrity. The people on the team will always define its level of success, but how they function together will also play a role.

The Eight Functions of Virtuoso Teams

Creating opportunities for team members to work together collectively is one of the requirements for building a strong team. Helping them realize exceptional results is the other. However, you won't accomplish either unless you know what the members think and feel. The surest way to find answers to your questions is simply to ask.

You'll be most motivated to spend time on this when your team faces a roadblock, but often that will be too late. A more proactive approach would be to do some teambuilding when things are going well. To do that, you simply ask the members of the team to discuss these eight functions, the strengths they need to leverage, and the weaknesses they need to mitigate. The eight functions should work in harmony to create a team of virtuosos, not a collection of egos:

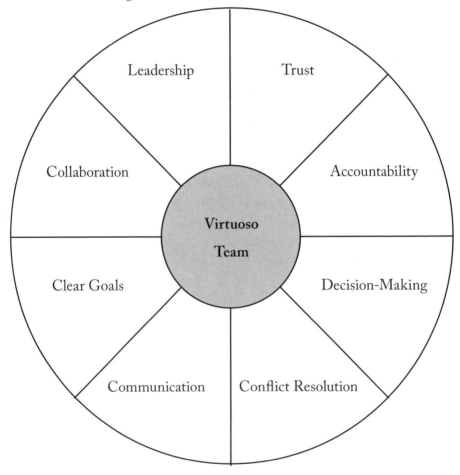

As you analyze the eight team functions, you may conclude that virtuosos working together are bound to experience anxiety. As I mentioned previously, usually virtuosos have made their mark through individual contributions. Collaborating may seem foreign to them. In general, you'll find that team members usually experience anxiety from one of two main sources: not accomplishing the task or faulty interpersonal relationships. In their solo work, they didn't have to rely on anybody else to accomplish the work, and they could control the quality of the results without anyone else's involvement.

When task issues create the problem, the team will identify difficulty with goal setting, accountability, or decision-making. Also they will disclose that they are worried about setting priorities, managing time, coordinating efforts, and distributing work. When goals are unclear or vague, or when members can't agree on the goal, strain is the inevitable outcome. Therefore, setting concrete, specific, measurable goals not only contributes to task completion; it also helps to circumvent one of the main causes of the tension and sets the stage for clarifying how to distribute the work.

When faulty interpersonal relationships are the problem, members will talk about not being able to trust one another, conflict, and the inability to work cohesively. Usually they haven't been communicating very effectively—at least they haven't been listening to each other too well. Some problems may be temporary, but some may have more permanence. Knowing what to expect will arm you with the information you'll need to determine the degree of difficulty the team experiences. Drawing from his classic work with teams, B.W. Tuckman offered some insight about what you can anticipate as teams go through the predictable stages of development: forming, storming, norming, and performing.[9]

During the forming stage, members try to determine if and how they will fit in with this particular team. They strive to discover what they have in common with each other and look for evidence that they belong in this group as they seek to understand and to be understood.

The storming stage frequently involves the members becoming disillusioned with the task and one another. You can expect unproductive behavior, arguing, defensiveness, and competition. Relationships that began during the forming stage may suffer, and negative feelings that were either suppressed or ignored during the forming stage may surface in the form of impatience, rebellion, domination, and open conflict. Often members feel uncomfortable and wonder how they ever got into this situation. This time might be considered the team's adolescent stage of development.

The team gains confidence and competence during the norming stage, so this becomes a time to share data and to explore solutions. The controversies that members settled during the storming stage help this stage run more smoothly. By now members have begun to establish systematic approaches to decisions, and the ground rules for acceptable behavior have become more apparent.

After days or weeks, the team can perform. There's no rushing the stages of team development. Each team must find its own cadence and balance. However, if the team can't perform by the end of six weeks, you may need to step in.

Because of the synergy that the team developed in the earlier stages, openness, trust, cooperation, and maturity reign. The team is now ready to exhibit high flexibility and maximum use of productivity. Energy is high because the team utilizes each member's strengths, and competitiveness does not hamper participation. They now show the maturity to start making their own decisions to move ideas to action.

Decision-Making/Problem-Solving

The most important task of a team is solving problems and making decisions—everything else hinges on these. Therefore, even when leaders turn decision-making over to a group, they retain the obligation to evaluate and influence *how* the group will proceed. Your role is to facilitate the team members' best thinking, to challenge them, and to help them think more effectively than if you weren't involved.

No one method for doing this works every time, so leaders should consider the pro's and con's of each approach before advocating a course of action. Usually the nature of the decision or circumstances will determine the process that will be most effective. As the leader, help them focus on solutions and stretch them to go where they've never gone before. The following are alternatives.

Consensus involves members agreeing to support a decision—not necessarily unanimity. Group members begin with different points of view, but after discussion, all members agree to support the same decision. People often confuse consensus decision-making with compromise, but the two differ. Compromise, by definition, involves a settlement of differences in which each side makes concessions—people give to get, in other words. We have to look no further than the political arena to see the trap doors of compromise!

Compromise involves more of a settling and negotiating than consensus does. Group members give in on some points in order to achieve their important goals. This settlement can result only in partial satisfaction and, therefore, questionable commitment to the outcome. By contrast, true consensus requires the highest degree of input and can take the greatest length of time, but it has the strongest chance for successful implementation. For your most important decisions, hold out for consensus.

Voting is one of the fastest methods for decision-making, but it presents other problems. Even *majority vote*, which involves more than 50 percent of the participants agreeing to a course of action, can create difficulties if the decision will require the commitment of each person, even the dissenting ones. A worse problem, *minority rule*, occurs when fewer than 50 percent of the members support a decision, a situation that most often occurs when there are three or more alternatives. This division of support can cause the final outcome to be without substantial advocacy. Both majority and minority rule can cause problems because, in either situation, a significant number of group members may not be motivated to implement the decision.

Sometimes an authority or expert in the group, after hearing discussion of the alternatives, will make the final decision. Typically, if the members recognize the expertise of the person and feel others have considered their contributions, they will support the decision. However, if these conditions don't exist, the group's acceptance of the conclusion will be tenuous. In all cases, as the senior leader, your primary responsibility involves deciding who decides. You can frequently leave the "how" to the person who owns the decision, or to the group, but you will need to create a system for deciding who has ultimate responsibility for the decision.

Trust

Without question, effective decision-making is the engine of the train that drives effective teamwork, but trust fuels the engine. Without trust, nothing happens. Lack of trust compromises the individual's effectiveness on the team, reduces team performance, and increases cycle time—which creates higher costs and lower productivity.

People talk about trust as though everyone agrees on the definition, but like "strategy," people use the word "trust" in so many different contexts that we've lost the ability to share a common meaning. Some use it to express their confidence in another: "I know he'll be able to do that." In another context, it means something more akin to a belief in another's loyalty, "I'd trust him with my life." In yet another, it denotes predictability, "She'll be here. She never misses a meeting." The definition of trust that so many overlook—but certainly feel—involves the faith people have in each other not to judge them.

Top performers almost uniformly dread criticism of their work. They want not only to deliver amazing results but also to know others can count on them to do so. Therefore, admitting limitations and asking for help are foreign behaviors to many virtuosos. Allowing themselves to stretch—which frequently invites failure—will happen only when they feel safe. When members don't trust, they conceal their weaknesses from each other and try to cover their mistakes. Instead of asking for help and constructive feedback from each other and those outside the group, they waste time trying to justify their actions. So, what can you do to create the safe haven they need to produce the kinds of results one would expect from a team of virtuosos?

In Chapter 1, I wrote extensively about the role of trust in positioning yourself as an F^2 Leader. In order to be effective, those whom you influence must trust *you* before they trust each other. Steadiness and predictability form the core of trust. This sort of reliability is not only ethical; it's practical. If your team finds you erratic or impulsive, they will experience so much anxiety that they will never begin to build trust in one another. Consequently, your first goal involves modeling the reliability and even-handedness you want them to emulate.

Fairness, one of the main constructs in F^2 Leadership, takes on a new dimension when you apply it to leading a team. Leadership theorist John Gardner noted that to win trust, leaders must exercise fairness when issues are being openly adjudicated and when they are being discussed in the backroom. As he notes, "Contending elements seek private access to the leader, and if it is widely believed that such offstage maneuvering works, the system is in a constant turmoil of suspicion. Nothing is more surely stabilizing than confidence that the leader is unshakably fair in private as well as in public."[10]

Challenging in the best of circumstances, building trust in geographically separated teams, when face-to-face communication rarely exists, can be daunting. Research suggests that when teams rely on teleconferencing and other forms of communication technology—especially when members do not already know each other—building trust can take two or three times longer than it would if the members met face-to-face. Therefore, the first favor you can do yourself and your team is to create and fund opportunities for members to work together in the same location, especially at the beginning of a project.

Trust among the team members all starts with you. But it doesn't end there. Leading a team of virtuosos demands something more from you. It requires that you trust your team and instill in them a trust of one another. Building this sort of confidence requires communicating your expectations that everyone will act with integrity, in the best interest of the team.

No one person's goals or agenda can supersede those of the team. They must have the confidence in one another's abilities and motives, and give each other the benefit of the doubt. They need to take risks, knowing that you and their fellow team members will support them. They need to have faith in the knowledge that each person of the team shares commitment to the team's goals and a dedication to the excellence that will continue to define this collection of people as a team of virtuosos. Sometimes a team contract can serve as a foundation for this. Simply put, this contract outlines the guidelines or rules on how the team will function. The creation of it provides reliability, predictability and consistency—all essential elements of trust. The members themselves negotiate "rules of engagement," such as how quickly members will answer e-mails, who will run meetings, areas of accountability, and role clarity. The team may need your help to begin the process, but then you'll need to leave it to them to draft.

Collaboration

When a team of virtuosos takes the time to dig deeply into issues to find underlying concerns, several things happen. First, they discover solutions that no one has ever even considered before, much less implemented. They stimulate thinking and create synergy. Often a win/win result becomes reality. Fully exploring alternatives and attempting to find solutions that satisfy all concerned create an environment in which team members can recognize and utilize others' talents and expertise. Collaboration that leads to consensus defines the ideal outcome, but the process is time consuming, a factor that causes many teams to opt for a quicker fix. But when all members of the team will be required to implement the group's decision, the time is well spent.

Consensus does not mean total agreement. Neither does it imply that members have capitulated. Instead, consensus is achieved when every team member can say, "I have had the opportunity to express my views fully, and they have been thoughtfully considered by the other members of the team. Even though this solution may not be the one I believe is optimal, I think it works, and I will support it."

Leadership

Because you are not a member of the team, your role must consistently remain that of external leader. Even though you exert influence over the individuals and the group, if you interfere too much, you will reduce the effectiveness of the team. Communicate your trust and then back up your words with actions. Refuse to play a role in their squabbles or disagreements. Develop the habit of responding to all requests to do so with, "I have complete faith in your ability to work this out in the group without my involvement." If you vacillate from this position, even once, you will encourage the team members to turn to you when they need a referee. Virtuosos clash. That's the nature of this particular beast. But by definition, virtuosos are the best of the best, so they possess the means to discover solutions among themselves, without your participation.

Teams need leaders, both from within the group and from the person responsible for the team's performance: you. Often leaders will emerge through the stages of the team's development. Sometimes members will rotate leadership responsibility, depending on the nature of the goal. In all cases, team members will look to you for feedback. They will rely on you to help them calibrate their actions—to reinforce the effective and discourage the ineffective—and to make decisions that affect them.

In 1995, I began my doctorial research on the Vietnam prisoners of war, which I discuss more completely in Chapter 9, to understand better the role leadership and communication play in bouncing back from adversity. The findings from this study illustrate the importance of the chain of command, but they also highlight the value in shared leadership responsibility. Because the POWs enjoyed such cohesion, their captors speculated that removing the senior leader would compromise their system and cause the POWs to be more malleable. They were wrong. The POWs, arguably a large system of many teams of virtuosos, took their leadership responsibilities seriously. When the captors removed the senior ranking officer, the next senior ranking officer took over. Leadership never waned.

When they were reachable, the senior-most ranking officers, James Stockdale and Robbie Risner, made the global decisions for the group. However, Stockdale and Risner spent large blocks of time in solitary confinement. No one could reach them—not even by tapping on the walls or flashing signals from across the campground. When these senior leaders could not communicate, those next in the chain of command supported the decisions that had been made and drew from the well-defined system the senior leaders had established to help them make new decisions.

Drawing from these lessons, you can create a culture of shared leadership among your team too. When people understand the priorities and values they need to address, making the decisions and accomplishing the tasks becomes much easier. But it all starts with a crystal clear understanding of what the team needs to accomplish.

Clear Goals

Virtuoso teams care about one thing above all else: results. Input and process pale in comparison to output—the achievement of clearly defined, specific goals. By definition, most virtuosos are strategists. The very nature of the individual will cause him or her to focus relentlessly on *what* needs to happen before detailing the *how* of the venture.

Goal-oriented individuals achieve impressive results because the satisfaction of a job well done satisfies their own best interest—they need to feel successful. Often a team of virtuosos will need their leader to help them redefine their success measures. Individualistic behaviors need to take a back seat to the team's success, but this doesn't happen automatically or easily.

The team needs to realize you value results above all else. If they sense otherwise, you will invite hidden agendas and self-aggrandizing behaviors. As I mentioned, teams go through predictable stages of development, but they should never lose sight of their long- and short-term goals. If they do, asking "What are we trying to do?" and "What's important now?" will help them refocus on objectives and priorities without becoming unduly distracted by process.

Communication

On a team of "A" players, message sending—talking—seldom defines the reason for communication breakdowns. Message receiving—listening—does. Smart people often overlook the fact that others have valid opinions that they need to hear. Frequently they prefer pontificating to entertaining alternative points of view.

What can you do to mitigate the natural officious tendencies of these people? First, when they try to engage you in off-line discussion, force them to prove they've heard each other: "What did Bob have to say when you put that idea on the table?" "Explain to me why Susan objects to your idea." They may not like articulating opposing viewpoints, but they should be able to. If they can't, it proves either they didn't listen to the argument, or they never considered it seriously.

Second, model the behavior you want them to replicate. Develop the habit of listening first and talking second. Don't interrupt, and ask open-ended questions to help the other person flesh out ideas. Offer your own ideas only after you have given the other people a chance to explore theirs thoroughly.

As Apollo 13 showed us, teams of virtuosos don't need face-to-face interaction, but it helps. Whenever possible, provide the resources for your team members to meet. When they can't, provide the technology for them to teleconference. Communicating via e-mail should be a last resort and used only to transmit information, not opinion. I tell my clients to follow the four-inch rule. That is, no e-mail can measure more than four inches. If it does, people need to phone each other.

Star performers realize they can't get their way all the time, and in fact, consensus building can waste valuable time and compromise results. But members must feel as though the other group members have heard and considered their opinions and ideas. Do what you can to make communicating easier and model the behaviors you want to see.

Effective Conflict Resolution

When communication and trust break down, conflict occurs. Sometimes it occurs anyway. Even though it won't make people feel good, you should expect conflict and even embrace it. On the one hand, team membership provides a way for relieving pressure because distributing responsibilities and talking with others who share our concerns can relieve tension and reduce stress. Research tells us that groups make more daring decisions than a person working alone would, primarily because of the shared responsibility and blame if something goes wrong. On the other hand, when we try to work with others to accomplish a goal, annoyance is a likely byproduct.

Not all tension is related to goal accomplishment. Often teams experience problems with interpersonal relationships. As the leader, your willingness to convey respect for each member, foster trust, and encourage two-way communication will set the stage for team members to adopt these behaviors in their interactions with one another.

Frequently virtuosos have short fuses. By nature, they are impatient people who want fast results. It's one of the reasons they succeed. However, their impatience often triggers anger. Anger, like tension, is usually seen as something destructive, something to be avoided. Managed effectively, anger can provide the energy that helps the team mobilize into action.

Healthy teamwork depends on the ability of the participants to give accurate feedback to each other, even when this feedback is negative. Anger helps to do that.

Although anger often prompts us to act, it is not usually the first emotion we feel. Typically, something causes the anger. We tend to ignore the first emotion and report the anger that follows. For instance, if the team is being distracted, not focusing on the task, and generally just wasting time, a member might become frustrated or impatient; but instead of reporting these emotions to the team, he or she will wait until anger has taken over before saying anything. Once someone expresses anger, the team will be more motivated to resolve the problem but only if the members have effectively addressed their emotions. Misdirected anger has a way of sabotaging the team's efforts and causing more disagreements.

What should you do? Put the issues on the table and have people talk about them. When conflict does occur among team members, it should be settled as soon as possible, because, if it is not negotiated to a conclusion, it will shadow all phases of the discussion process and will interfere with the team reaching its goal. This can be particularly troublesome when the team tries to operate under time restraints.

Conflict can be either constructive or destructive. Much will be determined by how members manage the discussion and by how they regard each other. Managed effectively, when the participants view each other with respect, resolving differences can actually help the team function more efficiently, because discussing problems increases awareness, encourages change, and increases motivation. If we don't know something is broken, we can't fix it.

Conflict can also serve to reduce small tensions among the team members. In fact, conflict resolution can enrich relationships. Many times, conflict intimidates us because we are afraid that it will cause a major breakdown in rapport. Once we learn the fallacy of that thinking, we become more confident about resolving future disagreements and moving on with objectives.

Accountability

A team of virtuosos commits to impressive results and holds itself accountable as a team without blaming "the weak link." All are in the same boat. Timeline- and deadline-driven, members measure performance by assessing collective work products, and everyone does real work. In short, virtuoso teams commit individually and collectively to results.

Perhaps the most significant cause of problems for teams is that members literally don't know what they or other members do or should do. Members haven't established clear lines of responsibility; they don't communicate and haven't clarified publicly exactly what the team needs to achieve and how everyone must behave. Ambiguity becomes the enemy of accountability, which compromises commitment. This lack of understanding creates barriers among team members that significantly impede efficient and effective teamwork, but with the right kind of help, team members can learn methods for removing these obstacles.

One of the best tools you can use to help a team overcome some of the discord so members can get back on track is to have a candid discussion about areas of accountability for task accomplishment and decision-making. Modifying the Accountability Chart introduced in Chapter 5, you can guide the members to discuss exactly what they need, want, and expect from one another.

The goal of accountability charting is to help the members operate more effectively by clarifying each team member's role, responsibilities, and expectations. Charting helps everyone understand who should participate in which decisions and identifies the right people for work assignments, projects, meetings, and task forces. It also helps people learn how not to step on each other's toes and how not to assume someone else will take care of a particular task.

Once you have created a culture of accountability and commitment, your role changes. At that point, you should leave the policing of behavior to the team. Peer pressure goes a long way on virtuoso teams. Each individual realizes he or she is playing in the big league and doesn't want to disappoint the other players. This fear alone will cause people to behave in functional ways. Similarly, tolerance of sub-standard performance or violation of team norms vanishes on this kind of team. You may be called upon to be the external arbiter, but when you do meet to discuss issues, reward and punish the team as a whole—not as individuals.

Conclusion

Understanding how to build a team of exceptional people involves appreciating how individual members' characteristics and personalities unite to form the unique culture of a virtuoso team. Satisfaction, performance, productivity, effectiveness, and turnover depend, to a large degree, on the socio-emotional make-up of the team. No two teams are alike—even if the two teams would both be considered teams of virtuosos. However, when we understand some of the universal factors that contribute to successful interactions among exceptional people, executives can adapt and adjust their communication to the situation and make choices that will benefit the team and the organization.

There is a saying: "Treat a person as he is, and he will remain as he is. Treat a person as if he were what he could be and should be, and he will become what he could be and should be." This notion of a self-fulfilling prophecy has a message for leaders. Under the direction of a competent leader, a successful team will evolve throughout a period of time. The leader who sees into the future and anticipates the team's productivity can take steps to ensure that outcome.

Chapter 8

Become a Star on the Board of Directors

Try not to become a man of success, but rather try to become a man of value.

—Albert Einstein

In parts of Indonesia Komodo dragons make unwelcome and unannounced visits to villages that border their habitat. Even though the giant lizards and humans lived in harmony for generations, contention exists now. Environmentalists have imposed new policies in a region where people perceived a sacred duty in caring for the Komodo dragons. Th e relationship between lizard and human has not been the same since.

Executives and boards of directors have experienced a similar loss of symbiosis. The Sarbanes-Oxley Act of 2002 and The Dodd-Frank Wall Street Reform and Consumer Protection Act of 2010 have caused executives, especially CEOs, and directors to examine the way they do business. Now, more than ever, directors are taking their responsibilities seriously, speaking up, and striving for results; but in many cases, the evolving relationship between the company's executives and the board has not found the right symmetry. Finding it will depend on several factors: investing in your professional development, surrounding yourself with knowledgeable peers, and doing your part to create a stellar board.

Put on Your Own Oxygen Mask First

Not all executives will interact with the board, but CEOs, CFOs, and General Counsels usually will. The skills, training, and experience that got you to the point of joining a board probably won't match the ones you'll need going forward. Like inept golfers at an exclusive country club, ill-prepared executives will double bogie every time they open their mouths. You will need to do things better and differently. But how?

First, start with professional development. If you haven't already done so, go to *www.nacdonline.org* to visit the Website for the National Association for Corporate Directors. This organization exists to educate executives and directors about how to improve both their interactions and their results. The association offers the Director of Professionalism class several times a year. I highly recommend it. In addition to learning fundamentals of financial reporting and governance, completion of the course entitles the participant to a listing in the association's directory.

Serving on a board other than your own will help you take giant leaps toward developing board skills. Sitting CEOs are the most sought-after directors, with CFOs following as a close second. If you know how to read a balance sheet or can make sense of most financial reporting, the other directors will build a statue in your honor. If you can chair an audit committee, they will seek Vatican approval for your immediate canonization.

A word of caution: Not-for-profit boards and advisory boards will not give you the same experience that a for-profit or publicly traded board will, but they are a good start. If you feel passionate about the cause of one such board, go ahead and accept. You will learn the basics of governance and then position yourself to assume the role of director on a privately held company. After that, the publicly traded companies will find you more attractive. But you have a limited amount of discretionary time, so be sure you are using it wisely. If you are a business owner and want to experience board interactions, consider establishing an advisory board for yourself. If you will be interacting with a board that already exists, consider the advice of the following experts.

Advice From Nell Minow

Nell Minow is the editor and cofounder of The Corporate Library, a leading source for corporate governance and executive compensation and analysis. Previously she served as a principal of Lens, an investment firm, president of Institutional Shareholder Services, Inc., and as an attorney at the U.S. Environmental Protection Agency, the Office of Management and Budget, and the Department of Justice.

In her various roles, Ms. Minow has had the opportunity to observe the behaviors that help and hinder executives. In her comments to me, she advised executives, especially CEOs, to surround yourself with people—directors and employees—who are smarter than you and willing to disagree with you. This will give you the opportunity to persuade them to your way of thinking or for them to convince you of theirs. Either way, through this process of disagreement, you uncover potential problems and mistakes.

As Minow pointed out, one of the biggest problems you'll face as an executive is that people quit telling you the truth. When she took the reins at ISS, her predecessor, Bob Monks, remarked, "Watch how funny your jokes get!" In her new role, Minow soon learned what Monks meant. Employees too often tend to tell the CEOs what they think they want to hear. Therefore, smart CEOs try to assemble a board of directors who will tell them what they need to know.[1]

Advice From Ken Duberstein

Former Reagan Chief of Staff Ken Duberstein currently serves as a director for The Boeing Company and The Travelers Companies and chairs the governance committees for both. In his address to the 2010 National Association of Corporate Directors, he advised executives to be independent but loyal to the mission of the organization. As he pointed out, executives should raise an eyebrow when they hear something troubling but not approach any discussion with an agenda. Further, executives need to make clear their commitment to the values of the company and reaffirm their personal ethics.

He also highlighted the importance of listening to understand. Too many executives think more about what they need to say than what they need to hear. However, listening to shareholders and stakeholders, according to Duberstein, will bring the board close and encourage them to open up. Ask follow-up questions until you understand what it will take for everyone to commit to the company's vision.

Advice From Norman Augustine

Retired chairman and CEO of Lockheed Martin, Norman Augustine, sat on the same panel with Mr. Duberstein at the 2010 NACD Conference. He began his remarks with a list of executives who had earned themselves prison time while running some of the nation's leading companies. Augustine's most notable advice to executives, especially new ones, was to conduct their personal lives in ways that reflect the values of the company. He mentioned how often smart people, like the ones he listed, do dumb things that ultimately cost them both their professions and their freedom. A focus on "we" instead of "I" can help executives concentrate on what's important for building the company.

Advice From Alexandra Reed Lajoux

Alexandra Lajoux serves as the Chief Knowledge Officer for the National Association of Corporate Directors. She is the author of *The Art of M & A Integration* and six other books that address corporate concerns. For more than 30 years, she has provided corporate directors with leading-edge research about how to improve their performance.

Lajoux's advice for executives involves using the time of directors wisely. As she pointed out, according to the respondents to the 2010 Public Company Governance Survey, directors typically meet only six times per year for board meetings (usually for a day) and four or five times per years for committee meetings (normally for a half day). Committees and boards often meet another two or three times by phone, but it all adds up to part time work. Therefore, according to Lajoux, executives do well when they prioritize information and present it in a succinct fashion. When they overwhelm directors with too much, critical issues can fall through the cracks.[2]

Advice From John Stroup

In the fall of 2005, 39-year-old John Stroup became the CEO of Belden, a $1.5 billion publicly-traded manufacturing company. In 2005 the stock price floundered around the $20 mark. Within two years of Stroup taking the helm, the stock price had tripled. Since that time, Belden has made major acquisitions in Europe and China and has expanded its footprint while so many competitors have erased or blurred theirs.

In August of 2010, I asked Stroup what he learned in those first months as CEO that he wished had known ahead of time. Here's what he said:

◊   Be aware of the weight of the job. Everything you say is remembered.

◊   When you run a large organization, you can't expect to have a good day every day.

◊   You have to select carefully those with whom you can brainstorm, and then announce clearly that this is truly a brainstorming session and not a decision-making meeting. Otherwise people worry about every far-fetched ideas that the CEO mentions or even entertains.

◊   Be careful about venting. It upsets people long after you've calmed down.

One of the specific challenges Stroup faced was his role on the board of directors. At first he tried to build harmony with the group of experienced directors, and 95 percent of all communication, written or spoken, was public. He sought to build cohesion and collaboration with a group but then realized, after three years, that there might be a better way.

Today Stroup takes a more balanced approach. He interacts with the group about 50 percent of the time, but then seeks out the directors individually the other half. Stroup realized that when he deals with each director individually, he gives them the individual respect and attention they want and deserve.

He also realized that not everyone is an equal contributor on every subject. As he came to know the directors as individuals, he learned who to talk to and depend on when he faced problems with people, acquisitions, risk, and the plethora of other issues that plague CEOs. He started approaching his "expert" directors first and then presenting their best thinking to the board as a whole.

He cautioned other CEOs not to alienate a particular director by not seeking his or her advice. If you find you never go to a specific individual, there's a reason. You may need a different dynamic or interaction than you have. You may also need a different discipline represented. But each director should hold the keys to some aspect of the CEO's role. Stroup gave other CEOs three other pieces of advice:

1. Recruit other sitting CEOs to be on your board. Only they will truly understand the challenges you face. Retired CEOs offer a great deal of value too, but only those currently at the helm will offer the unique real-time perspective.

2. Top grade. Look for better candidates who offer the insight and area of expertise you need.

3. Communicate.

When Stroup began his role as the new CEO on the board, he viewed interaction with directors as "about them." It didn't take him long to realize the tremendous benefit these interactions offered him. He didn't learn this lesson right away, but he's never forgotten it.[3]

Advisory Boards Make Sense

There is no substitute for soliciting the opinions of the executive team, the people who will be most affected by change or its absence. Often, however, the answers to complicated questions don't lie within those most affected. Frequently the CEO will need to look outside the organization for advice and wisdom. Sometimes this comes from a Board of Directors, a body of individuals that has the duty of influencing a company's direction. Members of this board have a fiduciary responsibility to represent the shareholders by making pivotal decisions.

Advisory Boards, on the other hand, do not vote, nor do they have fiduciary obligations. Rather, as the name implies, they exist for the sole purpose of advising the CEO and executive team. Small companies, family-owned companies, and organizations that do not have a board of directors often find that advisory boards can be helpful in assisting the leadership, but sometimes companies find that they benefit from both kinds of boards.

In the last decade, advisory boards have been rather commonplace in the Silicon Valley, particularly for new ventures. However, even though they are relatively inexpensive and easy to form, outside this arena, advisory boards, though valuable, are a much underused asset in helping companies handle change. Advisory boards are unencumbered by compliance and other business issues specific to boards of directors, and they can provide the CEO and executive team the benefits of experience, expert knowledge, contacts, and credibility that will help them navigate the future of their companies. An effective advisory board can provide expertise that a small company cannot usually afford to hire in its full-time employees, and it can offer ongoing personal support to those who have the lonely position of CEO.

How do they get started? Because they are free from the regulatory restrictions that shape a board of directors, advisory boards vary greatly in composition and function. CEOs usually choose advisory board members for their expertise, experience, and knowledge. A well-balanced advisory board will include four to seven individuals who have a background in one of the critical areas that affects the business: finance, operations, human resources, business development, marketing, sales, and industry issues. They will be people who are candid, objective, and independent—not friends who will tell the leader what he or she wants to hear.

Recruitment of qualified members often occurs through acquaintances—people the CEO knows directly or whom existing advisory board members know. Some members contribute their time for the pleasure of the stimulation of being involved in cutting-edge discussions, but more often, participants are compensated by an annual stipend, stock options, or an hourly fee. Research indicates the main attraction for being on a board is the intellectual adventure, the chance to meet with outstanding peers and to discuss issues of the future. It is an honor to be invited, and high-quality people attract other quality people.

The purpose of an advisory board is self-evident: it gives advice. So, the members should be good listeners who offer dispassionate analysis about the challenges the company faces. They should be sounding boards for the

CEO when he or she struggles with decisions related to anything and everything that touches the company. If they can quickly get to the core of complicated problems, they can offer the leadership a new perspective for understanding implications and consequences.

For best results, the members' advice needs to be both strategic and tactical. They can assist by anchoring decisions in the company's vision, mission, and values, but they can also offer specific, step-by-step instructions for carrying out plans. They need to be able to separate important from unimportant issues so that they can encourage the leaderships to focus their energies, time, and resources on those initiatives that will have the most impact. In short, a successful advisory board will be able to help the CEO see a bigger picture when the temptation is to be distracted by the day-to-day problems of running a company.

This relationship is not one-sided, however. CEOs have responsibilities too. First, they will need to involve themselves in the recruitment of qualified members.

Then, the CEOs will need to set meetings well ahead of time and set agendas for the meetings. Most advisory boards have two to three meetings a year, but others meet every quarter. With a start-up venture, the board may meet monthly until things are under way. Usually the meetings of the entire board will be half a day or a full day, but often CEOs find that they need specific advice from individual members more often. Whatever the needs of the company, the effectiveness of the advisory board will improve when expectations are clear on both sides, and the board and leadership can concentrate on the challenges of helping the company's employees handle change, even if it is unexpected or unwelcome.

The Stellar Board

Whether you're creating an advisory board or learning to work with a board of a privately held or publicly traded company, the real challenge for directors and executives isn't regulatory compliance—it's high performance. To achieve it, directors and executives need to systematically examine the five constructs of a successful, stellar board.

Stellar Boards

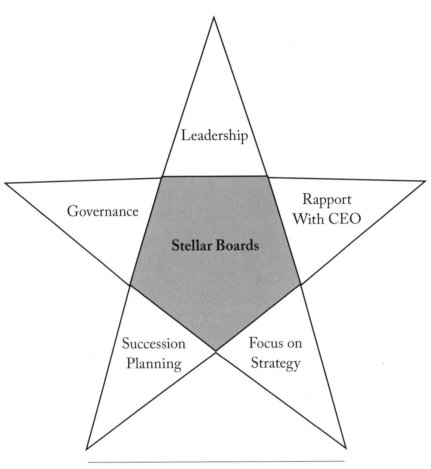

Leadership

Governance

Rapport
With CEO

Stellar Boards

Succession
Planning

Focus on
Strategy

Leadership

Thought leaders do not share a common opinion about the best way to lead a board. Some steadfastly hold to the notion that the CEO and board chair should be the same person. Others think the roles should be split. A third camp posits that the CEO should have the chair responsibilities with a separate lead director position designating the top director position. In my opinion, the chair and CEO roles should remain separate. Both directors and the CEO can be more effective when the roles and duties of the chair differ from those of the chief executive. Also, when these roles are held by different people, the chair can act as a lubricant between the two entities, especially when inevitable conflict occurs.

Shareholder activists strongly support this position, but in practice, it remains less than 50 percent in larger corporations. Each argument has its merits, but you probably won't get to vote unless you own the company. Usually the existing board hires a new executive to fill a seat that has been vacated, and the new person soldiers on with the established tradition.

Unless you are a CEO who also serves as the chairman of the board, you probably won't have board leadership responsibility in an overall sense. However, even if you are a non-chair CEO, the CFO, or general counsel, you will have duties related to keeping things on track. Your primary leadership responsibility then will be to develop a relationship with your counterpart on the board. For instance, the CFO should work closely with the chair of the audit committee.

Executives who find themselves interacting with the board have the leadership responsibility to keep the group focused on the right issues. To do that, draw from Alexandra Lajoux's previous advice to keep things succinct. When you present information, whenever possible, do it in a summary or bullet format. Directors have learned to hate the sound of the Power Point ginning up, so use it sparingly. If you must, limit the number of slides.

Too often directors assume the role of sponges who simply absorb that which you put in front of them. Part of your leadership duties requires you to prepare questions that will stimulate dialogue. If the data remain in their heads, what good is it? You need to guide the process of making the implicit explicit—of making knowledge pragmatic advice.

If you can do that, your next duty is to move the discussion to consensus. The discussion should uncover all kinds of differing points of view, but ultimately the board needs to ask itself, "So what?" What will directors support, if the decision is theirs? And how will executives use the insights they have gained from the debate to influence the decisions they will make?

Rapport With the CEO

Board success starts with the relationships between the directors and the CEO. As mentioned previously, the CEO should regularly disagree with the board, and robust debate should occur but never at the expense of good rapport. Embrace tension. Move beyond the outdated thinking that the board is a necessary evil and realize that a certain degree of tension is both healthy and desirable. Contention, however, is not productive. The CEO should ask questions and question answers but all in a climate of candor and responsiveness. Trust, respect, and open communication form the foundation of any strong relationships; board relationships are no exception.

I've addressed trust at several other junctures, but when building rapport with the board, the CEO should keep top of mind the importance of predictability, excellence, and honesty. Directors need to trust you to do what you say you will do, to uphold the values of the organization at all times, and to conduct your personal and private life with the utmost integrity. Gone are the days of CEOs expecting directors to trust them in business decisions when they have clearly not represented the highest ethical standards in their private lives.

Open communication holds the keys to the kingdom of good rapport. Naturally you'll need to be on the same page with regard to the company's vision, mission, values, and strategy. But you'll need to go beyond that. Do you agree about what success will look like? Can you routinely bring the conversation around to priorities?

One tool that many CEOs find helpful is a template for formal conversations and briefings. When you present information in a pre-determined way, directors become accustomed to hearing issues in a predictable format. They will follow you more closely and know what to expect. If you present bad news with the same equilibrium and dispassion as you do good news, they will learn that they can trust you not to hide information or to tell them what they want to hear.

Executives tend to worry too much about what they will say instead of concentrating on how much they listen. In general, be quiet every chance you get. Most CEOs make the mistake of talking too much during meetings. If the directors in the room are not worth listening to, you have the wrong people on your board. A meeting is your chance to hear what they have to say and to benefit from their collective knowledge and expertise.

Remember, you communicate at all times. You cannot not communicate. Your behavior in and out of board meetings will speak volumes about who you are as a person, and each nugget of information will give directors reason to build rapport with you—or to avoid doing so.

For instance, do you feel threatened by directors talking to others in your chain of command? If you don't encourage directors to go to the source of information, you appear to have something to hide. If you put up roadblocks, you compromise trust.

Of course, boundaries should exist. Encourage the nose in/fingers out model. Negotiate the levels of involvement on critical issues, and have clear lines of accountability for making decisions and for director involvement. For example, no director should approach one of your people without notifying you. And certainly, no one should reprimand one of your people without you being in the loop. If a director does one of these things, you should express your displeasure, but don't try to limit access. Trust is a two-way street, as is communication.

Focus on Strategy

Too often boards of directors don't understand when and how they should be involved in strategy. When earnings decline, a competitor makes a sudden move, or a merger or acquisition looms, they come to life. But often it's too late. By not getting involved earlier in the game, directors deny executives and the company in general the value of their input.

Stellar boards do better. They don't formulate strategy, but they maintain a clear focus on it. They assess and critique it. Like the princess in the story about the pea, directors need to detect flaws deep in the strategy—not to execute, but to detect and report. The challenge for executives, therefore, is to make sure directors have all the necessary information to do their job.

Sounds simple. Why then is strategy such a source of angst? One reason is that too often boards and executives don't take a systematic approach to how they will interact with regard to strategy. The board discusses strategy piecemeal during a period of time, often in relation to something else. Or, when executives present the strategy as a finished product, directors sit idly and contribute little.

Contrast these practices to the process that the Stellar Board uses, not only to reach full agreement on the strategy but also to shape it. Executives articulate the strategic direction and clarify the measurements, criteria, timelines, and standards for evaluating it. Then, directors ask questions and offer opinions. This list offers a starting point for this discussion:

◊ Does the company have the resources, financial and human, to execute?

◊ Have they considered the full range of external factors?

◊ Have they sufficiently examined risk?

◊ Are the assumptions valid?

◊ What is the company's competitive advantage?

◊ How does this strategy leverage it?

◊ Will customers benefit?

◊ How will we make money with this strategy?

When directors ask these questions, they ensure that management has not made a major market entry or other strategic decision based simply on instinct, historical experience, or guesswork. Executives should anticipate these questions and prepare answers for them. If directors don't ask them, put them on the table yourself.

As the board reshapes and improves the strategy, directors and management reach a common understanding about what future success will look like. Once the strategy is set, solicit the help of the governance committee to ensure the directors' skills and talents are aligned with the strategy. Executives and directors working together on strategy is like a dance. Sometimes you lead, and sometimes you follow. But you try to avoid stepping on each other's toes, because when the music stops, you want to make sure you still have a chair.

Succession Plan

In Chapter 6, I outlined the steps you will need to take to ensure a healthy leadership pipeline. Many of the same principles apply to how you will work with the board to help them determine your replacement. However, you'll need to know some of the specifics of how to work with the board on succession planning. Here are my recommendations. Some are specific to the CEO, but most pertain to any executive who regularly meets with and relies on the board.

1. Openly discuss your plans for retirement. This isn't an easy topic for directors to broach with you, so take the lead. If your plans change, let them know that too.

2. Map out the specific role you will play in finding and preparing your replacement.

3. Working with the board, develop selection criteria. Instead of putting together a list of currently needed attributes, keep a future orientation. Think about what will be required of executive positions in the future, not what you or anyone else has done in the past.

4. When you find yourself two years away from retiring, identify an internal replacement, or oversee the recruitment of one.

5. Identify high potential candidates for each executive position 10 to 15 years before any one of them is likely to reach the executive level. Let the board know them and interact with them.

6. Encourage a discussion of emergency replacements. Sometimes this replacement will be a director. When that's the case, work closely with that person so the company can recover from the sudden loss of any executive.

7. As you consider the future of the company, consider what groups you might not have represented in the current C-suite. For example, if you plan to expand in Latin America or Mexico, having a bicultural, bilingual executive or director might help you serve your growing market.

8. As I mentioned in Chapter 6, consider the experience of your successor, but don't over-emphasize it. If someone had required ceiling painting experience to paint the Sistine Chapel, we might have missed one of Michelangelo's greatest works. Seek proof of excellence, but don't fixate on industry or specifics. Remember, amateurs built the ark.

9. If you're the CEO, encourage the executives in your C-suite to spend time with each director. Suggest each executive initiate a private dinner with one director each quarter. In a year's time, each executive will have had one-on-one time with four directors. It will strengthen relationships and increase confidence on both sides.

10. Finally, work with the board to define the stages of transition. First, create a list of likely candidates for each executive position. Then place each in a series of expanding roles that give candidates the opportunity to learn and the board the chance to assess them. Don't publicly announce who the candidates are, even when people start to become aware of who is being developed. Promote the top contenders with expanded roles or titles. What you don't want is what people commonly refer to as a "horse race." Setting up a competition causes people to express loyalty to friends and perceived winners. The tension can cause damage to morale and nervousness among investors. Also, you can lose valued talent if that person doesn't win the race. Keep in mind that a dead horse can cause quite a thud just by falling!

Governance

"Governance" is another of those all-encompassing words that people use but that few can explain in concrete terms. The dictionary defines governance as supremacy, domination, power, or authority. When used for corporations, it usually means general board oversight.

Governance underpins the board's ability to do all the aspects of its job. While strategy and succession planning address specific "what" questions, governance deals with the "how." It includes but is not limited to decisions about the board's size, frequency of meetings, director selection, shareholder relations, and social responsibility. When a board has a governance committee, those directors initiate action plans with specific timelines for implementation of recommendations. This committee should have the authority to shape and recommend policy and structure.

The existence of a governance committee doesn't let the CEO or other executives off the hook. To be part of a Stellar Board, executives need to play an active role in how things happen. Have strategy drive the agenda. Regulatory issues will control a considerable portion of each meeting, but you and the chair can collaborate to control the rest.

Of course an agenda will guide the actual meeting, but you can do more to streamline governance. For instance, when the board meets, tackle important, difficult, and unpleasant issues immediately. If you wait several hours, everyone will be tired and impatient. You'll get a better caliber of discussion earlier in the day, and the energy will be higher once you've made the tough decisions.

Most boards hold executive session meetings *following* the board meeting. Once again, if this meeting occurs late in the day, people will be spent. You can benefit, therefore, from what I call an "executive session sandwich." In other words, meet *before* the general meeting to address critical issues and then use the low-energy time after the session to tie up loose ends.

Another energy-zapper is the board book. Often these epics make *War and Peace* look like *CliffsNotes*. Use the board book to inform, not persuade. If the book includes mountains of data with little salient information, directors will overlook key issues. Lead with a summary page, the questions you'd like to discuss, and the topics that merit debate. In short, discuss, don't present the book.

Whenever possible, enrich committee reports too. Typically, these reports include a detailed description that lacks relevant information or that rehashes an entire committee meeting or topic. Directors are busy people. Aggregate the critical information, present it in summary form, and offer analysis, not just information.

Above all, avoid death by Power Point. At a recent convention of the National Association of Corporate Directors, people actually snarled when someone mentioned the use of Power Point. Too often the slide presentation offers little more than the book in electronic format, and the presentation eats up valuable meeting time. Dialogue, not more slides, holds the key.

Another key to good governance lies in better leveraging your directors' contributions. Encourage directors to communicate regularly about their experience and expertise. You should know how to pull this from the directors when you need it, but if you have never formally gathered this kind of information, it won't exist in a time of emergency or decision-making.

Constantly evaluate whether the directors' skills, talents, and experience support the current strategy. In general, you will want directors that exhibit integrity, good judgment, strategic skills, financial literacy, confidence, and high performance standards. But occasionally you might also need an industry authority, an international expert, a turnaround specialist, or a government procurement professional. Play an active role in the selection of new directors, and work closely with the governance committee to choose the best and brightest that will bring diversity of thought to your board.

Unless you are the chair, evaluating the board won't be your primary responsibility, but you can still drive it. Encourage regular evaluations of directors. Have a clear, agreed-upon purpose for conducting the evaluation. Do you want to improve overall performance? Individual performance? Drive shareholder value? Eliminate someone from the board? If it is the last, a formal evaluation might not be the best route. Clarify how information will be collected, who will have access to it, and how it will be presented to the directors collectively and individually.

When doing board evaluations or committee evaluations, both interviews and surveys work. However, all records should be paper and pencil, so they can be shredded to protect confidentiality. The minutes will represent a summary of the process, forms, action steps, and ratings, but only in general terms, such as "using a 5-point scale, all members of the governance committee received a 4.0 or higher on their ratings." Any papers distributed at meetings should be collected and destroyed.

Include an assessment of committees in a board evaluation. What is the quality of their reports? Are they transparent? What is the overall relationship to the board? Does the committee drive shareholder value? Make evaluations complete, thorough, and efficient. Asking each director to complete an exhaustive survey—or even worse, an exhaustive survey on each peer—is an enormous use of time, and many of the directors will either not do them or will not do them in a timely fashion. When using a survey for the entire board or committees, customize it to your needs. Measure *only* those categories that are directly applicable.

Routinely evaluate the composition of the board, not just the performance of the directors. As the direction and strategy of the organization shift, so should the skills and experiences of the directors. Present the balanced findings to the board, encourage discussion, identify ways to leverage strengths, spotlight areas where adjustments need to occur, and formulate an action plan and timeline for moving forward.

In a confidential format, have directors evaluate their peers based on observable behavior that highlights how this person can add more value. Then, provide one-on-one, private feedback to each director, preferably delivered by a third party.

Ask the board to conduct separate evaluations of key executives at least once a year, but seek timely feedback in executive sessions or private conversations. Above all, *don't create materials that can be subpoenaed*. Doing these things won't guarantee you'll have a well-run board, but you will have taken significant steps in the direction of goodness.

How Executives Help Well-Run Boards Make Decisions

The key to better board performance lies in the working relationships between directors and executives, in the dynamics of board interaction, and in the competence, integrity, and constructive involvement of individual members. Most people understand what boards should be: sources of challenge and inquiry that add value without meddling—champions of the organization that make CEOs more effective but not all-powerful.

The high-performance board, like the high-performance team, is competent, coordinated, cohesive, and focused. Such entities do not simply evolve, however; an exacting blueprint must guide their construction. The challenge of board building is enormous, but most executives don't know how to play a bigger, more valuable role in making that happen.

To help you get started, consider this 2 × 2 model that further develops David Nadler's work with board building.[4] This model addresses how directors and executives need to view director involvement and its role in overall effectiveness. As you will note, sometimes boards can enjoy effectiveness, even with low involvement. Boards that have their fingers in when they shouldn't will be only minimally more effective than boards that stay out of everything. The key lies in *appropriateness* of involvement.

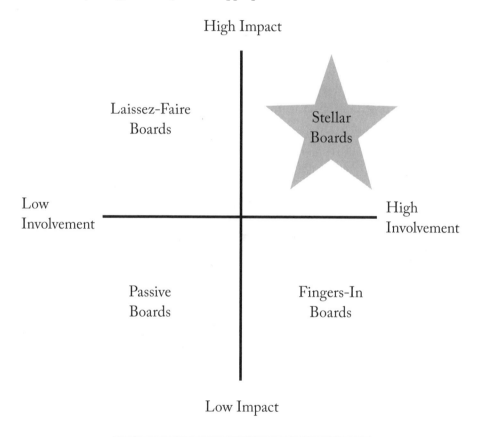

High Impact

Laissez-Faire Boards

Stellar Boards

Low Involvement

High Involvement

Passive Boards

Fingers-In Boards

Low Impact

The Passive Board

Until current legislation and awareness surfaced, many boards found themselves in this quadrant. When involvement is inappropriately low, effectiveness will be low. The board's activity and participation are minimal and at the CEO's discretion. The board has limited accountability. Its main job is ratifying the CEO's decisions.

Passive boards meet at scheduled times but seldom schedule anything outside of those meetings. They overlook or ignore opportunities to meet with internal and external auditors, general counsel, or key managers. They don't seek active participation in strategy formulation or attend to the leadership pipeline. Members fail to make themselves available to the executives in the company, so the experience and expertise of the directors languishes.

The Laissez-Faire Board

Boards operating in the laissez-faire quadrant manage to enjoy some effectiveness because they have learned to be involved on critical issues. For instance, they may devote time and attention to strategy formulation, but then leave implementation to the company's executives. Directors oversee CEO succession planning but trust most of the rest of the leadership pipeline to management. If the company has hired strong executives, directors don't need much more engagement than the Laissez-Faire Board offers.

Directors on these kinds of boards maintain credibility with shareholders because they know the difference between the important and the unimportant and show up for the important. The board certifies that the business is managed properly and that the CEO meets the board's requirements. Many CEOs have come to appreciate and desire a Laissez-Faire Board, even though it's not the most effective of the four general kinds.

The Fingers-In Board

The expression among executives is that directors should be "nose in, fingers out." In other words, these executives want directors who know what goes on but who stay out of the day-to-day management of the company.

Fingers-In Boards can exist in any situation, but they tend to surface during crisis. The board becomes deeply involved in making key decisions about the company and holds frequent, intense meetings. They intrude inappropriately, compromising both morale and effectiveness. They bother people. Frequently the Fingers-In Board focuses on tactics, not strategy. They can waste an entire meeting discussing a new label or brand—something that even the VP of marketing wouldn't ordinarily spend time on.

These kinds of directors have been known to bypass the CEO and give direction to employees. They want deep involvement with decisions. They convene frequently, often without a clear purpose in mind. They lack effectiveness, primarily because they squander their time and energy on the noncritical instead of zeroing in on the critical efforts they should be addressing.

The Stellar Board

Directors on Stellar Boards serve as the CEO's partners. They provide insight, advice, and support on key decisions. They recognize their responsibilities for overseeing CEO and company performance. The board conducts substantive discussions of key issues and actively defines its role and boundaries. They fill gaps in executives' experience and expertise, so they serve as a constant source of advice and wisdom.

When Stellar Boards meet, their agendas limit presentation time and maximize discussion time. Directors and executives take advantage of informal interaction among directors. Board members are honest and constructive. They stand ready to ask questions and are willing to challenge leadership, and they oversee CEO and organizational performance. Directors tell executives what they need to know and hold them accountable for results. Board members also actively seek out other directors' views and contributions. They prioritize well and spend appropriate time on important issues.

So what's a CEO to do? If you realize you'd like to create a Stellar Board, but past performance and tendencies indicate you don't have one, what should you do? Start with a wake-up call.

To determine the directors' perceptions of their level of involvement and effectiveness, the CEO can ask them to rate each of the elements of a Stellar Board. Using a five-point scale, the CEO and each director assigns a number to the current level of involvement and one to the desired level. The CEO can also use these five areas as global topics and subdivide each into the specific challenges or situations of a particular board. If you're working with a Fingers-In Board, you might find the desired level of board involvement is actually less than the current level.

Assessing Involvement

Using this form and a scale from one to five, board directors and the C-Suite executive can rate the existing and optimal levels of board involvement for each Stellar Board activity. One represents areas where the board is not engaged and five represents areas where members are highly engaged.

Sample	Current Level	Desired Level	Gap
Focus on Strategy	1 ② 3 4 5	1 2 3 4 ⑤	3
Governance	1 2 ③ 4 5	1 2 3 4 ⑤	2

The higher the gap between the two numbers, the more likely effectiveness is being compromised. To maximize effectiveness, executives and directors should negotiate the appropriate level of involvement in each of the five major areas of Stellar Board performance.

	Current Level	Desired Level	Gap
Leadership	1 2 3 4 5	1 2 3 4 5	
Rapport With CEO	1 2 3 4 5	1 2 3 4 5	
Focus on Strategy	1 2 3 4 5	1 2 3 4 5	
Succession Planning	1 2 3 4 5	1 2 3 4 5	
Governance	1 2 3 4 5	1 2 3 4 5	

Examining the averaged scores of the directors and comparing it to the CEO's score will illuminate the largest gaps and the most significant improvement opportunities. This exercise will surface gaps between where the board needs to be focused and where it is actually spending its time and resources. It will also uncover perceptions of appropriateness. In other words, directors may continue offering the level of involvement they have always offered unless someone points out that the current level is not the desired level.

This sort of gap analysis helps quantify the perceptions of the CEO and the directors. By comparing actual and desirable levels of involvement for each area, the board and CEO can plot in great detail where to concentrate needed change. Second, juxtaposing directors' and executives' views of the board's role may surface disagreements that otherwise act like submerged mines.

This exercise has other applications too. As the directors consider all the scenarios that might require changes to their involvement, they're forced to consider the future. They can use this to evaluate how well they have been addressing their self-defined mission and to discuss whether meetings have devoted the appropriate amount of time to the right topics. Finally, it is a starting point to determine whether directors possess adequate skills, experience, and knowledge in the areas that matter most. Establishing an overarching agreement about the appropriate level of engagement helps board directors set expectations and ground rules for their roles relative to senior managers' roles.

Conclusion

Each year, new regulations surface to protect consumers and hold boards and executives accountable to shareholders. Corporate governance is on the move. Meltdowns and regulations cause change, but some things remain the same. We have come to demand more of our executives and directors. No longer can either group languish in a role and expect to keep it for life—not even in privately held companies. A volatile economy has shown us not to rest on our laurels too long or we won't have any glory to rest on.

Active, compliant boards and executives no longer offer organizations enough. Companies need and demand stellar performance from both individual contributors and the board as a whole. Today's *Wall Street Journal* does not report another string of company meltdowns or bad CEO behavior. Perhaps they have subsided for the present. Ultimately, however, the discovery and reporting of problems did us a favor. They brought to light some of the issues executives and boards need to face. Avoiding fraud will keep you out of prison, but it won't drive success. Your success depends on your taking a more active role in your own development and finding symmetry and symbiosis for all concerned.

Chapter 9

Become an Agent for and a Champion of Change

It is not the strongest of the species that survives, nor the most intelligent; it is the one that is most adaptable to change.

—Charles Darwin

People don't fear change; they fear the unknown. As the senior leader, shining the flashlight into the darkness so others can see their way through the transition will define a prominent and recurring role for you. During turbulent times, those around you will count on you to present a confident, self-assured demeanor. They will want you to let them know they can trust you—trust you to take charge and to stay in charge. In short, they will want you to show no fear.

As with all fears, those associated with change are due largely to the *perception* of what might happen rather than to the likelihood of it actually happening. The perception that failure will occur, therefore, immobilizes people at the exact time that they need to spring to action. If you were to ask 100 people for an antonym for "success" at least 99 would say "failure." I submit that the opposite of success is not failure: it's the unwillingness to try again and to learn from setbacks. Thomas Edison, arguably one of the most successful inventors of all time, wrote this about his numerous attempts to invent the light bulb: "I have not failed. I've just discovered 10,000 ways that don't work." (Apparently he wrote this in the dark, however.)

In 1993 Apple introduced the Newton, a personal digital assistant. The project missed its original goals: first, to reinvent personal computing, and then, to rewrite contemporary application programming. Also, in initial versions, the handwriting recognition gave extremely mixed results and was sometimes inaccurate. The project fell victim to project slippage, scope creep, and a growing fear that it would interfere with Macintosh sales. In short, the Newton was not a success. Yet Apple went on to introduce the iPhone and iPod, both huge success stories. For Apple, reality changed when their much-loved Newton project did not prove to be successful. Yet senior leaders did not allow the fear of another failure to keep them from developing ever-evolving technology. They responded to changes that would ensure the company's success for years to come. Today, the president of Apple probably doesn't even own a Newton, unless it's in one of those boxes in a corner of the corporate basement.

Your role, then, in times of change is to do what senior leaders at Apple did: to create perceptions of hope and optimism within your organization. Will you serve your team as a Paul Revere who gathers intelligence but sounds the alarm only when necessary? Or Chicken Little, a foul fellow whose only skill involved spreading pessimism? If the sky ends up falling, no one will thank you for predicting it. But if strong economic times follow the tough ones (as they always do), and your team saw you as having been unresponsive to their needs during the bad times, they won't forgive you. So, what can you do? How can you help others navigate the uncertain waters of change, especially change that comes more by imposition than invitation? First, understand why people resist change and the stages they will go through, and then recognize what you need to do to help them with the change.

The Reasons People Won't Change

Every executive who has attempted a major change initiative has encountered people who simply wouldn't change or who resisted to the point of distraction. As mentioned, the overriding and most obvious reason for the change is fear: fear of loss of power, fear of failure, fear of rejection, fear of the unknown, fear of fear itself. Annoyance accounts for another portion of the resistance. People don't want to learn the new skills associated with the change, form the new relationships required, or join a new team.

Embarrassment, a close kin of fear, occurs when the proposed change implies that whoever owns the status quo showed bad judgment. In other words, people frequently cleave to the status quo because to do otherwise would mean they erred in the first place. In these cases, in an attempt to preserve their position and sense of security, individuals will become defensive. When confronted with evidence that a traditional approach needs to change, these people look outside themselves and often outside the company, blaming the stupidity of the customer, the vagueness of strategic goals, or the unpredictability of the environment. *Organizations* don't defend against change; insecure individuals within the organization do.

Also, these same people often don't make the most of new opportunities because they're making the most of old ones. When leaders understand this and the underlying causes of the fear that has everyone immobilized, they have taken the first steps in ensuring the success of the change initiative. The second step involves examining the collective history of the issue—the legitimate reasons that led to the status quo approach, understanding all the while that they will gain control of the future only by examining the past. These leaders will move forward only when they and their direct reports look *in* non-defensively, not *out* cynically.

In my work with organizations in transition, a focus on *tactics* rather than *strategy* accounts for another major reason people don't want to change. They justify their existence by their willingness to work long hours, often on activities that don't support the overall strategy of the company. Instead of concentrating their efforts on tasks that would drive the strategy, they do three things: what they do well, what they like to do, or what they've always done. The wise executive does well to understand this phenomenon and to recognize the peculiar ways their company's practices provide fertile ground for inertia.

Consider Helen, the director of HR at a mid-sized company. The company, owned by equity partners, faced some unprecedented changes related to years of inadequate leadership and a changing economy. In working with the owners, I concluded that the CEO, COO, and at least two others on the leadership team needed to be replaced. In addition, the reporting relationships didn't make sense—too much redundancy of effort and not enough accountability. This company faced serious problems related to its overall strategy and succession plan, but what Helen wanted to talk to me about was implementing a leadership training program. Don't get me wrong. I have delivered many hours of leadership training and think it has a place in the overall scheme of things. But while the ship floundered, Helen, in essence, wanted to take time to wind the clocks. Not surprisingly, Helen wanted to justify her existence in the organization and aggrandize her importance in the unavoidable changes.

Helen's reaction is, unfortunately, too often typical. However, successful change depends on the collective actions of the individual people in your organization who will support the change. When you show your trust in and respect for the people who report to you and understand the fears that stand in the way of progress, you will strengthen the foundation of the change. As Martin Marietta's former president, Tom Young, observed, "No one shows up in the morning thinking, 'I guess I'll see how badly I can mess up today.' but an unenlightened management can put them in that frame of mind by 9 a.m." Similarly, people don't really want to thwart the change efforts just because they can. They do so because of emotion. Your job, as the leader, is to make sure you understand those emotions so they don't derail the process before 9 a.m.

How People Respond to the Stages of Change

Why do some people conquer change when others are devoured by it? I wanted to know the answer in order to understand why some executives can lead others through change, but others can't. So I decided to study leaders who had helped people overcome some sort of huge adversity and emerge healthy and hardy. I wanted to draw from their experiences in order to advise leaders about ways they can help themselves and others weather the storms that inevitably affect organizations. To find these answers and to better understand how resilient people handle adversity, I moved to Pensacola in 1995 to study the repatriated Vietnam Prisoners of War at the Robert E. Mitchell POW Center. The lessons I learned were surprising, almost shocking.

In 1973, 566 Vietnam POWs were repatriated to the United States. Evidence about prisoners from prior captivity situations indicated high incidences of Post-Traumatic Stress Disorder. Of the WWII POWs who participated in the studies, 50 to 82 percent, particularly those who were imprisoned in the Pacific Theatre, received a diagnosis of PTSD. More than half of the Korean POWs in the studies received a similar diagnosis. Because of these staggering numbers, in 1976 the Navy began to study 138 repatriated Vietnam POWs. In the 1996 20-year follow-up, the researchers found surprising results: fewer than 10 percent of the Vietnam prisoners of war had received a diagnosis of PTSD. The researchers expected better results than POWs from previous war had experienced, but they had no idea that the findings would be so much better.

The data are astonishing when comparing the Vietnam group to the other captivity situations, but they are also shocking in light of the implications of these numbers. To give a frame of reference for understanding this, at any given time in a metropolitan area, about 1 to 4 percent of the population experiences symptoms of PTSD because of violent crime, natural disasters, or other kinds of trauma. Yet his group of people, who had been imprisoned, tortured, isolated, and beaten, had no significantly higher incidence of PTSD than the average people in the average city in America. How can that be? As many of my study participants told me, they owe their lives and mental health largely to the leadership of then-Captain James Stockdale and Colonel Robbie Risner, the two senior leaders of the POW community. Through their policy-making, role-modeling, and true grit, these two men influenced the safe return of hundreds of men and their resilience for decades after.

Researchers and theorists have defined the predictable stages of change or loss. Some describe five stages, others four. My research with the POWs indicated they went through three. Typically, people experience these same three stages when a change occurs in their lives: awareness, adjustment, and readiness to move forward. If we adapt and choose to go through the stages in a healthy, purposeful way we earn the rewards of mastering the challenges of the change. As the POWs proved, the three stages can become stepping stones to success as we learn to empower ourselves and others to move toward triumph.

However, just as we can learn empowerment, we can also learn helplessness. When we become angry or resistant to the inevitability of the change, we become victims of it, get stuck in one of the stages; and the stages then become a process that leads *away* from success. Executives who want to keep the best and brightest can benefit from understanding these stages so that they can meet their direct reports wherever they are and help them through the steps that lead to moving on.

Stage I: Awareness

During Stage I we become aware of the change, which leads to one of two reactions. We deny it and resist the new reality, or we face the new challenges it presents. The POWs had little opportunity to deny. They quite literally soared above Hanoi one minute and lay facing a hostile crowd of villagers the next. Once captured, they endured torture, starvation, and isolation. Those who refused to accept their new reality met a worse fate than those who acknowledged their fears, accepted their fate, and focused on the future.

Similarly, when leading others you can help them with their responses to change by managing your own reactions more successfully. Often you won't welcome the change. Circumstances will force it on you. You might be angry; you may be scared; you might even be immobilized. Whatever your initial emotions, you will need to put them aside in order to help your people with their feelings. This control over reactions occurs only when you better understand what is going on, so that you can go through this stage with a sense of challenge instead of denial.

For the POWs, the awareness came in sudden ways; more often, awareness creeps cat-footed into consciousness. However awareness presents itself, during Stage I your direct reports will need you to be a true change agent, which means you will need to influence them to accept the change by offering reassurances and support, whenever possible. Open and honest information offers the surest way to reduce anxiety at any stage of the change process, but it is particularly crucial during the initial phase. Explaining timelines, processes, rationales, and anything else you know will help to ease people through this difficult time.

Too often executives assume that communicating is something for human resources or management to take care of. In reality, communication must be *your* priority. Your direct reports will look to *you* for the answers, so try to have as many as you can. If you don't attend to this function of your job, rumors will run rampant, and the grapevine will hum with damaging information. The single most important gift you can give your people is consistent, clear, and endlessly repetitious communication—all components of trust.

Paradoxically, establishing trust is most difficult when it is most needed. In times of change, the people in your organization will base their trust on two things: predictability and consistency, both of which you'll find in short supply during a transition. However, your direct reports will look to you to provide them. As much as possible, they will want you to let them know what to expect and to reassure them that things will be okay. Sometimes you'll be able to do that; sometimes you won't. In all cases, they will want you to avoid jumping on the bandwagon of uncertainty. They will want you to make declarative statements about what you know to be true, instead of inserting invisible parenthetical question marks in your speech. (I refer to the dreaded "upspeak" that is sweeping the nation, causing many otherwise impressive leaders to appear disarticulate and uncertain—irksome traits during the best of time, dreadful habits during times of change.) No matter what set of circumstances present themselves, your understanding Stage I and the two typical responses, denial and challenge, can help you recognize what's happening and what your direct reports are experiencing. Here's how the two reactions can be contrasted:

Stage I: Awareness	
Denial	Challenge
Behaviors and Feelings	Behaviors and Feelings
◇ Confusion.	◇ A willingness to struggle.
◇ Focus on the past.	◇ Focus on the future.
◇ Immobilization.	◇ Drive to succeed.
◇ Missed meetings or deadlines.	◇ Acknowledging the range of feelings.
◇ Withdrawal, shutting down.	
◇ Worry and uncertainty.	◇ "Wait and see" attitude.
◇ Paralysis.	◇ Flexibility.
◇ Shock and fear.	◇ Ability to identify opportunities.
◇ Anger and frustration. Asking "Why me?"	
	◇ Belief in own abilities.
◇ Disorientation.	◇ Acceptance of reality.
◇ Shunning friends and family.	◇ Focus.
	◇ Closeness to family and friends.

Coping Strategies for Stage I

How can you help your direct reports through this stage? Obviously, if they react with a sense of adventure and opportunity, you won't have to do too much except listen to their ideas. However, if they respond with denial, you will want to be more involved. First, make sure you communicate your acceptance of the change, even if your enthusiasm is somewhat forced and counterfeit in its early stages. Next, ask open-ended questions that will help people discover what they want to do:

- ◊ "What are some options for making this easier?"
- ◊ "What opportunities will we have now that we wouldn't have had before?"
- ◊ "How might you take an active role in this transition?"
- ◊ "What might you gain personally from this change?"

Keep in mind that no matter what you do, many people will experience this as a tough time.

The length of time most people will take to go through this stage will vary greatly. Some will breeze through in a matter of days, but more typically, people will need a few weeks to let the reality sink in. If your people become mired here for more than two months, there may be significant issues at play that will require more help than a leader can give. In those rare cases, referring the direct report to the Employee Assistance Plan or another clinical professional might be advisable. Winston Churchill offered some sage advice for people going through Stage I: "If you're going through hell, keep going."

Stage II: Adjustment

Usually by Stage II, people have finally accepted that the change won't go away. They may recognize the unavoidable nature of the change, but they won't all react to it the same way. Some will build obstacles to resist the changes and reject personal responsibility, and some will cope and explore opportunities. Even if they have not skated through the first stage too well, once several months have passed, people start to live in harmony with their changed world. Strong leadership becomes even more important during this stage.

When the POWs entered the adjustment stage, the senior leaders challenged them to keep their minds active by teaching each other skills, communicating regularly with each other through the walls in their cells, and exercising daily. Through these simple instructions, the leaders encouraged the POWs to build relationships with one another, to take control of the few things they could control, and to live one day at a time while never losing their focus on the future. Just as the POWs relied on their senior leaders, so will your people need your help to make wise decisions to reinvent their worlds, or they will be tempted to retreat from adjustment, to resist rather than adapt.

Stage II: Adjustment	
Resistance Behaviors and Feelings	Adapting Behaviors and Feelings
◊ Confusion. ◊ Anxiety. ◊ Withdrawal. ◊ Exaggerated need to control. ◊ Shifting of responsibility. ◊ "Arguing" with new reality. ◊ Commitment to "go it alone." ◊ Resisting new ideas. ◊ Refusing to try new ideas. ◊ Tunnel vision on the *one* solution. ◊ Inability to feel joy.	◊ Curiosity about future. ◊ Willingness to confront change. ◊ Building relationships. ◊ Ability to live one day at a time. ◊ Development of responsibility. ◊ Courage to understand change. ◊ Willingness to ask for help. ◊ Openness to learning. ◊ Willingness to take risks. ◊ Willingness to explore. ◊ Ability to celebrate success.

Coping Strategies for Stage II

Adjusting to a new reality means developing new skills or honing existing skills so they can be applied to a new set of circumstances. Specifically, your direct reports will need your help with problem solving, relationship building, and flexibility, the same three skills that you will need yourself to maintain your equilibrium.

Problems solving involves the ability to deal directly with the difficult situations we face and to make positive changes to resolve them. Effective problem solving requires critical thinking, a global perspective, strategic planning, and the ability to anticipate consequences. When you eagerly probe for understanding, go beyond the obvious, and prioritize effectively, you help your direct reports to see the future as open and malleable. Together you will be able to paint a credible picture of opportunities and possibilities and communicate your enthusiasm for making them happen. Here are some ways you can help others cope with change by improving their problem-solving abilities:

◊   Encourage people to solve problems as soon as they become aware of them.

◊   To make problems more manageable, ask your direct reports to separate them. Put each in one sentence by saying, "The problem is...."

◊   Separate emotions from the problem. Decide *what* is right, not *who* is right.

◊   Help people determine their desired outcome. Start with the end in mind.

◊   Brainstorm. List a variety of creative and practical solutions.

◊   Don't let them get trapped into thinking that there is only *one* solution to any problem. See options as having pros and cons rather than being "right" or "wrong."

Effective communication is the single most important ability you're going to need. It will help your direct reports build relationships, share thoughts and feelings with you and each other, and promote mutual understanding, even during difficult circumstances. As the POWs learned, when ordinary men welcome closeness and develop a supportive social fabric, they can withstand extraordinary adversity.

For example, in his book, *The Hanoi Commitment,* former POW Jim Mulligan recalled the devastating effects he experienced after he succumbed to torture and, for the purpose of the captors' propaganda, confessed to "crimes": "'I'm broke,' I cried. 'I'm a traitor. I've disgraced my family, my country, and myself.' I despaired at being alive and cursed the effectiveness of the automatic ejection system."[1] Captain Mulligan's tragic comments represent the same feelings others expressed. Many of the men wrote that, with the support of the other POWs who also admitted they had capitulated under torture, they were able to restore their sense of worth.

Like the POWs, when the people in your chain of command combine communication and closeness, they gain the necessary tools for building the relationships that will help them stay connected and supported during difficult times. But this connection doesn't happen automatically. On the contrary, the closeness that engenders effective communication hinges on a willingness to listen, the capacity to convey respect for others' ideas, and a genuine interest in people.

Making relationships a priority, building time into our lives for the people who are important to us, laughing together, and having fun with each other all create interactions that are characterized by joy and fun. Sharing our feelings and concerns enhances these relationships and encourages more closeness. An upward spiral of cohesion and connection starts to build on itself when we communicate with one another in our attempts to focus on the positive. As a result, we deal more effectively with the stressors in our lives.

These things can't be forced, however. You can only create an environment in which they are allowed to flourish. During times of change, the wise leader does well to realize that people will need to spend more time building a sense of connection to people both at home and at work. Permission to dress badly one day of the week won't help with this, but the availability of more flex time may. In general, flexibility in both time and thinking will serve you well.

Flexibility is the degree to which we feel comfortable with unstructured and unpredictable situations. Life is unpredictable, so our responses to the problems we face need to be adaptable, rather than rigid. Flexibility provides one way for us to respond more favorably to circumstances we can't control. Mental agility has another important payoff: it stimulates creativity. By being open to a variety of creative and imaginative alternatives, we avoid getting trapped into thinking only one resolution exists. When you encourage your direct reports to avoid rigidity in their thinking, to experiment with innovation, and to seek the input of others, they can become more open to new ways of solving problems.

Once you help people to stop fighting the currents and learn to flow with them, they can approach decision-making with new dexterity and energy. No one can control change, yet if we're not careful, it will control us. When people are forced to adjust to new, uninvited changes, feeling out of control is a common, normal response.

As the renowned Holocaust survivor Victor Fankl taught us, and the Vietnam POWs reinforced, finding humor in difficult situations is one way of controlling what we can control, even if we can't have power over the events that required us to marshal our coping behaviors in the first place. Much evidence exists to support the idea that humor is a determinant of resilience. People have learned to rely on it, not in spite of crisis but *because* of it. Recognizing the value of humor to expand coping behaviors increases our understanding of the powerful role it and laughter can play in helping us bounce back from the hardships that unwanted changes often bring. Then, consciously and actively helping others to find humor in their daily lives can make them *feel* better until things *get* better. As entertainer Victor Borge said, "Laughter is the shortest distance between two people." When we use laughter and humor to tackle problems effectively, build strong relationships, and explore new ideas, we control what we can to turn challenges into opportunities. Even though the second stage of adjustment may take your direct reports two or three months, with your help they will emerge from it equipped to move forward.

Stage III: Moving Forward

Stage III is the stage during which most people are truly ready to identify with new goals and clearly focus on how to reach them. They have experienced the transformation of transition and are ready to commit. For the POWs, reaching this stage quickly probably accounted for their ongoing mental health. They accepted the change, adjusted to it, and then put into place the requisite behaviors for moving on. They began to see themselves as professionals, still on active duty, whose job it was to be the best POWs they could be. From this, they found meaning in their experience, grew as men, gained a sense of mastery over their circumstances, and ended up with a feeling of accomplishment. But reaching this stage does not happen automatically. Sometimes people get stuck in a previous stage, and the change will not be successful for them—they regress instead of committing to the new reality.

Stage III: Moving Forward	
Regression Behaviors and Feelings	Commitment Behaviors and Feelings
◊ Inability to cope with change.	◊ Adaptation to the new world.
◊ Powerlessness.	◊ Acceptance of reality.
◊ Sense of failure.	◊ Sense of accomplishment.
◊ Feelings of helplessness.	◊ Sense of control and mastery.
◊ Doubt.	◊ Confidence.
◊ Focus on loss and regret.	◊ Feelings of satisfaction.
◊ Confirmation of regression.	◊ Evidence of personal growth.
◊ Inability to find purpose in life.	◊ Ability to find meaning in life.
◊ Incapacity for experiencing joy.	◊ Willingness to experience joy.
◊ Angst, uneasiness, and distress.	◊ Achievement of peace.

Strategies for Stage III

Your primary responsibility during Stage III is to offer ongoing support. If you see regression, you will need to determine what caused it. Usually a regression in behavior implies the person never really coped with the change. He or she might have attempted moving forward, but if you sense that there has been no real progress, this might indicate that the person needs more help. People can compromise weeks or even months of progress if they can't truly move on with the altered reality. Sometimes too many changes coming too close together can cause people to regress. At other times, changes in the personal lives of your direct reports can seemingly gang up on them. Whatever the cause, your reaction should be the same: Determine where they are, and then offer them the guidance and support they need, provided they will let you. Even if you're the best leader in the world, you can't protect your people from unexpected events that rock their worlds. The best you can do is to develop the skills for helping them when this kind of change does occur—that and plan change every chance you get.

Because they were cemented in a strong social structure, the Vietnam POWs had a buffer against fragmentation of self or of the system. They showed us that control is central to people's health, their personal benefits, and in their case, their actual survival. As the leader, you have the responsibility for taking care of yourself during times of change so that you can help others. You need to put on your own oxygen mask before you can help anyone else with theirs. Only then can you approach a major change initiative with the confidence it will take to make it successful.

The Four Steps of a Successful Change Initiative

Many people are uncertain about the appropriate degree of change, so in the absence of guarantees, no change becomes the default position. As the leader, one of your jobs is to make sure this doesn't happen. To understand clearly what you'll need to do to walk your team through the transition, use the following four steps:

1. Set the stage. To start and drive any change initiative, you will need to establish the importance of the undertaking and identify the people with enough power to lead it. You and they will then want to recognize and discuss potential problems and major opportunities in order to achieve a coalition of supporters.

    As you set the stage for the transformation, remember that without question, *logic* makes people think, but *emotion* makes them act. Knowing this, you can help to move people away from their comfort zones by encouraging them to examine the consequences of stagnation and the opportunities of change—to think analytically about the changes. But then honor the emotions tied to threats and opportunities.

In my work with companies in transition, the most dramatic change efforts have been tied to a new leader taking the helm; a major shift in power, such as an acquisition or merger; or a change in the market, such as the merger of two rivals or the loss of a major customer. This kind of change sets off a series of reactions that move things forward. When this happens, you'll want to harness both logic and emotion, to make sure you create a sense of urgency without producing panic. You can do both by defining the path.

2. Create and communicate the vision. Identify the vision, communicate it succinctly, and then create a sense of urgency about it. If you want only to treat the symptoms of your current condition, you probably aren't really committed to a change effort. But if you truly want to reinvent your organization, you need to let others know what that will look like. Reinvention involves more than altering the status quo; it demands the creation of what hasn't ever been before. For example, at some point a caterpillar transforms itself into a butterfly. It doesn't become a bigger or better caterpillar; it changes into a different living being. Humans start out as 20-inch long, bald, toothless creatures who can't walk or talk. As we grow and change, we don't become bigger babies; we become drastically altered beings. The DNA stays the same, but the organism evolves. Similarly, if your vision involves transforming what your organization was into what it needs to become, you as the leader, will need to understand and communicate what that creature is going to look like.

As I mentioned in Chapter 4, a vision clarifies the direction in which the organization needs to move. People don't need a 3-inch binder that painstakingly describes the details of the change; they need a compelling statement that describes what things will look like when they complete the change. The absence of such information fuels the fear people already have. As the comic strip philosopher Pogo once observed, "The certainty of misery is better than the misery of uncertainty." The biggest favor you can do for the people in your organization is to remove the misery of uncertainty about where you're leading them.

3. Create a culture of change. One of the founders of organizational psychology, Edgar Schein, drew from a wide range of contemporary research to define corporate culture and to demonstrate the crucial role leaders play in successfully applying the principles of that culture to achieve their organizations' goals. Schein defined culture as "A pattern of shared basic assumptions that the group learned as it solved its problems of external adaptation and internal integration, that has worked well enough to be considered valid and, therefore, to be taught to new members as the correct way to perceive, think, and feel in relation to those problems."[2]

If an organization's culture, therefore, has stabilized because of a long history of success, leaders may discover that changing deeply embedded assumptions requires more than a change in the organization's goals; it necessitates a shift in the company's basic culture from one of traditional approaches to one that embraces innovation.

Truly great companies understand the difference between what should never change and what should be open to change, between what is sacrosanct and what is not. A well-conceived change effort, therefore, needs to protect core principles, the enduring character of an organization—the consistent identity that transcends trends, technology, product line, or services. Core principles provide the glue that holds an organization together through time. Throughout history we can see examples of how people captured and exemplified their fundamental beliefs. The Declaration of Independence, the Uniform Code of Military Justice, and the Bible all offer examples of how people have written and adhered to their core creeds. Even when the organization grows, diversifies, or changes location, these beliefs provide enduring tenets and a set of timeless principles.

Successful leaders don't confuse, and don't let their direct reports confuse, a change in operating practices with a change in core ideology. The root of culture is "cult," a testament to the kind of thinking that can often guide decision makers to adhere to a mindset that no longer works. But just as senior leaders can encourage cult-like thinking, they can stimulate a culture of change. A change in operating practices or strategy does not constitute a desertion of all that is "holy," but only those organizations that create a true culture of change can help their people understand the difference.

Imagine if Walt Disney had limited his company's purpose to the creation of cartoons. The world would have been denied Disneyland, EPCOT Center, and countless hours of family film entertainment. By definition, culture is a stabilizer, a conformist force, a way of making things predictable. Therefore, only when leaders manage the contradictions and define the very culture of the organization as one of learning, adapting, and innovating, can they stabilize perpetual learning and change. These leaders serve up sound thinking, optimism, and a future that is malleable—never Kool Aid. One of the ways they accomplish this involves removing the barriers to the transformation they espouse.

4. Remove the barriers to change. Once you have set the stage, communicated the vision, and begun the process of creating a culture of change, the final step in your change initiative will be to remove the obstacles that stand in its path. Sometimes the barriers exist in people's heads, but at other times they are real and problematic—sometimes even human.

    For example, narrow spans of control, the antithesis to empowerment, undermine efforts to increase productivity or to move ideas to actions. Those in your chain of command who either don't know what decisions they should make, or who hesitate to make them because they fear consequences, will impede progress. Therefore, you and all those who report to you can jump start your change effort by delegating decisions and the power to carry them out to the lowest possible level in the organization. This means delegating entire, important parts of the change initiative, not just pieces of it, along with the authority to execute. No one will be fooled by your willingness to let him decide where to put the Coke machine.

The issuance of an order might bring compliance, but commitment will still elude you if people don't understand their own role and importance to the change. In other words, people need ownership, not just real estate. If you allow politics to trump progress, you will inadvertently develop a culture of "no way." A word of caution: Empowerment does not mean abandonment. Encouraging people to do something helps no one if they lack the skills or experience to do it. So, set expectations for your people, watch them, give them feedback, and help them if you see them headed for failure or a barrier.

Sometimes the barrier is a person who never wanted the change. These people can undermine the transformation process when their behavior does not match the lip service they pay to it publicly. If, however, you tie performance during the transition to evaluations and compensation, you will probably see this sort of passive/aggressive resistance grind to a halt. The reasons people block change are numerous and complex, but they don't really matter. The *behaviors* that indicate a commitment to the proposed change do. Finally, you need to identify "We've never done that before" as the mantra of the enemy, and begin to support your change allies.

How to Encourage Your Change Agents

Discouraging your enemies is the first step; encouraging your allies is the second. Your most vocal adversaries will often take the form of perfectionists. They will advocate making sure you have 100-percent accuracy and precise data before moving an idea to action. Some things, like brain surgery, have to be perfect; for most other things, 80 percent right works. The goal should be success, not perfection. As we learned in physics, a body at rest tends to stay at rest; a body in motion tends to stay in motion. So start moving, and hearten those who also champion the change. Here are ways you can do that:

1. Encourage independent thinking. If you communicate the vision and delegate entire parts of the change initiative, those in your chain of command should have no trouble knowing what the right thing to do is. It's when you change your mind with every flavor-of-the-month idea, waffle on your values, and focus on tactics rather than strategy that people don't know what they should do. If you hold out for popular opinion, you will waste time and compromise momentum. Conversely, if you support self-reliance and resourcefulness by rewarding it, you will see more of it.

2. Listen to someone who is outside the box. In the 1980s, NASA challenged Lockheed Martin to cut the weight of the huge fuel tank that forms the structural backbone of the space shuttle. The effort stalled at the last 800 pounds. As the blue-ribbon engineering team turned its attention to increasingly exotic lightweight materials, one of the line workers suggested they stop painting the tank. The 200 gallons of paint that covered the tank added 800 pounds to a device whose life span in flight was only about eight minutes and whose fate was to end up at the bottom of the Indian Ocean.[3] Similarly, Southwest Airlines cut significant costs when they responded to a suggestion from a flight attendant that they stop putting the company logo on trash bags and to use the much less expensive generic ones. And Taco Bell thought outside the box when its marketing executives devised the slogan to "Think outside the bun." Those in the box often can't think outside it. You'll actually need to learn from those who live outside it and then give them the confidence to speak up.

3. Make learning safe. By its very nature, change involves a journey into uncharted seas. You and your team won't know what to expect—except the unexpected. I guarantee, everyone will make mistakes, but you won't know when or where they will

occur. If your team fears retribution for their mistakes, however, they will be too cautious. They won't learn quickly. Conversely, if you have created a true learning culture, one that contains a core shared assumption that the appropriate way to behave during the change is to be proactive problem solvers and learners, you will better your odds of success. As the leader, you will need to portray confidence that active problem solving leads to learning and that the *process* of learning must ultimately be part of the culture, not any given solution to any given problem. This orientation will help you navigate the waters of the current change effort, but it will also do something more dramatic: it will set the stage for a quick response to future changes.

4. Address *behaviors*, not minds and hearts. So often leaders approach change with the idea that they need the organizational equivalent of a religious conversion. This is wrong-minded and unrealistic. Many, many people in your organization may never agree with you that the change should occur. That's their right. But you will want to see *behaviors* that indicate their support. For example, in the late 1970s I was involved with Social Action for the United States Air Force. At that time the senior Air Force leadership had decided to put women in positions they had not previously held. For many, it was an unpopular decision. My job was to help the Air Force develop the guidelines that would establish how the transition would occur. Although many resisted the principles, they complied with the required behaviors, and the subsequent changes for women spoke volumes about the success of the change efforts. Remember, people are much more likely to *behave* their way into a new way of thinking than to *think* their way into a new way of behaving. Consequently, today people take for granted that women will hold these positions, and little resistance is apparent.

Conclusion

People change when the pain of staying where they are overcomes the fear of change. Sometimes, however, people don't perceive the pain before significant damage has occurred. Like insidious heart disease, symptoms of impending destruction may go unnoticed. As the senior leader, your job is to build a culture of change, one that supports the long-term strategy of your company. There are two kinds or organizations: those with a strong strategy and culture of change, and those going out of business. In other words, what got you here won't necessarily get you to the next level. The Pony Express did not become the railroad, and the railroad did not become the airlines. Vanguards in their days, both the railroad and airline industries thrived. Today, however, both industries suffer from decades of bad management. Unlike the leaders in these two industries, you will need to excel at reading the tea leaves. What opportunities and threats loom on your horizon? How can you leverage your strengths and mitigate your weaknesses to ready yourself for them? You can start by replacing large-scale, amorphous objectives with results-driven goals that focus on quick, measurable gains. After all, as former British Prime Minister Harold Wilson once said, "The only human institution which rejects progress is the cemetery." The formula is simple: reinvent, reengineer, and become the architect of your organization's future.

Chapter 10

Ten Lessons for Leading During Crisis

A smooth sea never made a skilled mariner.
—English Proverb

Tragic circumstances, like the terrorist attacks of September 11, often come as a terrible surprise. Sometimes Mother Nature deals a cruel blow, as she did on August 29, 2005, when New Orleans suffered losses of lives and property after Hurricane Katrina. More often, disaster occurs at an individual level—an employee is diagnosed with cancer or a family member dies suddenly. In any scenario, adversity causes pain—at least in the short run—and that pain spills over into the workplace. When that happens, people need strong leaders.

Crisis defines leadership. As Abigail Adams wrote to her son John Quincy in 1780, "The habits of a vigorous mind are formed in contending with difficulty. Great necessities call out great virtues." Leaders don't seek or welcome crisis, yet by its very serendipitous nature, it offers an inestimable gift to leaders who rise to the challenge and reinvent themselves and their organizations. Almost anyone can lead where others want to go, when the seas remain smooth and the weather calm. True leaders, however, understand that they must use their power and position to be something other than powerful and in charge. They take responsibility and build confidence and trust instead of blaming fate, the economy, or anything else. They control what they can control and cope with the rest.

247

Great leaders seem to know or learn that a sense of control over our destinies defines one of the most basic of human needs. When we feel in control of a situation, we feel empowered and focused. When we don't, we get discouraged, and in the worst-case scenario, we start to feel like victims or aggressors.

Often you can't control significant things at work. In fact, you probably don't hold sway over most things, but you can control your own *reactions* to unfortunate events. No matter what happens to us, no one else can tell us what to feel about it. When you realize you have power over how you respond, you have taken the first step in helping direct reports feel authority over *their* reactions to unpleasant and unexpected changes. You can also show compassion and empathy when others hurt. When your employees know they can express their pain at work, they no longer have to expend the energy to suppress it, and they heal more quickly.

No MBA program, training simulation, or case study will teach you everything you need to know to handle crisis. As the leader, however, if you fail you may not get a second chance. So, like parachuting, you need to get this right the first time. The trouble is that you won't know when that first time will be. It's usually a nasty surprise. Preparing and arming yourself with knowledge, therefore, stacks the deck in your favor. Once you understand the nature of crisis and the behaviors that will worsen or mitigate it, you will be better equipped to help others navigate the stormy seas.

When hard times rear their ugly heads, leaders have to be the heroes, the rescuers who look after others and help them keep from losing their perspective and their coping resources. Nearly every crisis contains within itself the seeds of success as well as the roots of failure. These 10 lessons will help you sow the seeds that will ensure your organization's triumph after the crisis has passed.

Lesson 1: Heed the Early Warning Signs

Where there's smoke, there's usually a fire, or there was a fire, or one is about to start. Sometimes the fire immediately rages out of control, requiring copious amounts of water to douse it, the involvement of trained firefighters, and loss of resources. At other times, the embers will glow, and leaders will fail to notice them until they have ignited into a full-fledged inferno. When crises start small, leaders often fail to recognize the threat.

By the time they figure it out, the crisis has grown to the point that containing it becomes impossible. The warning signals will take many forms, depending on the nature of your business, but if you're alert to these, you will recognize problems before they become disasters:

◊ Persistent customer complaints.

◊ Persistent employee complaints.

◊ A preponderance of rumors.

◊ High potentials leaving the organization.

◊ No one ready for promotion.

◊ Significant changes in technology.

◊ Internal or external resistance to innovation.

If you don't spot any of these warning signs in your organization, you may wonder how a reasonably bright executive could overlook any one of them. Easy. Never underestimate the appeal of inertia. Doing nothing becomes the default position for many leaders, especially the ones with hubris, excessive pride. Self-satisfaction and a perception of invulnerability blind leaders to the signs of imminent peril. They ignore the rumors, make excuses for their high potentials leaving, and overlook complaints.

Turning this sort of blind eye also causes leaders to minimize the scope of the problem and to fail to discern patterns. The breakdown in the mortgage and banking industries of 2009 provides possibly the most dramatic and far-reaching example of the consequences of overlooking the warning signs. Of course, we should probably factor in greed at some point—no small contributor to this debacle either. If you fail to connect the dots or heed the warnings, you're likely to crash and burn, which leads to the next lesson.

Lesson 2: If You Can't Prevent a Crisis, at Least Contain It

Left unchecked, a small disturbance in the atmosphere can quickly escalate to genuine crisis status. Therefore, you need to add crisis containment to your crisis management tool kit. After an event, once you have the requisite information, you'll want to act quickly and decisively, communicate copiously, and above all else, behave ethically.

A pervasive tendency I've have noticed lately involves a propensity to defend inappropriate behavior if the perpetrator happens to represent a person we hold dear or a group we usually admire. When evidence comes to light that someone has done something wrong, out of loyalty, perhaps, we defend the poor behavior. Bad form in the best of times, during a crisis, this reaction can cost you enormously, both in tangible losses, such as customers, and in intangible losses, such as credibility.

For example, because I am a Vietnam POW researcher, people tend to ask my opinion about topics relevant to POWs in general. Therefore, when Abu Ghraib Prison abuse dominated the news, people asked for my reaction. I tend to be very pro-military, but I cannot defend the atrocities committed at Abu Ghraib Prison. The data point to numerous examples of individuals behaving badly, but it also evidences a breakdown in both leadership and the system. It shouldn't have happened. Period.

In response to my observations, one man commented: "At least we never decapitated anyone on a video for the Web," to which I responded, "Since when does the American military allow terrorists to write their code of conduct?" Senior military leaders recognized the seriousness of the abuses and took steps to correct the wrongdoing, even though a few radio commentators remarked that they didn't see what all the fuss was about— clearly an attempt to defend the military, even when it had been wrong.

Senior leaders face this kind of decision frequently. A valued direct report, an esteemed colleague, or a political office-holder you've supported does something wrong, and people turn to you for direction. As I tell my clients, don't defend bad behavior, yours or anybody else's. When you uncover a mistake, admit it and move on. When you behave badly, apologize and move on. This sort of consistency will do more to build trust in your organization than any other singular activity. People want to know what you stand for. If you send conflicting messages and defend those who have done damage, you compromise good will. Organizations, political parties, and religions aren't perfect, largely because each employs flawed people. You won't be perfect either, but you don't have to try to make two wrongs a right. And you don't have to fuel the crisis with an ill-advised defense of who or what caused it.

Lesson 3: Never Run Out of Altitude, Airspeed, and Ideas at the Same Time

Like accomplished, safe pilots, leaders need to maintain altitude, airspeed, and ideas—the three main ingredients in the formula for ensuring success, or at least a best-case scenario outcome. In a physical sense, altitude relates to the elevation of an object above a certain level, usually the earth. Therefore, altitude, as it applies to leadership, involves a global perspective, a realization that a bigger picture exists, and no one person is the center of the universe. When leaders indicate that they have altitude, they usually exhibit these behaviors:

◊   Vision, an ability to see the future and to anticipate consequences.

◊   Critical thinking, the capability to go into uncharted territory. Managers have the ability to do the right thing well; leaders have the ability to figure out what the right thing is.

◊   The ability to prioritize, to do first things first, and to separate important from unimportant uses of time.

◊   The motivation to look beyond the obvious.

◊   The skills to paint credible pictures of possibilities, to see the future as open and malleable.

◊   An eagerness to create competitive strategies.

Psychologists tell us that human beings want power and authority over their future. We want to feel that we have a say in how things will go for us. When we perceive that our actions will make an outcome likely, we feel optimistic and secure. When we don't, we feel insecure. We feel like victims. Sometimes people stay in a victim's frame of mind after a loss or disappointment. They doubt their capacity to make their lives happen according to their own aspirations, so they wait to be rescued or blessed by good fortune. They start to feel undermined and overwhelmed, and they can become totally immobilized.

To maintain your altitude during a crisis, recall the words of Will Rogers: "Even if you're on the right track, you'll get run over if you just sit there." The fear of making mistakes, however, often compromises our altitude and causes us to get run over. We imagine dire consequences instead of objectively seeing mistakes as setbacks, not disasters. During times of adversity, there is much we can't control, but our global perspective, our altitude, is one thing we can take charge of. Looking out for each other is another.

When we think of airspeed, we think of velocity and the forces that make us go forward. Countless studies indicate that getting the job done describes only part of the leader's job; building relationships to keep the right people doing the job defines the other part of it. Relationships provide one of the main sources of fuel that helps successful executives accelerate their productivity and that of others. The leader who avoids running out of airspeed tends to have these traits:

- A knack for building relationships.
- A good sense of humor.
- A strong motivation to follow through.
- A willingness and availability to listen.
- A genuine interest in people.
- The capacity to convey respect for people and their ideas.
- The confidence to tell people what they need to know, not just what they want to hear.

Relationships, communication, closeness, and humor all fuel us and provide the airspeed that keeps us going through adversity and enables us help others. Communicating with those that we care about or who rely on us allows us to keep this perspective. Altitude and airspeed, two critical elements for any leader's success, need a critical third to handle crisis: ideas.

Creative problem solving captures one of the most essential talents a leader can possess. Leaders who can look at diverse information and see relationships, reason abstractly, make logical connections, and think of the future as open and malleable bring an invaluable asset to their organizations: the capacity to generate ideas. When leaders have ideas, they can solve unfamiliar problems and make decisions that are in the best interest of their direct reports and the organization, skills that are tied to the following:

- An openness to brainstorming and creativity.
- The motivation and enthusiasm to challenge existing processes.
- A knack for inviting input from a variety of perspectives.

◇   A willingness to experiment with novel approaches and champion innovation.

Having ideas makes us mentally flexible, which in turns equips us to see things from several perspectives, tolerate uncertainty, adapt to change, and solve problems in new ways. When people don't value flexibility, tragic things happen. Think of the tragedies of history. Look at the Greek tragedies, the Shakespearean tragedies, and the Sopranos—all tragic because people were inflexible. When people opt to overlook alternatives or to see the future as open and malleable, they condemn themselves and their futures to misfortune. Catastrophe makes for good drama and schmaltzy television series, but it's no blueprint for running an organization.

To draw from US history, one has to look no further than the Cuban Missile Crisis, which was *actually* named a crisis at the time, to understand the importance of maintaining altitude, airspeed, and ideas. While contending with the Civil Rights Movement at home and recovering from the botched attempt to overthrow Cuban dictator Fidel Castro in the Bay of Pigs invasion in April 1961, Kennedy faced the central crisis of his presidency—and perhaps of the entire Cold War. In October of 1962, Khrushchev, emboldened by Kennedy's failure at the Bay of Pigs, sent Russian ships carrying nuclear warheads to Cuba in an attempt to establish a Soviet nuclear presence just 90 miles off the coast of Florida.

Kennedy resisted calls for direct engagement and ordered, instead, a naval blockade around Cuba. The move prevented the Soviet ships from gaining entry to the island and bought time for cooler heads to prevail. On October 22, Kennedy declared that any missile launched from Cuba would warrant a full-scale retaliatory attack by the United States against the Soviet Union. On October 24, Russian ships carrying missiles to Cuba turned back, and when Khrushchev agreed on October 28 to withdraw the missiles and dismantle the missile sites, the crisis ended as suddenly as it had begun.

Even though the United States faced a real threat of destruction, Kennedy did not lose his perspective. Presidential advisor Ted Sorensen would recall that Kennedy insisted on knowing all his options. He did not do anything rash—did not panic or overreact. He remained calm and never lost his sense of humor, perspective, or modesty.[1]

Lesson 4: Face Reality

Acknowledge the crisis, get everyone else to acknowledge it, and respond to the early warning signals. Don't deny the urgency or severity of the adversity; don't blame people, external events, or the elusive "they" that seem to contribute to most of the world's mischief. If you played a role in creating the crisis, admit that too.

Pharmaceutical giant Merck offers a perfect example of doing the opposite. In spite of evidence that the painkiller Vioxx contributed to heart attacks, the senior leaders at Merck decided to continue marketing the product while the company sponsored its own research. In 2004, Merck CEO Ray Gilmartin pulled the drug from the market, but the damage had been done. Vioxx had been linked to 27,000 heart attacks. In 2007, Merck announced a $5 billion settlement and ended the crisis, but not before the disaster had claimed both dollars and public good will.

Contrast Merck's experience to the Tylenol crisis of 1982, in which seven people died in the Chicago area after taking pain-relief capsules that had been laced with potassium cyanide. Because the tampered bottles came from different factories, and the seven deaths had all occurred in the Chicago area, investigators ruled out the possibility of sabotage during production. Almost immediately investigators concluded that the culprit had entered various supermarkets and drug stores over a period of weeks, pilfered packages of Extra-Strength Tylenol from the shelves, adulterated their contents and then replaced the bottles. Yet, senior leaders at Johnson & Johnson knew they had to do whatever it took to protect its clients, so they went above and beyond what they probably would have had to do legally.

Johnson & Johnson distributed warnings to hospitals and distributors, halted Tylenol production, and ceased advertising. The leaders issued a nationwide recall of Tylenol products, with an estimated $100 million value, and offered to exchange all Tylenol capsules with solid tablets.

The company's mission statement that they would be responsible to consumers using their products explains why Johnson & Johnson leaders reacted so quickly and positively. These leaders' accountability to its customers proved to be its most efficient public relations tool and the key to the brand's survival. It probably also offers the most dramatic example of executives facing reality. In this, as in most cases, the reality wasn't pretty; the decision involved pain, and the short-term loss to the company proved to be astronomically costly. Yet it defined the right thing to do and ultimately ensured the continuation of the company and the product.

Denying reality has probably destroyed more organizations than incompetence ever could. A sudden catastrophe like 9/11 was impossible to ignore, but the ones brewing in your organization probably aren't. In fact, the future calamity might now present itself as an annoyance, an inconvenience, or a benign problem. The lion's share of facing reality, therefore, involves perceiving the emergency before it becomes one. Bad news never gets better with age. It all starts with you. If you acknowledge the present or emerging crisis and your role, if any, in creating it, you will be able to guide your organization to face the reality too.

Lesson 5: Prepare; Don't Practice Bleed

"Practice bleeding" is the term I use to describe the propensity to suffer before the pain begins. In an ideal world, crisis management begins long before a crisis actually occurs—in a calm and objective environment in which no one is physically or metaphorically bleeding. It starts with a thorough audit of organizational risks—not a hand-wringing, floor-pacing attempt to control the future. Listing every potential organizational crisis would be impossible. However, understanding some of the major categories of risk can help you identify the types of crisis you need to avoid and for which you should prepare. The nature of your business will determine the risks you will face, but some universal perils exist:

◊ Natural disasters.

◊ Product tampering.

◊ Accidents.

◊ Technical breakdowns.

◊ Economic changes.

◊ Aberrant employees.

No one has ever gained from suffering before a tragedy or practice bleeding. If the time comes to suffer, you'll know how. Like rocking in a rocking chair, practice bleeding will give you something to do, allow you to pretend you're doing something important, and impress people with your stoicism. But the activities associated with practice bleeding will take you no further to preparing for crisis. Preparation, on the other hand, will make all the difference. Here are some ideas for planning for crisis:

1. Monitor your cash. It is the lifeblood of any business. Without it, all your great plans to have a product you're proud of or a culture where people like coming to work are worthless. If you can't pay those good people on payday, the time clock will run out before you attempt to throw the Hail Mary, and you will lose the game. In most situations, cash is king. In crisis, it is more of a demanding emperor: not earnings per share, revenue growth, or return on equity—cash. Do you have sufficient cash reserves to get through the worst crisis you can imagine? What do you need to do immediately to prepare for this worst-case scenario?

   Even companies that go to great lengths to devise strategic plans for financial growth and success fail to recognize that strategic planning that does not include crisis management strategies is like sustaining life without guaranteeing life. No organization can prepare for every single crisis event. This would be an impossible task and a tremendous misappropriation of financial and human resources. However, now, not at the onset of the disaster, is the best time to prepare for as many contingencies as you can imagine—and then some.

2. Establish a crisis response team. This group should represent the major areas a crisis would likely affect. For example, if you run a manufacturing company, product recall may present the biggest threat to the company. Which operations people, legal minds, marketing professionals, and public relations experts will need to participate? Don't wait until you face a disaster to assemble this team. Go outside the organization if you must, but build the team you need now. As the senior leader, you will lead the crisis initiative, unless you can't. This team, therefore, needs to function independently of you under those circumstances.

3. Evaluate potential crisis situations and decide on appropriate responses to the most likely ones. Simulate crisis and the

procedures to get through it. One of the most dramatic examples of leadership during crisis occurred on January 15, 2009, over the Hudson when Captain Sullenberger landed a crippled US Airways plane and saved the lives of all the passengers and crew on board. He accomplished this heroic rescue for one reason: he had prepared over a period of time with mock simulations, often in a simulator, of similar emergencies.

In your organization, how can you do something like this? What would your company's equivalent be to hitting a bird during flight? On that flight the flight attendants chanted, "Brace! Brace! Heads down! Stay down!" as the plane careened to water. What do your employees need to chant during a time of crisis? Practice it, and make it your mantra for survival. A crisis is no time to search for answers or direction. Put it all in place beforehand. The leadership at Johnson & Johnson didn't have to search for a code of conduct at their time of crisis; their mission steered them in the right direction. Think about a "crisis drill" the way you would a fire drill. Have a plan, communicate it, and then practice it when people aren't expecting it to happen. Build in contingency plans in case technology doesn't work (as it didn't on 9/11).

4. Build relationships outside the organization that can help you when you falter. In 1941, Franklin Roosevelt went before Congress seeking support for Great Britain in its fight against the Nazis. Many Americans opposed him with a "keep out of the war" mantra. Roosevelt, however, believed the US needed to aid their desperate allies. Roosevelt reminded America that you do not ask your neighbors to pay you for a fire extinguisher when their house is on fire. He convinced the vast majority, which led to a turning point in the war that affected the history of the world and mankind. Who are your allies who would lend you a fire extinguisher in a time of need? Do they know they could count on you for the same?

5. Create a list of the 10 worst things that could happen and what the organization would do about those situations. Who should be the point person on each disaster, assuming you are not

available? Who should be the backup if the point person isn't available? Prioritize the list and discuss both the likelihood of the risk and the seriousness of it. If you make products, someone, other than you, should have recall authority and know the relevant stakeholders to notify.

6. Cathy Dunkin, the president of Standing Partnership, a St. Louis-based reputation management firm, tells her clients that they should know how they'd want to respond to a crisis well before one occurs. She recommends preparing a list of contact information for your key audience—shareholders, media, employees, the community, customers, elected officials, vendors—anyone you'd want to send accurate information immediately. The point person, not just the CEO, should have this information available at all times.[2]

7. Make the learning from a failure visible. An absolute catastrophe is one that you don't learn from, and inevitably repeat. Rush to find the cause of the failure, but forget assigning blame. When you unearth the cause of the problem, put systems in place to avoid something similar in the future. The Ford Edsel provides perhaps one of the biggest product failures of all time, but Lee Iacocca learned from this setback. He realized that the motoring public no longer bought cars simply because of brand loyalty or their need for transportation. He determined from this experience that a segment of the population wanted a "lifestyle" purchase, which led to the production of the Mustang, which immediately became an unexpected success. Don't fix the "weak link." Ask yourself, "What products, services, or relationships can we create to exploit what we've learned?"

Lesson 6: Be Realistic but Optimistic

When facing the early stages of adversity, declaring victory too soon or underestimating the severity of the problem do not prove prudent. Think of former President Bush standing on the aircraft carrier *Abraham Lincoln* in a military flight suit in front of a giant "Mission Accomplished" sign on May 1, 2003, declaring that the war in Iraq was over. More than seven years later, the war persists; soldiers and civilians continue to lose their lives; and the debates in Congress rage. In the throes of a full-fledged crisis, don't assume that rearranging the chairs on the Titanic will do anything important. Be realistic, and communicate a genuine, sensible assessment of the situation. And whatever you do, don't tell people or yourself that it can't get any worse! In addition to tempting fate, this sort of non-pragmatic observation will brand you a liar or a fool.

Optimism, on the other hand, offers its own rewards. But how do you get ready for the worst case while holding hope for the best? It's a tricky balance, but my research of the Vietnam POWs taught me that sometimes you fake it until you make it.

In 1965, for example, according to US reports, no troops fought in Laos. But one of the participants in my POW study, Gary, was there. An Air Force captain, he was shot down in May of 1965. In spite of his youth and junior rank, he was the senior ranking officer in charge of a group of enlisted personnel. As Gary told me in our 1997 conversation, he had "no hope of repatriation...I was dead, never going to come out." He observed, "They all seemed to think they were coming back, and I didn't want to bust anybody's bubble. But no, I didn't believe we were coming back." He said he was "absolutely pessimistic," yet he decided, "It didn't hurt anything to have hope. I knew better, and I knew what I had to do, help the others and continue giving Charlie hell."

Gary's attitude might not seem optimistic. In fact, he called it "absolutely pessimistic," yet it appears to have served the same purpose as optimism. He felt a sense of responsibility to his troops to hold on to hope for their sake. "I was already dead," he explained to me, so doing what he thought was important drove his actions and influenced his team. Gary provides an important clue about the coupling of positive attitude, even when it does not truly involve optimism, and finding a purpose in the experience.

Striking a balance between realism and optimism won't be easy during a crisis. You won't know what the future holds, and you might not even be certain what your best guess is. Above all else, you can't use others for your own therapy. Direct reports won't want to reassure you, and they probably couldn't if they wanted to because they will be too caught up in their own worries. You won't be able to look to anyone else in the organization for comfort. Looking outside the company, however, makes great sense. Family, friends, trusted mentors, and therapists can give you the help you will need to put on your own oxygen mask first. Only then will you be of any use to anyone else.

Lesson 7: Take Charge of Communication

During times of adversity, those in the organization look to senior leaders, especially the CEO, to communicate—to tell them the facts, to define the situation, and to give them hope. Yet, if you want to know why so many companies sink into chaos during times of crisis, you need look no further than the CEO's mouth.

Instead of transmitting loud and clear, too often senior leaders create static. They either don't communicate enough, or they rely on worn-out platitudes like "Let's focus on the priorities," and "We need to hunker down." Static of this ilk masks the real message and substitutes for the essential one. To keep your eye on the critical, consider these questions:

◊　What needs to happen today to mitigate the crisis?

◊　What vagueness can we clear up?

◊　What do I need to communicate?

◊　What are people most afraid of?

Contrast the situation in a typical organization in chaos with a SWAT team or an emergency room staff. Employees in typical organizations often nod in apparent agreement when the CEO uses fuzzy terms and then later react with panic, uncertainty, or inertia. Dissimilarly, leaders of a SWAT team or an emergency room—those who handle crisis each day—use concrete, specific language. They may bark orders in a seemingly aggressive manner, but no one stands around wondering what to do, afraid of overstepping, and scared of a misstep. Executives can learn much from those who are in the crisis business. Everyone speaks the same language and knows his or her role. If they don't, people die. When you fail to take charge of communication, perhaps no one at your organization dies; they just wish they could.

Industries that deal with life-or-death situations have learned through the years the critical role specific messages play, but they have done something else. They have discovered the critical role of internal communication. Important during the best of times, effective internal communication becomes vital at the time of a crisis.

To better understand the crucial role this plays, I talked with Mark Abels, TWA's former VP of Corporate Communication. On the fateful day in July of 1996 when Flight 800 crashed, Mark was one of the people in charge of media relations for the company.

As most tragedies do, this one came as a surprise, so he was not in place to handle the emergency. Instead, a phone call to London awakened Mark informing him of the incident. Mark then informed the CEO, Jeff Erickson, of the disaster. Even though the two were overcome with sadness, both men knew the crisis planning would go into gear in their absence until they could fly back to New York to do what they could.

The airlines provide a shining example of what other companies can do to prepare for crisis. First, there are no industry secrets in this arena. Airlines willingly share lessons learned after any crash. Second, each airline has a plan that others can execute whether the senior leader is available or not. Third, they understand they must take care of the unnoticed victims, the people whose job it is to handle crisis and the volunteers who help them.

Many remember that 230 people lost their lives on Flight 800. Most, however, don't realize that 50 of those people were TWA employees and their families. Virtually everyone employed at TWA knew one of the people on that ill-fated flight.

The tragedy of July 17, 1996, did not teach Abels and the others involved too many new lessons about handling crisis, but it reinforced many—some of them related to taking care of employees. Here's what Abels thinks others can learn:

⬥ Outsiders will seem to be your priority, but you'll need to pay attention to your internal audience. When the "sharks" quit circling, the employees will remain.

⬥ Shield your people from the media or anyone else who might hurt them further.

⬥ Keep them informed. Don't let them hear news from the media. It's insulting.

⬥ Attend to the employees' needs. TWA leaders provided counselors for the employees, arranged prayer services, approved time off, and made people feel useful.[3]

Remember, the most important messages you send won't be the verbal ones; they will be the nonverbal ones. People will *listen* to your words and hope to hear clear, straightforward, honest answers. However, they will *watch* what you do and notice whether you send consistent, congruent messages—and they will ask themselves whether your actions support your words. If they do, you will move the organization forward, even though you struggle through a crisis. If you don't, your people will suffer more from the disaster and will never forgive you once it's passed. Strong leadership like Jeff Erickson's can go a long way in restoring the organization to its former self in the shortest length of time.

Lesson 8: Encourage and Listen to Impolite Candor

On August 5, 1997, a Korean pilot, the recipient of a flight safety award with 8,900 hours of flight time, crashed into the side of Nimitz Hill in Guam, killing 254 people. This was not an isolated event. The loss rate for Korean Air in the period between 1988 and 1998 was *17 times higher* that than of United Airlines. The reason? Some say politeness. The Korean language has different levels of conversational address, depending on the relationship between the addressee and the addresser. The co-pilot would not have dared use a familiar or forceful tone with the captain, even though he realized they should not make a visual approach in the rainy weather.

Seven years prior to the Korean Air crash, a Columbian airliner ran out of gas because the captain was too polite to declare an emergency and demand Air Traffic Control at Kennedy give him priority landing. Apparently neither the captain nor the first officer wanted to assert himself with the arguably forceful JFK controllers.

The black box recording of the 1982 Air Florida crash outside Washington DC indicated the first officer tried three times to tell the captain that the plane had a dangerous amount of ice on its wings. Instead of assertively issuing a command to the captain, however, the first officer *hinted* at the problem. The first officer's last words just before the plane plunged into the Potomac River: "Larry, we're going down."

Even though the captain usually has more experience, historically crashes happen more often when the captain flies the leg of the trip. When the captain flies, others don't issue orders. When the first officer flies, the captain doesn't hesitate to speak up when something looks amiss.[4]

Since these historic crashes, airlines have improved their safety records throughout the world. Cockpit Resource Management now teaches crew members how to address problems, when to speak up, and when to ratchet up. Many in corporate American should take heed.

As the senior leader, do you quash debate in favor of politeness? Or, do you encourage robust dissent? If you do the former, you may crash and burn. If you embrace opposition and put conflicts on the table, you will improve your communication with your team, but you will do something even more important: you will take the responsible first step to ensuring the efficacy of your ideas and strategy.

Throughout my career I have addressed the importance of listening, but when addressing the leader's role in handling crisis, it merits another nod. You may be the smartest CEO ever to grace your company's doorstep. You might be highly experienced, with a knack for influencing others. But if you can't put your ego aside during times of crisis and draw the answers from others, you'll miss the single most important coping behavior for helping you soar through the storm.

People must feel free to speak their minds—to you and to those above them in the chain of command. Often employees will see a crisis brewing long before senior leaders ever find out about it. If you punish whistle-blowers, if those in your chain of command shelter you from negative feed-back, or if management dismisses warnings, people will learn to keep their observations and opinions to themselves.

I've said it repeatedly: if you want solutions, be quiet every chance you get. People tend to parrot strong leaders in the best of times. In crisis, you can count on a cacophony of squawking echoes. Your people might not immediately know the right answer or even some good ones, but if you stay quiet long enough, you just might hear some brilliance start to surface. There will be time for you to talk later (unless the building is on fire or something equally dire occurs) but if you don't encourage others to talk, you may lose their ideas forever.

Lesson 9: Exude Powerful Vulnerability

During crisis, leaders often feel overwhelmed with responsibility—as though they carry the weight of the world on their shoulders. Hundreds, perhaps thousands, of people's livelihoods depend on you, shareholders or investors count on you to honor your commitments to drive value, and customers rely on you to continue to deliver the product or service that accounts for your current success. When you face a pending crisis, therefore, you might tend to take the whole burden on yourself. Your default position might be to retire to your office to ruminate about the problem.

Admitting limitations has counterintuitive benefits. When you level with people, they are more likely to forgive your mistakes, and you'll make stronger connections with them that ultimately increase your ability to persuade and influence. That, in turn, will strengthen your leadership. No one expects you to have all the answers—just a willingness to discover them. The people in your organization don't want you to turn in; they want you to turn to them and others who can help. They want you to show your vulnerability because they know you are experiencing it. This doesn't contradict my earlier advice not to look to your direct reports for reassurance. They probably won't be able to offer that, but they can usually provide information and ideas. When you open yourself up and share your limitations, you connect on a level that doesn't exist in non-crisis times. Further, exposing your own vulnerability invites your people to admit theirs. When this level of candor exists, cohesion and renewed respect will follow.

Former POW Robinson Risner provides one of the most dramatic examples of how to lead during crisis—all the while admitting limitations and strengthening cohesion and loyalty. After the 1970 Son Tay Raid and the late shoot-downs during the Christmas bombings of 1972, the prisons in North Vietnam proved too small to house all the prisoners in the single or double cells the captors had previously used. Then groups of prisoners filled large dormitory-sized rooms. In addition to enjoying each other's company and engaging in daily educational seminars, the POWs derived great pleasure in their Sunday church services, which often included the recitation of memorized scripture, hymns, and the singing of either the National Anthem or "America the Beautiful."

The captors had finally released then Colonel Robbie Risner, the senior ranking officer of the POWs, from his years in solitary confinement. He joined the large group for a church service during which the POWs wanted to sing the National Anthem. When the POWs began to sing, the captors warned them to stop or they would put Col. Risner back in solitary confinement. Realizing his group's need for cohesion and control, Col. Risner ordered the men to continue singing. They did, and the captors dragged him back to his tiny, solitary cell.

In 1998, at the 25th anniversary of their repatriation, Ross Perot, who had long been a champion of the POWs and their causes, hosted a gala in Dallas that included a magnificent performance of the Dallas Symphony. At the conclusion of the event, Mr. Perot took the microphone and invited all the POWs who had been in that church service to come to the stage to sing the National Anthem so Robbie Risner could finally hear them. As we all rose to our feet for the tribute, a humble but proud now-retired General Risner walked to the stage to hear the anthem he had missed 25 years earlier.

In 1972, Colonel Risner understood the importance of exuding a powerful vulnerability during crisis. His action the day of the church service galvanized the POWs, augmented their determination, and ultimately contributed to their returning resilient and hardy. In 1998, General Risner once again exhibited his understanding of the concept. At the gala in Dallas, he united the POWs and those who had gathered in their support and honor with his powerful vulnerability.

Machiavelli advised his followers, "Never waste the opportunities offered by a good crisis." Even though you may not perceive this reality at the time, a crisis provides a unique opportunity to create transformative change in your organization. Sometimes these opportunities will present themselves in the form of your relying on others, at least for a while. You cannot get through most crises alone, so don't try. Learn to accept support from your team and realize that the very trait that explains your success to date—your independence—will prove to be your worst enemy in a crisis. Overused, any asset becomes a liability—none more obviously than exaggerated self-reliance during a disaster.

Lesson 10: Respond Appropriately to the Media

Conventional wisdom suggests, "Never argue with people who buy ink by the barrel." Old saying, current relevance. You shouldn't argue with them, but you'd better understand them. The higher you go in your business or industry, the more likely you will have occasion to deal with the media. The business of the journalist is to detect duplicity and disguise. Your goal is to make sure you don't supply either. Sometimes you'll need to seek counsel from others in how to do this.

Lawyers are a critical component of any effective crisis communication team. However, they invariably focus on protecting the company from lawsuits more than on enhancing the company's reputation. Lawyers typically counsel silence in times of crisis, but often silence can have a devastating effect on the company's credibility. Think of Boeing reeling from a succession of scandals. Jim McNerney, a veteran of General Electric and 3M, pulled Boeing out of its nosedive both by instituting clearer rules of ethical conduct and by launching an effective public relations strategy. He ended Boeing's traditional silence and invested in reputation management. He is, unfortunately, the exception to the rule. Many CEOs have run the noblest of intentions onto the rocks with blundering helmsmanship because they failed to receive the help they needed, largely due to the fact that they hadn't recognized its value. Consequently, when crisis occurred, they responded in ways that they later regretted. So, what can you do instead?

1. Cooperating with, not obstructing, the media will help you get your message out. Build a reputation for yourself and your organization, and let media representatives know they can count on you to be responsive to reporters who are working on a story. Be a source of information, call them back immediately, and make yourself available for interviews when they are doing a story related to some knowledge you have.

2. Establish a relationship with a PR firm *before* you face a crisis so they will know enough about your business to give you solid advice. Dunkin suggested senior leaders hire or appoint someone to take charge of their reputation management in order to "earn trust equity with those who matter most to them."

She also mentioned the importance of someone monitoring the internal and external messages about the company so senior leaders can anticipate issues and respond early to a brewing disaster. This kind of ongoing diligence, which includes offering to serve as a resource for the media and making oneself available for interviews during non-crisis times, will build a legacy of transparency and openness that will pay huge dividends if and when crisis strikes.

3. Try to minimize the lag time between the first signs of trouble and an appropriate response from the company. The sooner you present the facts, the sooner the rumors disappear.

4. Don't respond to unfounded stories. It only gives them credibility.

5. Be transparent and avoid "no comment." If you don't know an answer, say you don't know but will find out. Don't encourage the media to go searching for another source of information. Be it and be accurate.

6. Executives should be accessible to the press and amenable to interviews during non-crisis times. Then, when and if a crisis occurs, the media are less likely to be unfair or too harsh. Have one official, not necessarily the CEO, present the big picture. Let other spokespersons address technical issues. They'll know more and have more credibility.

7. Don't attempt to minimize the situation. Don't compare your current situation to worse ones.

8. Even if someone did something stupid that put your company in a bad light, don't blame the victims.

9. Before crisis strikes, build a strong reputation for social responsibility in the community and trust among your employees. Trying to backpedal during the crisis can never have the same effect that proactive efforts produce.

10. Communicate a small number of carefully chosen messages. Too many will confuse people.

Conclusion

Crisis involves change—either sudden or evolving—that results in an altered reality. Often this reality presents urgent problems that the senior must address immediately. In some instances the crisis causes death. In business, more often the crisis involves sudden or serious damage to people, reputation, or financial stability.

In too many cases the lessons from the crisis slip away. Many organizations spend thousands of hours planning for a crisis and millions of dollars implementing contingency plans for one, but precious few in developing a systemic way to approach learning from it. "Lessons learned" should follow any sort of major challenge you have faced—whether or not you'd categorize the event as a true crisis. Here are some questions that may help:

⬧   Knowing what we know now, could this crisis have been avoided? How?

⬧   What were the early warning signs and how could we have heeded them sooner?

⬧   How could we have contained the situation better?

⬧   In what ways did our plans work and not work?

⬧   Did we have the right people in place?

⬧   How should we improve communication in the future?

⬧   Did we involve the media appropriately?

⬧   What was our biggest mistake? How will we avoid this next time?

The U.S. Army has maintained a Center for Army Lessons Learned for decades. Its mission is to turn every incident into practical advice that can be disseminated to future generations of soldiers. Their function does not involve assigning blame or punishing. Rather, this center exists to evaluate options for the future.

You can create the same function in your organization. Gather input from everyone who participated in the crisis or emergency. Encourage their candor and express your appreciation for their involvement. Then, as the senior leader, provide closure to the event. Move on. There's work to do and people relying on you to make sure it gets done.

Appendix

Know Your People

On a scale from 1 to 10, with 10 meaning you completely agree, rate the following:

	1	2	3	4	5	6	7	8	9	10
I understand expectations.										
I have the resources to do my job right.										
My boss recognizes and uses my talents and skills to their fullest extent.										
My work challenges me.										
I have the chance to learn new skills.										

	1	2	3	4	5	6	7	8	9	10
I have the chance to advance in responsibilities and position.										
My boss gives me recognition and praise when I deserve it.										
I know that my boss cares about me.										
I can trust my boss to tell me the truth.										
This company is committed to excellence.										

Succession Planning Grid

Decision-Making/Problem-Solving

Solo Contributor	Manager With Direct Reports	Manager of Other Managers	Multi-Business Leader	CEO
◊ Technical expertise. ◊ Capacity and desire to learn quickly.	◊ Capability to separate tactics from strategy. ◊ Knack for zeroing in on critical issues.	◊ Strategic focus. ◊ Well-developed critical thinking skills. ◊ Talent for evaluating strategies of other managers. ◊ Ability to anticipate consequences. ◊ Talent for prioritizing seemingly conflicting goals. ◊ Proven track record for solving unfamiliar problems. ◊ Ease of multi-tasking. ◊ Solid track record for making high caliber decisions. ◊ General business acumen. ◊ Facility with budget decisions. ◊ Ability to create order during chaos.	◊ Aptitude for making sophisticated financial decisions related to profit and loss. ◊ Skills for blending specific business strategy with overall enterprise strategy. ◊ Aptitude for critiquing strategy by asking questions and requiring support data. ◊ Complex thinking to manage more than one business. ◊ Three- to five-year vision. ◊ Decisiveness. ◊ Global perspective. ◊ Creative problem-solving	◊ Visionary thinking—five- to 10-year focus ◊ Ability to handle ambiguity. ◊ Knowledge of how to grow the business organically and acquisitively. ◊ Insight to create policy that will affect everyone in the enterprise.

Task Orientation

Solo Contributor	Manager With Direct Reports	Manager of Other Managers	Multi-Business Leader	CEO
◊ Strong achievement drive and bias for action. ◊ Systematic approach to work. ◊ Time mastery. ◊ High energy level. ◊ Strong commitment to meeting deadlines. ◊ Results focus, even when the work is hard or demands long hours.	◊ Capacity to satisfy achievement needs through work of others. ◊ Focus on short term objectives. ◊ Willingness to delegate. ◊ Knowledge of goal setting. ◊ Ability to define roles for and with others.	◊ More pronounced tendency to feel accomplishment through others' efforts. ◊ Capacity to overcome obstacles. ◊ Preference for working independently, neither wanting nor needing close supervision. ◊ Eagerness to bring about continuous improvement by questioning the status quo.	◊ Value of and responsibility for unfamiliar functions. ◊ Focus on both short- and long-term objectives. ◊ Risk orientation. ◊ Resourcefulness to be alert to opportunities. ◊ Talent for working under time constraints.	◊ Change orientation. ◊ Focus on stock price, shareholder value, and financial solvency. ◊ Portfolio management.

Leadership Skills

Solo Contributor	Manager Wirect Reports	Manager of Other Managers	Multi-Business Leader	CEO
◊ Integrity. ◊ Reliability.	◊ Dominance. ◊ Motivation to give candid, balanced, developmental feedback. ◊ Readiness to make unpopular decisions and influence firing decisions. ◊ Ability to discipline without destroying. ◊ Emotional maturity. ◊ Knowledge of how to build cohesion. ◊ An understanding of how to structure work for and with direct reports.	◊ Emotional toughness, especially when making unpopular decisions. ◊ Ability to establish and articulate performance standards. ◊ Willingness to fire when necessary. ◊ Confidence and self-assurance. ◊ Coaching/mentoring orientation. ◊ Competence in serving as a sounding board for others. ◊ Resilience.	◊ Ability to trust others in the chain of command to handle the day-to-day decisions related to running the businesses. ◊ Talent for asking the right questions to draw out the ideas of others. ◊ Obvious maturity in use of power.	◊ Leadership of disparate entities, often geographically dispersed. ◊ Capacity to set the pace of change and to orchestrate it well. ◊ Capability of serving as a trusted exemplar. ◊ Skill for articulating vision. ◊ Crisis management. ◊ Ongoing learning. ◊ Management of top and bottom lines. ◊ Emotional fortitude. ◊ Courage. ◊ Ability to handle failure.

People Skills

Solo Contributor	Manager With Direct Reports	Manager of Other Managers	Multi-Business Leader	CEO
◊ Strong interpersonal skills. ◊ Teamwork orientation. ◊ Respect for peer group.	◊ Knowledge of how to build teamwork. ◊ Skill for identifying talent and influencing hiring decisions. ◊ Openness and tolerance, especially for people whose ideas, customs, and beliefs are different. ◊ Insight into the underlying agendas and motivations of others. ◊ Ability to get to the core of conflict. ◊ Capacity to build trust. ◊ Empathy.	◊ Gift for spotting and developing talent. ◊ Insight about own strengths and weaknesses. ◊ Social poise and astuteness.	◊ Succession planning—ability to select and develop leaders of leaders. ◊ Source of advice and wisdom. ◊ Cross cultural awareness. ◊ Agility to balance the different needs of various stakeholders. ◊ The ability to put others at ease in social situations.	◊ Board of director relations. ◊ Investor relations. ◊ Community orientation.

Development Plan

Goal	Development Activity	Specific Task	Start Date	Review Date	Person to Review
	Attend senior-level meetings				
	On the job training				
	Job rotation				
	Job enrichment				
	External training				
	Education/degree				
	Task force assignment				
	Mentoring/ coaching				
	Shadowing				
	Job scope increase or change				
	Start-up project				
	Fix-it project				
	Project team leader				
	Project in another area				
	International experience				
	Budget experience				
	P & L responsibility				
	Self-study				
	Industry involvement				

Notes

Chapter 1

1. Bronwyn Fryer and David McCullough,"Timeless Leadership: A Conversation with David McCullough," *Harvard Business Review* (March 1,2008): 2.

2. "From the Battlefield to the Boardroom," *Success* (Nov./Dec. 2006): 23

3. Interview with General Richard Myers. August, 2008.

4. "The Heroes of July; A Solemn and Imposing Event. Dedication of the National Cemetery at Gettysburgh," *The New York Times* (November 20, 1863): 1.

5. Peter Drucker, "What Executives Should Remember," *Harvard Business Review* (Feb. 1, 2006): 3.

Chapter 2

1. Taiichi Ohno, foreword by Norman Bodek, *Toyota Production System: Beyond Large-Scale Production* (Portland: Productivity Press, 1988), 17–20.

2. A. Lowy, and P. Hood, *The Power of the 2 × 2 Matrix* (San Francisco: Jossey-Bass, 2004), 2–3

3. Irving L. Janis, *Groupthink* (Boston: Houghton Mifflin, 1982), 8.

4. G. Moorhead, R. Ference, and C.P. Neck, "Group Decision Fiascos Continue: Space Shuttle Challenger and a Groupthink Framework," *Human Relations* 44 (1991): 539–550.

5. M. Bazerman, and Dolly Chugh, "Decision Without Blinders," *Harvard Business Review* (January 2006): 90

6. C.R. Anderegg, *Ash Warrior* (Hawaii Office of PACAF History, Hickam AFB: 2000), 9.

Chapter 3

1. Interview with General Carlson. March 4, 2010

2. Interview with Dr. James Dennis. March 2, 2010

3. R. Goffee, and G. Jones, "Leading Clever People," *Harvard Business Review.* (March 2007): 72-79.

Chapter 4

1. M. Freedman, and B. Tregoe, *The Art and Discipline of Strategic Leadership* (New York: McGraw-Hill, 2003), 15.

2. R. Buzzell, and G. Bradly, *The PIMS Principles: Linking Strategy to Performance* (New York: Free Press, 1987), 7.

3. M. Robert, M., *The Strategist CEO: How Visionary Executives Build Organizations* (New York: Quorum, 1988), 20.

4. D. Halberstam, *The Reckoning* (New York: William Morrow, 1986), 544.

5. W. Churchill, *The Grand Alliance*. (New York: Houghton Mifflin, 1950), 371.

6. E. Lawler, "Business Strategy: Creating the Winning Formula," *Organizational Development* (San Francisco: Jossey-Bass, 2006), 553.

7. Interview with Navy Commander (Ret.) Trish Beckman. February, 2008.

8. B. Tregoe, and J. Zimmerman, *Top Management Strategy* (New York: Kepner-Tregoe, 1980) 20.

9. B. Tregoe, and J. Zimmerman, 43–54.

10. R. Kaplan, and D. Norton, *The Balanced Scorecard* (Boston: Harvard Business School Press, 1996), 43–47.

Chapter 5

1. O. Gadiesh, and J. Gilbert, "Transforming Corner-Office Strategy into Frontline Action," *Harvard Business Review* (May 2001): 10-11.

2. S. Gwynne, "Flying into Trouble," *Time* (Feb. 24, 1997): 4.

3. Interview with Tom Philips, CEO of Weekends Only Furniture.

4. T. MacCraw, *Prophet of Innovation: Joseph Schumpeter and Creative Destruction* (Cambridge, Mass.: The Belknap Press of Harvard University Press, 2007), 151.

5. D. Sull, and C. Spinosa, "Promise-Based Management: The Essence of Execution," *Harvard Business Review* (April 2007): 45-46.

6. M. Mankins, and R. Steele, "Turning Great Strategy into Great Performance." *Harvard Business Review* (July/August, 2007): 32–35.

7. F. Roethlisberger, and W. Dickson, *Early Sociology of Management and Organizations*. (London: Routledge, 2003): 408-421.

8. G. Neilson, K. Martin, and E. Powers, "The Secrets of Successful Strategy Execution," *Harvard Business Review.* (June 2008): 3–4.

Chapter 6

1. B. Groysberg, L. Sant, and R. Abrahams, R. "How to Minimize the Risks of Hiring Outside Stars," *The Wall Street Journal* (September 9, 2008).

2. R. Charan, "Ending the CEO Succession Crisis," *Harvard Business Review* (Feb. 2005): 3.

3. J. Menkes, *Executive Intelligence* (New York: Harper Collins, 2005): 27.

4. Interview with General Richard Myers. August, 2008

5. J. Cohn, R. Khurana, and L. Reeves, "Growing Talent as if Your Business Depended on It," *Harvard Business Review* (Oct. 2005): 68–69.

6. R. Charan, "Ending the CEO Succession Crisis," *Harvard Business Review* (Feb. 2005): 74–75.

Chapter 7

1. Interview with Maestro Anthony Pappano, Director Covent Garden. Oct. 7, 2010.

2. NASA History Program *http://history.nasa.gov*

3. Audio recording from Apollo 13 mission. *http://www.youtube. com/watch?v=0vZa7g14F-Y*

4. D. Goodwin, *Team of Rivals: The Political Genius of Abraham Lincoln.* (New York: Simon & Schuster, 2005), 7–15.

5. C. Nelson, *The First Heroes: The Extraordinary Story of the Doolittle Raid—America's First World War II Victory* (New York: Viking, 2002), 3–7.

6. Interview with Lt. Col. (Ret) Richard Cole, co-pilot to Jimmy Doolittle during the Doolittle Raid. Oct. 6, 2010.

7. Interview with Tom Casey, manager for Doolittle Raiders. Sept. 28, 2010.

8. *http://www.historynet.com/jimmy-doolittle-and-the-tokyo-raiders-strike-japan-during-world-war-ii.*

9. B. Tuckman, (1965). "Development Sequence in Small Groups," *Psychological Bulletin* 63 (1965): 384–399.

10. J. Gardner, *On Leadership* (New York: Free Press, 1990), 33.

Chapter 8

1. Interview with Nell Minow, editor and co-founder of The Corporate Library. October 2010.

2. Interview with Alexandra Reed Lajoux, Chief Knowledge Officer for the National Association of Corporate Directors. October 2010.

3. Interview with John Stroup, CEO of Belden, a St. Louis-based, publicly traded manufacturing company. August 2010.

4. D. Nadler, "Building Better Boards," *Harvard Business Review* (May 2004): 3.

Chapter 9

1. J. Mulligan, *The Hanoi Commitment.* (Virginia Beach, Va: RIF Marketing, 1981), 37.

2. E. Schein, *Organizational Culture and Leadership* (San Francisco: Jossey-Bass, Inc., 1992), 12.

3. N. Augustine, "Reshaping an Industry," *Harvard Business Review on Change* (Boston: Harvard Business School, 1997), 174.

Chapter 10

1. M. Updegrove, *Baptism By Fire* (New York: St. Martin's Press, 2008), 185–213.

2. Interview with Cathy Dunkin, President and CEO of Standing Partnership, a reputation management firm headquartered in St. Louis with offices in Virginia. November 2009.

3. Interview with Mark Abels, former VP of Corporate Communications for TWA and current Senior Vice President for k-global, a Washington, DC-based public affairs firm. April 2010.

4. M. Gladwell, *Outliers* (New York: Little, Brown and Company, 2008), 177–223.

Index

A

Accessible, make yourself, 18
Accommodator, the, 23-24
Adjustment, 232-236
Advisory boards make sense, 206-208
Afraid to make people angry, don't be, 18
Agent for and a champion of change, become an, 225-246
Aggressor, the, 23
Altitude, airspeed, and ideas at the same time, never run out of, 251-253
Angry, don't be afraid to make people, 18
Assessment model, talent, 74
Awareness, 230-232

B

Barriers to change, remove the, 241-242
Behaviors, address, 242
Blinders, making decisions without, 67-70
Box, listen to someone outside the, 241

C

Cash, monitor your, 256
Change agents, how to encourage your, 241-242
Change initiative, the four step of a, 238-242
Change,
  create a culture of, 240-241

how people respond to the
stages of, 228-238
remove the barriers to, 241-242
Coach, what it takes to be a, 79-97
Coaching and mentoring, proven
techniques for, 87-90
Coaching your high potentials,
97-100
Communication,
robust, 147-149
take charge of, 260-262
Competitive advantage, strategize
to leverage your, 101-128
Consumer protection act
of 2010, 201
Containing crisis, 249-250
Create and communicate the
visions, 239-240
Crisis and checking with clients, 258
Crisis response team, establish
a, 256
Crisis situations, evaluating
potential, 256-257
Crisis,
containing, 249-250
if you can't prevent, 249-250
ten lessons for leading during,
247-268
Culture of change, create a,
240-241
Culture of indecision, how to
conquer a, 54-57
Culture, create an
action-oriented, 138

D

Decision making and problem
solving, 43-70
Decisions without blinders,
making, 67-70
Derailers, 32
Destiny, control the hinges of, 43-70
Dodd-frank Wall Street
reform, 201
Doolittle raiders, 185

E

Early warning signs, heed
the, 248-249
Empathy, lack of, 37-38
Encourage and listen to impolite
candor, 262-263
Encourage independent thinking,
241
Evaluating potential crisis
situations, 256-257
Execution, turning great strategy
into great, 129-150
Executive, what does it take to be
an executive, 16-20
Exude powerful vulnerability,
264-265

F

F^2 Leader, the, 24-29
F^2 Leaders, 15-42
Face reality, 254-255
Fair, why it's tough to be, 29-30
Fingers-in Board, 220-221

Forward, moving, 237-238
Four steps of a change initiative, the, 238-242
Functions of a virtuosos team, eight, 188

___

G

GLAD communication model, 91
Growth in strategy formulation, the role of, 119-120

___

H

Hanoi commitment, the, 235
Heed the early warning signs, 248-249
Hidden traps, how to sidestep, 57-67

___

I

Indecision, how to conquer a culture of, 54-57
Independent thinking, encourage, 241

___

L

Laissez-faire board, the, 220
Leadership, a new model for, 20-29
Leading during crisis, ten lessons for, 247-268
Learning from failure visible, make, 258
Learning safe, make, 241-242
Lessons for leading during crisis, ten, 247-268

List of ten worst things that could happen, 257-258
Listen to impolite candor, encourage and, 262-263
Listen to someone outside the box, 241

___

M

Media, respond appropriately to the, 266-268
Monitor your cash, 256
Moving forward, 237-238

___

N

Narcissism, 34-36
NASA, 105

___

O

Optimistic, be realistic but, 258-259

___

P

Passive board, the, 219-220
People respond to the stages of change, how, 228-238
People won't change, the reasons, 226-228
Perfectionism, 41
Pipeline, ensuring the, 151-174
Pipeline, steps in leadership, 162
Prepare, 255-258

Q

Quit 'n' stay, the, 23

R

Realistic but optimistic, be,
    258-259
Reality, face, 254-255
Reasons people won't change, the,
    226-228
Recklessness, 36-37
Relationships outside the
    organization, build, 257
Remove the barriers to change,
    241-242

S

Safe, make learning, 241-242
Sarbanes-Oxley Act of 2002, 201
Self-awareness, lack of self, 33-34
Self-worth versus position, 18
Set the stage, 238-239
Stellar board ,221, 208-218
Steps of a change initiative, the
    four, 238-242
Strategy formulation, the role of
    growth in, 119-120

Strategy,
    foundations of, 101-102
    nature of, 108-113

T

Talent assessment model, 74
Talent assessment, a new model
    of, 72-76
Team, establish a crisis response, 256
Ten lessons for leading during
    crisis, 247-268
Thinking, encourage
    independent, 241
Top talent, build magnets to
    attract, 71-100
Top it will be lovely at the, 17
Tough, why it's fair to be, 30-32
Transforming solo contributors into
    magnetic bosses, 76-78
Tregoe model, 110
2 × 2 Matrix, 46-48

V

Virtuosos, lead a team of, 175-200
Visions, create and communicate
    the, 239-240
Vulnerability, exude powerful,
    264-265

About the Author

For more than 30 years, Dr. Linda Henman has helped executives in military organizations, small businesses, and Fortune 500 companies define their direction and select the best people to put their strategies in motion. She has helped clients in the retail, financial services, food, medical, hospitality, manufacturing, and technology industries. Some of her major clients include Tyson Foods, Emerson Electric, Kraft Foods, Boeing Aircraft, Estee Lauder, and Merrill Lynch. She was one of eight experts chosen to work directly with John Tyson on his succession plan after his company's acquisition of International Beef Products. Through thousands of hours of coaching with hundreds of corporate clients, Linda has observed what it takes to move from middle manager to magnetic executive.

Linda holds a PhD in organizational systems, two Master of Arts degrees in both interpersonal communication and organization development, and a Bachelor of Science degree in communication. By combining her experience as an organizational consultant with her education in business, she offers her clients selection, coaching, and consulting solutions that are pragmatic in their approach and sound in their foundation.

A former university professor, she served on the adjunct graduate faculty at Washington University and belongs to the National Speakers Association, the National Association of Corporate Directors, and the Air Force Association. She holds numerous certifications, including Director of Professionalism, a designation given by the National Association of Corporate Directors.

She is the author of *The Magnetic Boss: How to Become the Leader No One Wants to Leave*, which Washington University uses in its graduate curriculum. She has also served as a contributing editor of two editions of *Small Group Communication: Theory and Practice*, has written peer-reviewed published articles, and authored numerous articles published in trade magazines.

As a professional speaker, Linda speaks about strategic leadership to large audiences throughout the United States. She recently delivered the opening keynote for Harrah's Leadership Conference, the Air and Space Technology Exposition, and the Banner Health Leadership Conference.

Serious about humor, Linda draws from her original research of the Vietnam Prisoners of War to help others cope with change and adversity so they can emerge from setbacks more resilient and hardy. She continues to associate with the Robert E. Mitchell Prisoner of War Center, a Naval research facility that has studied the Vietnam Prisoners of War since their 1973 repatriation. She has given interviews for radio and television regarding the POWs and their resilience during their captivity and the more than 35 years since their repatriation.

Whether working with executives or members of boards of directors, Linda helps develop strategic leaders and solve critical problems. Her academic and corporate credentials enable her to improve individual performance and increase overall organizational effectiveness.